Kava
in the Blood

Peter Thomson

TANDEM PRESS

First published in 1999 by
Tandem Press
2 Rugby Road
Birkenhead, Auckland 10
New Zealand

Copyright © 1999 Peter Thomson

Reprinted 2000

ISBN 1 877178 54 3

Cover design by Sue Reidy
Production by M & F Whild, Typesetting Services, Auckland
Printed in New Zealand by Publishing Press Limited

Contents

Fijian Pronunciation   4
Foreword   5

The Source   6
Coup d'Etat   10
Makuluva   18
Dum Spiro Spero   23
Mongoose on the Lawn   27
Great Council of Chiefs   34
Vaturekuka Hill   39
He Knows What To Do   45
Suva Rain   50
Cold Comfort Kava   55
In Praise of Kava   66
Taukei Movers   75
Fields of Vunidawa   83
Death Threats   94
Lautoka Cane Fires   103
Salvaging the Economy   107
Taveuni   115
The Governor General's Path   123
The Never Simple Truth   134
Fiji Patois   146
Buckingham Palace   153
The Deuba Accord   161
Bali Hai Profiles   173
Arrest at Musket Cove   177
Return to Navua   184
Mountains Tower Up   194
Imprisonment   204
Declaration of the Republic   215
Lay of the Land   220

Map of Fiji   227
Fijian Glossary   228
Afterword   233

Fijian Pronunciation

Standard Fijian is a phonetic language with the exception of the following letters:

B is pronounced MB as in remember
(thus *bula* is pronounced mbula)
C is pronounced TH as in mother
(thus *Cakobau* is pronounced Thakombau)
D is pronounced ND as in tender
(thus *Nadi* is pronounced Nandi)
G is pronounced NG as in singer
(thus *turaga* is pronounced turanga)
Q is pronounced NG as in finger
(thus *yaqona* is pronounced yangona)

Vowels are pronounced as follows:
A as in father
E as in let
I as in sing
O as in got
U as in flute

Fijian words used in the text are printed in italics and a glossary is provided at the end of the book.

Foreword

THIS BOOK BEGAN as a result of my last conversation with the late Ratu Sir Penaia Ganilau, the last governor general and the first president of Fiji. When I said my final farewell to him, he looked me in the eye and told me I should write a full account of what had happened at Government House in 1987, to keep the record straight. After my father, he was the man I respected and admired most in this world, and I told him I would. So over the last eleven years, when will and whimsy have allowed, I have written this book; and with allowances for my rampant subjectivity and the limitations on information available to me, I believe I've kept faith with him and with Fiji.

It has been suggested to me that I should have written two books rather than the one that is presented here. One story is about what went on in Fiji in 1987 between the two coups d'état, from the perspective of the permanent secretary to the governor general, the post that I filled at that time. The other is about growing up in Fiji as a fifth generation Fiji Islander of Scottish descent and the love that experience inspired. But to me the first book is not relevant without an understanding of the second, so to keep myself happy I've stuck to my plan. Bear with me, dear reader, if the years appear jumbled, and think of one story as the narrative and the other as dreaming time. Sometimes I too wonder which is which.

Perhaps I dwell too much on what *was* in Fiji, for people say we shouldn't live in the past. However if the latter were to be so, writing would be confined to futuristic genres. Even as I scribble these words in the present, their time will already be well in the past when they are read by you. So where is the line to be drawn to my retrospection: yesterday, last year, last decade? At this point in time I've just passed my fiftieth year, yet the times in which the events of this book are set are so clear, just a snap of a synapse away for me, and most of the business of living in the interim just a blur.

THE SOURCE

WHEN YOU LIFT your eyes landward from the sunburnt undulations of the Ra coast, you see the Nakauvadra mountain range rising nearly 1000 metres above you. Your eyes run along its rocky spurs and ridges in a westerly direction and there is a speck of white on the escarpment's ridge. It is the hill station of Nadarivatu.

The station was built in 1892 by the colonial government of Fiji, initially as a demonstration of its presence to the independent hill tribes who had long repulsed the authority of coastal leaders and clung to the old Fijian traditions of warfare and cannibalism. The hill tribes had acquiesced, and soon after the hill station's inception, Nadarivatu's cool air and fresh mountain streams began attracting visitors who wanted to escape the humid tropical conditions of the coastal capital. Wooden villas were built by the government for its officers, and these and other privately-owned wooden bungalows were spread along the hill slopes near the old fort erected at the time of the station's establishment.

Around the turn of the century, the governors of the colony would spend the hot season up at Nadarivatu. Drawing precedence from the habits of the Raj in India, governance of the colony would be despatched from the hill station during the summer months of January and February. The vice-regal parties sailed up the east coast from Suva and made their landings at Tavua. There they were met by Mr Brewster, who was the divisional commissioner at Nadarivatu from the years 1892 to 1910. Mr Brewster supervised the procession of horses, rickshaws, porters and ox-carts bearing the gubernatorial niceties as they moved across the Tavua foothills and ascended the Nadarivatu escarpment. The journey was 23 kilometres in length and over the last stretch the track gained altitude by 610 metres. Reed torches had to be lit, as nightfall would overtake the last few hours of the trek.

The sanative properties of the hill station were worth the effort of getting there, and these beneficial effects were demonstrated by Mrs Brewster, who after many years of Nadarivatu life retired to England, where she went on living to the age of 111, making her the oldest woman in Britain in 1982.

When my father arrived in Fiji in 1941 and took up his duties as aide-de-camp to the governor, Sir Harry Luke, they went on regular trips to the hill station in order to enjoy its cool climate. In those days Nadarivatu was still dominated by the fort, the divisional commissioner's residence and the governor's *bure*. The latter was a traditional Fijian house with reed walls, no ceiling, and a thatched roof soaring ten metres above the occupants. My father slept within the thick limestone walls of the old fort, which had by then been converted into a comfortable rest house.

My mother was born by the sea at Vatuwaqa in Suva and had often joined the colonial pilgrimage to the hill station during the hot months of January and February. On separate visits to Nadarivatu, shortly before they met in Suva, my mother and father each made the long climb to the top of Fiji's highest peak, Tomanivei, better known by the name given it by Mr Brewster, Mount Victoria. This cloud-enshrouded mountain, rising over 1200 metres through dense rain forest, was at that time seldom visited.

After my parents married, they continued to visit Nadarivatu during the hot season whenever they could. From childhood to adulthood their seven sons and one daughter would holiday there with them in one of the Nadarivatu rest houses. The temperatures were low enough for log fires, so evocative for us tropic people, to be lit in the hearths at night, while thick mists slid through the cool forests outside.

There were contemplative, fern-lined walks to be taken along the edge of the escarpment and horses to ride through the forest. Some time earlier a tumbling stream had been dammed with a cement retaining wall to form a swimming pool. A rope hung from a branch of one of the huge trees that blocked the sun from the dark pool, and we'd swing out on the rope and drop screaming into the icy water. As we walked back to the rest house, the sight of wood smoke from the kitchen chimney heightened youthful appetites and the final kilometre was taken on the run. Then steaming cups of tea would be drunk and mountains of scones consumed on the front veranda, sometimes with my father's friend, Semi Ketewai, from the nearby village of Navai.

On one occasion before Marijcke and I were married, Marijcke's parents, with their six daughters and one son, came to Nadarivatu to spend the holidays with us, and we all climbed Tomanivei together. This time my mother had to be pushed much of the way up. She and my father sat exhausted on a mossy mound on the summit they had each visited thirty years before, but on this occasion they were together and surrounded by their offspring. A lot had changed in thirty years, not least their responsibility for the sweating legion sharing the mountain top with them. As we surveyed the tumbling valleys of the Wainibuka below us and squinted out at the misty islands of Lomaiviti and Vanua Levu, they talked of the old days and of how Fiji had moved so calmly and purposefully from colonial times to independence. By their example they instilled in us a quiet pride and sense of blessedness at being party to the principles that had now made a nation of us all in independent Fiji.

After Marijcke and I had married, we were once more holidaying with my parents at Nadarivatu when one day my mother and I were driving past the old Forestry Department rest house and, pointing up at it, she said, 'That is where you were conceived.' I was quite stunned. My mother was not given to revelations of intimate detail and her remark was like a flashed glimpse through a curtain. Maybe I should have delved further, but I satisfied myself with contemplation of this new information. So this was where I began my luck-filled voyage along the liquid lip of the unknown. It is only now when I write about these things that I realise I owe my existence to Nadarivatu. For I was born in November 1948, and nine months before that was the hot season, the reason for my parents' presence at the hill station.

Strangely, while I was given life in the spiritual valleys of Nadarivatu, I came closest to prematurely losing it there. On one occasion, when I was in my early twenties, Marijcke and I were driving up the steep slopes of the winding dirt road approaching the hill station. We were unaware that, on the way up the rough Wainibuka section of the Kings Road, the engine of our old Valiant automatic had become disconnected from its chassis. Approaching Nadarivatu, we saw a Fijian lady struggling up the road with some firewood on her back and stopped to give her a lift. She politely declined, as she was about to take a side-track. So I put the automatic gear back into forward drive and touched the accelerator. The accelerator flopped to the floor, the engine roared at full throttle and the car threw itself into reverse with gravel and dust flying out from under us. We were out of control and heading at speed towards the yawning cliff behind us. It all happened so quickly there was nothing we could do. But sitting there on the edge of the precipice was our lifesaver, a rock of sufficient size and with a firm enough grip on the mountain that when the rear axle of the Valiant struck and rose upwards on the stone, the wheels of the car spun madly in the air and I was able to reach for the key and switch off the crazy motor. We threw ourselves out of the car, bodies shaking with adrenaline, and I went down on my knees in the dry brown grass looking under the car at our saviour, my namesake Petros, staring back at me.

In Fijian mythology, when the soul departs the body at death, it travels upon spirit paths, one of which passes through the very centre of Nadarivatu, on its way to the departure point for Paradise. *Dari* means dish and *vatu* means stone, and in the bottom of the glen in which the hill station nestles there sits a dish-like stone, the indentations on the top of which are supposed to be the source of the Sigatoka river which flows off in a southwest course for some 240 kilometres. Right past this boulder runs the spirit path, heading for the nearby Nakauvadra mountains, which are holy in the legends of Fiji because they are the earthly repose of the creator god Degei.

There is a fissure in the Nakauvadra mountains in which Degei lies in snake form, the rear half of his body set in stone; and into the coils of his reptilian pile, some poor souls are sucked. Lost in his reverie, Degei cares little for his creation, but when his serpent eyes slink open, legend says it is to assert once again his latent power over the scattered islands of Fiji.

Coup d'Etat

SHORTLY BEFORE 10am on May 14, 1987, my colleagues and I were serving kava to a group of foreign journalists in the media room at the Ministry of Information in Suva. I was at that time the Fiji government's permanent secretary for information. The journalists had come to Fiji to write stories on the changes that were occurring as a result of the election a month previously of a government which, for the first time in our history, was dominated by representatives of the Indian electorate. They were keen to hear stories of pending strife and were visiting us at the ministry in the hope of obtaining insights in this regard. I was enjoying pouring cold water on their proposals of unrest.

'This is Fiji, not Angola. You parachute journalists drop in here, become instant experts on the country and then produce half-truth, bad-news stories. Only a few months ago Pope John Paul stayed here and told us that Fiji was a symbol of hope for the world. Just relax a bit. See this country through our eyes. Come on, let's have another round of kava.'

'*Talo!*' The announcement of more kava produced stifled sighs from the journalists. They had been told it was impolite to refuse a bowl of our national drink, but you could see from the looks they exchanged that their patience for cultural respect was dwindling. To those not used to it, a kava session can have similarities to Chinese water torture, but with kava the water is muddy and acerbic.

As the kava was being served, one of my colleagues came into the room and whispered in my ear, 'Peter, you'd better have a look outside. There's something funny going on.'

Our visitors were engrossed in the rituals of the kava ceremony — when and how often to clap their hands in acknowledgement of the drinking, and the necessity of draining the half-coconut shell contents in one swig — and wondering when, if ever, they were going to feel kava's promised tranquillising effect. And always, on the tip of their numbed tongues, was the unasked question of why, in a free country, we chose to drink this stuff. All very diverting. I slipped out of the office.

The Ministry of Information was twenty metres away from the Parliament chambers across a quadrangle surrounded by the three-storeyed Government Buildings. As I came out into the quadrangle I saw armed Fijian soldiers with gas-masks over their faces moving briskly along the veranda opposite me towards Parliament.

'*Na cava oqo?*' I asked a Fijian bystander.

'*Sega ni macala*,' he shrugged.

As I watched the soldiers enter the Parliament foyer, I figured it was some sort of civil defence exercise. I turned and went back to the kava circle in the media room, unaware that I had just witnessed the launching of a coup d'état against the democratically elected government of Fiji.

One of the journalists was expounding on the symptoms of brewing trouble: the recent massive Taukei movement march through the capital calling for the reins of government to be returned to indigenous Fijians; the equally massive counter-march of government supporters; the fire-bombing of the offices of one of the prominent leaders of the Fiji Indians and the arrest the previous day of the Fijian senator Jona Qio on charges of being the fire-bomber. This journalist had also heard from one of our staff that members of our ministry were receiving anonymous death threats because our office was the mouthpiece for the new government.

We were countering with kava and explanations of cross-cultural tolerance, respect for Commonwealth principles, and the peaceful Pacific nature of problem-solving in Fiji, when the door was kicked open and gas-masked soldiers burst into the room. They formed a half circle around the open door and trained their guns on our stunned gathering. Through the door and into the protective half circle formed by his soldiers stepped Lieutenant Colonel Sitiveni Rabuka, wearing a grey lounge suit with *sulu vakataga*, polished military sandals and striped tie, and sporting a handlebar moustache. He lifted a hand-gun and said, 'Where is Peter Thomson?'

The open-mouthed faces of journalists and ministry staffers turned as one from the scene at the doorway to where I stood. I stepped forward and Rabuka motioned me down the corridor past a line of rigid typists to my office. Once in my office he said, 'Take this down.' As I sat down at my desk I noticed he turned his revolver away from me towards the floor.

He dictated while my fingers flew across the paper, 'The Royal Fiji Military Forces have taken control of the Fiji government to prevent any further disturbance and bloodshed in the country. I am on my way to Government House to seek recognition. I ask that the public remain calm and continue with their daily work. In particular I ask that the Fijian community do not take advantage of the situation.'

He told me to get this message broadcast on Radio Fiji and released to the media. Then he was gone. I looked at the treasonous scrawl on the paper in front of me. No-one could read that handwriting, I thought, so I called in my still dumbstruck personal assistant, dictated it into a third person format and asked her to type it up for me in the format of a Ministry of Information news release. Call it a bureaucratic reflex, playing for time or maybe too much kava.

In the meantime the media room had emptied. They'd all run across to Parliament to see what was going on. As my personal assistant gave me the typed-up release, some breathless ministry staffers returned with local journalists who had witnessed the numbing scene in Parliament. We drank kava in a state of shock. They told us that in the middle of a parliamentary debate Rabuka and about a dozen gas-masked soldiers had halted proceedings at gunpoint and, standing up on the Speaker's podium, Rabuka had announced a military takeover of government. They said all the government members of Parliament had been herded up by the soldiers and had been taken away in a truck.

More people arrived in the room. More breathless accounts of what had happened. More kava. Journalists running in and then running out to see where the action was now. Parliamentarians being herded into trucks by anonymous soldiers! As it started to sink in, this news was chilling. We'd only ever seen that sort of thing in Nazi war movies down at Suva's Regal Theatre.

I looked at Rabuka's message again and said to myself, 'I can't release this!' So I took it up to the prime minister's office to get some advice from the top. I entered the outer office and, looking through the open door to the prime minister's room, saw Rabuka seated behind the prime minister's desk giving instructions to someone. He had returned from Government House, and he certainly looked cool and in control.

I turned to leave the office and met Bill Cruickshank, the chairman of the Public Service Commission, coming in. Bill was a Scot whose wide experience had included getting half his jaw shot off when he was crewing aircraft in the Second World War. He was married to a Fijian woman from Lau. I had gone to him for his advice a month earlier when the Bavadra government had won the elections. That had been the first time since Independence that Fiji had effectively had a change of government leadership, and I wanted to be clear on certain announcement procedures involved in the changeover. The election results had come through just after dawn, and a short while later I was knocking on the door of Bill's house. He was open-mouthed when I gave him the news, and then he said, 'Welcome to the Third World, Peter. The Fijians will not accept this.'

And here we now were on the day of the coup, in a decidedly Third World situation. I asked Bill what he thought I should do about the release in my hand. He said that the civil service would have to cooperate because the military was clearly in control and all permanent secretaries were going to be called to a meeting later in the day to be briefed accordingly. Rabuka walked into the room, and I showed him the release. He approved it, and I had the message despatched to Radio Fiji.

In between these two meetings I had with Rabuka, he had been involved in an unexpected set-back. From our building Rabuka had driven up to Government House, the office and residence of the governor general, Ratu Sir Penaia Ganilau. He was anticipating a sympathetic reception from the governor general. Ratu Sir Penaia was the high chief of the province of Cakaudrove to whom Rabuka owed fealty. In previous years Ratu Penaia had been the deputy prime minister of the Fijian government that Rabuka's coup now sought to return to power. He was the manager of the Fiji rugby team when Rabuka played for the national side and, as a younger man, he too had played for the national team. As governor general, Ratu Penaia was commander-in-chief of the Royal Fiji Military Forces, he was Fiji's most respected old soldier, and above all he was the epitome of Fijian customs and values. It could be taken for granted that, on a personal level, Ratu Penaia would have been deeply disappointed with the results of the recent elections.

But Rabuka did not get the backing he expected at Government House. Ratu Penaia later recounted to me how he had told Rabuka in no uncertain terms that his actions were illegal and that he would not recognise Rabuka's military regime. Later that day the governor general confirmed his stand by proclaiming a state of public emergency and publishing it in the *Fiji Royal Gazette*.

Ratu Penaia then recorded an interview which was broadcast in the evening by the private radio station FM96, but not by the government-owned Radio Fiji. The transcript of the interview was published the next day on the front page of the *Fiji Sun* newspaper. In it he describes the 'unlawful seizure of the members of my government' and says that 'in the temporary absence' of ministers of the Crown he has assumed the authority vested by the Constitution of Fiji in Her Majesty the Queen. He said that the Constitution was the supreme law of Fiji and that duly appointed public officers remain in office. 'As commander-in-chief in Fiji, I now call upon all officers and men of the Royal Fiji Military Forces, the Royal Fiji Police and members of the public service to return to their lawful allegiance in accordance with their oath of office and their duty of obedience without delay.'

The scene was set for a tense stand-off between the young colonel committing high treason and the man he admired most, the elderly governor general defending the Constitution of the nation. But if Rabuka was shaken by this rebuff, it wasn't showing on his return from Government House, when I saw him again at the prime minister's office.

The next contact I had with Rabuka was at 11.30am, when he rang me from the Queen Elizabeth Barracks to dictate another news release and to say that a press conference should be organised at the cabinet office at 3pm. The news release was to assure the next of kin of all 'ex-government members' who were in the custody of the army that they were safe. As soon as the army found more comfortable accommodation for the ex-government members, they would allow their next of kin to visit them, and as soon as the 'caretaker government' was formed, the ex-government members would be released.

Next came the diplomatic corps. The British high commissioner, Roger Barltrop, chanced upon Rabuka outside Parliament just after the coup. Barltrop was dean of the diplomatic corps and asked that a meeting be held between the colonel and the corps. Rabuka agreed to see them at 2pm. I was subsequently rung by James Maraj, the permanent secretary for foreign affairs, who asked me to get Rabuka to reschedule the venue for the meeting with the corps from Queen Elizabeth Barracks to the Ministry of Foreign Affairs.

Why didn't Maraj contact Rabuka himself? I was beginning to get the feeling that I was getting too close to the flame and was uneasy about what others' perceptions might be. The only alternative I could see was to develop a really bad headache and go home for a few days, but I felt responsible for the welfare of the staff at my ministry and cared about my own sense of worth in a time of crisis. I decided that for the present it was better to be in the know than not, and to proceed with caution and conscience along this ragged path for the time being. I arranged for the meeting with the diplomatic corps to be rescheduled and then attended it with Maraj and the deputy secretary for foreign affairs, Dr Jona Senilagakali.

Not many members of the corps were there. The high commissioners from Australia and New Zealand were under orders from their governments not to attend. Barltrop pointed out that those in attendance were accredited to the legally elected government of Fiji and their presence at the meeting did not imply they had taken any position in relation to Rabuka's government. All very diplomatic. He said Rabuka had said to them that he assumed the corps had all informed their respective governments about the situation in Fiji, but he said this had not been possible because Rabuka had cut all international telecommunications. He asked that these be reopened, and Rabuka replied, 'That will be done.'

The American representative made a comment along the lines of their respect for democratic traditions and processes. Then the Indian high commissioner said that India expected that Indian nationals in Fiji would have their lives and property protected. Rabuka replied, 'Yes, sir.'

From the gathering of the diplomatic corps I went with Rabuka to the prime minister's office for a meeting which I had organised at the request of Nemani Delaibatiki, the editor of the Fiji Sun. The meeting was with the Fiji media bosses to establish what the new rules of the game would be.

Rabuka thanked the bosses 'most sincerely' for attending. He said that by now they would be well in the picture as to how the Royal Fiji Military Forces had at 10am that morning taken over the government. He said they had 'neutralised the government and instituted semi-military rule'.

He then said, 'Your role cannot be over-emphasised. During the past few weeks I am sure you have been monitoring the events that have been taking place around the country. No doubt you can see how these events could lead to a situation that would threaten law and order, life and property. A declaration of a state of emergency would have eventuated and the RFMF would have been called out to fight against our own people.'

'That being the state of things I would beg that you in your responsible posts give me and the Council of Ministers a fair go and fair coverage to keep the tension down. I believe if the public is well informed about what is going on, that calm will prevail. It is your responsibility to pass on information, but be sure that none of the releases would inflame racial tension. As a Fijian I am concerned about what the Fijian community can get up to. It would ruin the nation. What I have done this morning is a pre-emptive move to stop Fijian groups developing into terrorism or the RFMF being used against the people.'

'This is an interim measure. We will soon be appointing the Council of Ministers and we will be recommending to Her Majesty the Queen that Ratu Sir Penaia Ganilau be reappointed as governor general. With the military government in place the Constitution has gone. Legal people are now drawing up the interim Constitution which will guide us until a new one is put up.'

'The Royal Fiji Police Force and the RFMF are capable of maintaining law and order. Our primary responsibility is law and order. Former government ministers are still being detained and will be released to house arrest tomorrow. They have not done anything wrong, and it is my responsibility to see that they are comfortably looked after.'

He said he was a soldier, that he didn't want to sit and run the government but that he would be head of government for the time being. He said that his caretaker government would be drawn from civilians and backed by the military. Some of its members would be from the former government, some from the opposition and some from outside of Parliament.

Delaibatiki asked if the press could still write editorial comments and Rabuka replied in the affirmative. *Fiji Times* Editor Vijendra Kumar then said, 'Critical of the regime?'

'Critical to what extent?'

'Fair and balanced comment,' countered Kumar.

'Will it fan the flame of animosity? You understand the wide cross-section you cater for. Intelligent appreciation of your editorials should not put my regime into jeopardy or cause it to be looked on as a bad thing. The common people might take it in a different vein.'

The publisher of the *Fiji Sun*, Jim Carney said there was bound to be opposition to the regime, and with freedom of expression people would speak out against it.

Rabuka's reply was, 'Go ahead, gentlemen, you have freedom of expression.' He wound the meeting up by saying that he had taken his pre-emptive move because his assessment of the Fijians' feelings at this time had caused him to act.

Kumar said, 'We accept that.' But as they filed out of the room you could see the mood of the media bosses was still one of, 'Why the hell did he do it?'

This was my first experience of the colonel's winning ways. It had been a mixture of bravado and realism. Above all it was a consummate performance of confidence from a Fijian soldier who had just raped, pillaged and plundered the Constitution of Fiji. More of the same was to follow at the 3pm press conference in the Cabinet Room next door. In the past few months I had briefed two prime ministers and many cabinet ministers prior to meetings with the media, so after the media bosses had left the room, Rabuka asked me rather coyly if I had any advice for him before he entered this, his first press conference. I was nonplussed. 'Just say what you have to say' was all I could come up with.

A star was born as soon as those cameras started clicking, flashing and whirring, and the testing questions were answered with firmness, clarity and a touch of humour. Sure it was tense and tragic, but the journalists lapped it up. The man was photogenic and spoke in clear authoritative terms. There was no political waffle. In subsequent press conferences, as the international media appeared in droves with their banks of TV cameras, there was an air of huge excitement. It was show time. Fiji had never had an international media star like him. Love him or hate him, there was no denying his charisma and what appeared to be bountiful qualities of leadership.

MAKULUVA

GOVERNMENT BUILDINGS IS adjacent to the Suva waterfront, and when I had time during lunch breaks I would go for a stroll along the seawall in the shade of its avenue of banyan trees. Above the far shore of Suva's deep harbour, the outline of the Korobasabasaga Range rises behind a foreground collection of volcanic plugs and jungle-covered foothills. At the foot of Korobasabasaga the Namosi warriors had dwelt for as long as history records, and in times gone by they had come down from the hills to visit bloody raids on coastal dwellers.

After Rupert Brooke had brooded on this same compelling harbour view on November 24, 1913, he returned to his room at Suva's McDonald's Hotel and wrote '…across the bay are range and range of strange black mountains, always misty and sinister, inky abodes of ghosts and demons.' They seemed to Brooke like an entry point to the netherworld.

Further along the shoreline at the apogee of Suva Point, the eye rises from the basalt rocks of the seawall across the shimmering lagoon to where empty fishers' punts float tethered to poles cut from the mangroves. The poles are pushed deep into the sandy mud beneath the waters, but currents have caused them to lie at haphazard angles. Beyond the shallows an azure channel runs all the way from Suva Harbour to Nukulau Island. The channel is plied by trading vessels with cargoes of copra, kava, taro, and travellers from the outer islands. On the other side of the channel, the main coral reef lies, dead flat and monolithic, dotted here and there with beacons and the rusting remains of wrecked vessels which never made it through the passage to their Suva destination. Across the broad plateau of the reef, women wade at low tide searching for octopus and shellfish, catching small fish on hand lines, biting behind their heads to kill them before placing them in coconut leaf baskets at their waists.

Growing up through much of my youth on the Suva Peninsula, I remember the outer edge of the main reef seeming like the lip of our world. The sound of surf riding across the reef at high tide, the smashing of rolling swells against the reef's ramparts at low tide, and the surge of water withdrawing down coral canyons, sets up a constant rumble. During the activity of the day this is an unnoticed background noise, but on windless nights it is the pervasive sound of Suva. Beyond the night noises of flying foxes in the fruit trees and the barked messages of street dogs is always the distant murmur of the ocean, leaning on the great sea reef some twenty-five kilometres in length that encloses the peninsula. And on such tropical nights, youthful imagination would fly out from mosquito-netted security to the source of the watery roar, and from that surf-rumbled barrier seek for intimations of what the outside world might offer.

Viewed from the seawall, the main reef appears as a long line of frothy whiteness set between the dark blue of the Pacific Ocean and the many shades of light blue of the lagoon. To the east, the line of the white reef is broken in two places by the low green shapes of a pair of reef islands. The closest, Nukulau, has long been a popular place to visit. A jetty and deep water approach make it easy for pleasure craft to moor there, and the lawns among the coconut trees have for several generations been the scene of picnics and beach cricket. Under the decking of the jetty nested big *dadakulaci* sea snakes, in their black and white zebra coats. Boys would grab them by their tails and chase screaming girls down the beach, holding the swirling snake out in front of them.

In the 1840s the American John Brown Williams built his trading station on Nukulau Island. As well as a trader, Williams was the US Consul and one fourth of July he put on a party with fireworks and cannon. In the course of the festivities a cannon blew up and set fire to the trading station. The Fijian guests helped to douse the flames and some took to a bit of looting to complete the day's action. Williams's subsequent claims for compensation, greatly exaggerated over the next twenty years, were backed up by visiting US naval vessels and were, perversely, one of the reasons behind the ceding of Fiji to the British Crown in 1874.

About a kilometre from Nukulau across a deep channel, sitting on top of the main sea reef, facing the full brunt of the southeast trade winds, is the island of Makuluva. Like Nukulau it is a flat coral cay about half a kilometre in length, fringed with coconut trees and white sand beaches. Unlike Nukulau it is seldom visited, for there is no boat approach to the island except at high tide, when a small boat can carefully cross the coral reef that surrounds it.

When I think of Makuluva I think in the past tense, for it is not now what it was. After the 1955 earthquake, when a huge crack opened down the length of the main Suva reef, the currents in the area changed and the old Makuluva was gradually devoured by the sea. The same currents that ate away at its northern end formed a sandspit at its southern end, and effectively over the space of some twenty years the island moved the length of itself over the top of the reef. During this process the buildings and gardens of old Makuluva slipped into the void of nevermore. I loved these gardens, and long before the death of my grandmother and mother, their disappearance provided me with my a first sense of the inevitable passing of all things.

My parents and their friends used to rent the island for a couple of weeks every year during our school holidays. It was Crown property and had served during the early colonial period as a quarantine station. In the 1950s, when we used to stay there, Makuluva had a mown lawn at its centre big enough for us to play cricket or baseball on. It was lined on the windward side by a tall grove of coconut palms, which provided a noisy windbreak.

Facing north to the mainland were the caretaker's quarters and gardens, and to the south were thickets of waxy-leafed vines and trees typical of tropical reef islands. On the leeward edge of the lawn were buildings in the colonial tropical style. One was a long barracks with lines of bedrooms on either side of a central corridor. The next was a sprawling central building that served as dining room and entertainment area, connected by a wooden walkway to a kitchen building equipped with a wood-fired stove.

The rainwater from all these buildings was fed into a massive round cement water tank. I suppose the tank's size was related to the island's earlier use as a quarantine station, when the population might rise from that of the caretaker and his family to a whole shipload of people disgorged from a ship flying the yellow flag of cholera. To this tank the island's caretaker had reputedly tied himself during a particularly fierce hurricane when the surf of a storm-tide washed across the width of the island.

From the lawn to the swimming beach a sandy path bent through the low *mulomulo* trees. The path was lined with large white clam shells, and in the dense foliage which crowded in and overhung the lane on all sides the scuttle of lizards and crabs and the screech of nesting reef herons was heard. The path was known as Lovers Lane, and we used to take great precautions not to be seen on the lane at the same time as one of the girls. If you were so seen, you were stigmatised as lovers, and with all the mental torture and foolishness that such status was held to entail, one was well advised to take precautions. You would pause before entering the leaf-tunnelled entrance to the path and listen for the sound of voices further down it before proceeding. If you were half way down the path when you realised girls were about to enter it from one of its ends, the only option was to dive headlong into the scratching undergrowth beyond the line of clam shells.

Once down Lovers Lane you emerged from the soft green light of the tunnel into the glittering white-blue glare of the beach. Standing in the fullness of that glare, long before days of sun screen and Ray Bans, you raised a shading hand to your forehead and, squinting through one eye checked out the tide and whether the beach was populated by any of the adults or girls. Usually it was not. Whether it was or not didn't really matter, it just changed the nature of the experience; let's say from amused observation if they were there, to imaginative adventure if they weren't.

I have always measured other beaches against the scale of the beach at Makuluva. The entire islet was surrounded by a narrow beach with coral reef hard up against the shore, but only at 'the beach' had prevailing currents and winds created a wide swath of sand above the high-tide mark and an expansive sandy-bottomed swimming space between the reef and the low-tide limit of the beach.

Snorkels had just arrived in Fiji at that time and we would swim through the narrow channels in the reef with mask and snorkel for much of the day. Little brown boys with flipperless feet kicking bubbles into the opaque waters, moving across the sandy bottom of the channels as sunlight dappled our submerged bodies with wavering stars. The channels were like a maze and would occasionally lead to the edge of the reef where we would stop, suspended, hovering in liquid flight, and stare down with awe at the blue abyss.

The southern end of the beach was the sandy point shaped by the current, which gradually grew longer and longer as the island crawled at a snail's pace southward across the reef. The current-carried sand was particularly pure, and at low tide this unsullied spit seemed like an exposed private part of the island. Around its smoothness the tangled coral reef crackled and snapped with its low tide noises, and always from across the reef's plateau the heavy rumble of the ocean breakers.

Some nights we would search for turtle eggs with the Fijian caretaker's family. Taking long reeds and a kerosene lantern we would look for turtle tracks on the beach and test the sand thereabouts with the reeds to probe for buried rubbery eggs. On such nights we would traverse the southern sandspit in silence. It was a place we respected. Like translucent alabaster the point glowed in the moonlight, extended out over the greenish blackness of the reef. Ghostly white terns sat on the back of its virginal protuberance, under the arching starscape of the southern skies.

Further down the beach hushed conversation would recommence and on one such occasion I recall the talk was of Buretu, the Polynesian island that human spirits travelled to after the death of the body they had resided in. Beauty and happiness pervaded all things on the paradise of Buretu. It had been seen by mariners on calm days, twinkling like a mirage on the ocean's horizon. After death, spirits travelled down known pathways on the main islands and set off from certain points, such as Naicobocobo on Vanua Levu, to cross the ocean to the paradise island. Was Buretu only for Fijians or was it possible for our souls to dwell there too? We conjectured whether our sandspit was such a departure point and imagined the spirits slipping by in silence on that beach, past us youths searching by lamplight for turtle eggs in the Makuluva night

Dum Spiro Spero

MAY 15, 1987, the day after the coup d'état, I was at my office early. The *Fiji Times* headline was 'Coup. Army Seizes Power'. A message from prime minister Bavadra was on the front page saying he expected a resolution to 'this impasse' in a very short time. The *Fiji Sun* headlines were 'Army Takes Over' and 'Ratu Penaia Saddened By Coup'. The *Sun*'s editorial said 'in one ill-conceived action the military has besmirched its proud record, each member has broken his Oath of Allegiance to our Sovereign Queen, and collectively descended to the level of a banana republic guerrilla force.'

Rabuka appointed his Council of Ministers and they met at 11am. One of the first things they decided to do was close down the newspapers 'for the time being'. Radio was allowed to continue, but broadcasts were to be 'vetted' by the Council of Ministers. So now we had censorship.

The Council of Ministers was made up largely of ministers from the former Alliance government with the inclusion of some radical Taukei movement leaders such as Jone Veisamasama and Reverend Raikivi. Most importantly Ratu Sir Kamisese Mara, prime minister of Fiji for all but one month of Fiji's seventeen years as an independent nation, had agreed to join the council in the position of minister of foreign affairs. He was to say later in defence of his quick decision to join the council, 'I had to do it, because my house was on fire with members of my family inside. Why should I wait? I must try and rescue them.'

One of the chief concerns of the council was their lack of support from the governor general, and thus they agreed that Rabuka and Ratu Mara should go henceforth to Government House to seek the governor general's recognition of the Council of Ministers. At the conclusion of the council meeting I was drinking kava in the cabinet secretariat office with Ratu Isoa Gavidi when Reverend Raikivi joined us. This was the first time I had met this fundamentalist Methodist preacher. He said 'the governor general will be the most unpopular chief in Cakaudrove if he goes against the coup.' Raikivi was from Cakaudrove and had a reputation as a hot-blooded *talatala*. He seemed hyperactive, had shifty eyes behind the thick glass and heavy frames of his spectacles, and his moustache bristled aggressively as he denunciated. Around that *tanoa*, listening to his inflammatory dogma, I shuddered at the thought of what lay ahead.

Rabuka held another press conference with his main message being that he was 'in complete control of the situation' and that the coup had been 'accomplished without a single shot being fired.' But as the US State Department said in a release that day, 'the situation in Suva is in flux'. It was too early for them to make a statement as to whether the US government recognised Rabuka's government.

Yes, we were in a state of flux. There was a three-way power-play going on. In one corner we had the judiciary, who were taking a strictly legal approach and were calling for the pre-coup situation to be restored. The second party was Rabuka's Council of Ministers, who claimed to be the government but wanted the governor general to swear them into office to give them legitimacy. The third party was the governor general, doing his best to carry out his duties as the Queen's representative. The governor general had called on former attorney-general and old colleague Sir John Falvey to give him legal advice at that time.

On the same day the governor general, Ratu Sir Penaia, asked me if I would be willing to assist him with his duties at Government House. His secretariat prior to the coup was a low-key office suited to his formerly ceremonial role. I was more than pleased to answer his call, on grounds not only of official duty but also of personal loyalty. In this hour of national emergency I felt up to the challenge. It was to me then as if I had been preparing for this test in the fifteen years of experience that I had had as a district officer and Fiji diplomat, so within a week of the coup I found myself officially appointed to the newly-created post of permanent secretary to the governor general.

I could see the governor general was in a cleft stick and the big squeeze was on. The judiciary's initial stand was of no real help to him in terms of a practical way ahead; Fiji would not have peace unless a middle path could be found. He was in no doubt that the great majority of ethnic Fijians and the army were with Rabuka and they were not going back to an Indian-dominated government. The threat of Fijian violence being visited upon the Indian community was very real at that time and was being relayed to Government House through various credible channels.

It was clear to me that Ratu Penaia intended to carry out his vice-regal duties in accordance with the oath of office he had taken, central to which was his loyalty to the Queen. As the Queen of Fiji was also the head of the Commonwealth it was also clear to me that the governor general was going to have to come up with a solution that was internationally acceptable.

During the power play over the next few days, one of the Supreme Court judges took me aside at Government House. Judge Richard Ambler (Peter) Kearsley was my maternal uncle, and he asked me very sternly if I knew what I was doing. Had he confronted me a few days earlier, I would have said that like most civil servants at the time I was very unhappy and ambivalent about my position, but I was now working with the governor general and as a result replied that I was 100 percent sure I was doing the right thing.

It was suspected in some quarters that I was some sort of Government House agent for the judiciary at this time. It was known that Judge Kearsley was adamant that the laws of Fiji must be upheld and as such was implacably against any legitimisation of the coup's claims. Conspiracy theories were rife, particularly in the hearts of those with a guilty conscience. The truth is that, other than this brief conversation with my uncle, I had no contact with the judges at all.

On Sunday May 17 Ratu Penaia swore in Rabuka as chairman of the Council of Ministers. I was not directly privy to the reasoning behind this decision, but know the governor general's mood at the time was that he would not take actions based solely on legality if those actions would lead directly to the communal violence. He saw that holding on to the loyalty of the de facto head of the security forces was critical to the control of the situation. Contrary to the strictly legal line, it was quite apparent that he had no real opportunity to return government to the state in which it had been on May 13. To do so would have led at least to the events of May 14, at worst to civil war.

Later that evening, the chief justice called on the governor general and presented a plan which had been written for him by his brother judges. Its basic points were that the governor general had the power under the Constitution to dissolve Parliament, proclaim himself the executive authority of government and call for fresh elections. It also proposed the formation of a council of advisers to help him run the country in the interim and a review committee to inquire into constitutional grievances and remedies. It insisted that the governor general not recognise Rabuka's Council of Ministers and keep at all times within the requirements of the Constitution of Fiji. It was the Fiji judiciary's finest hour. Their advice placed an immense burden on Ratu Penaia's shoulders, but it provided him with an acceptable way ahead as governor general. And so the die was cast.

I then sat down to draft the first of many state-of-the-nation speeches which Ratu Penaia was to broadcast over Radio Fiji in the course of the next four and a half months. On the evening of May 18 he came over the air to say that it was constitutionally impossible for him to recognise Rabuka's Council of Ministers and that they should set about dismantling their regime, restore the free press, and release all political detainees. He also quoted a message from the Queen wishing him to know how much she admired his stand both as her personal representative in Fiji and as the guardian of the Fiji Constitution.

Further press releases from Government House on May 19 stated that the governor general was dissolving Parliament and taking the other measures outlined to him in the judiciary's advice. He emphasised that the laws of Fiji were in place and operative and called on the people of Fiji to be patient, calm and keep the faith. As these messages went out, the unanswered question was how the Fijian activists would react to the governor general's stand. With the shock of the coup, the floodgates which had held back the surge of indigenous nationalism, swollen with the resentment of electoral defeat, had burst open in the minds of the Fijian community. Would Ratu Penaia's *mana* and the Fijian's trust in the Crown be enough to shore up the floodgates? The critical test was upon us in the shape of the Great Council of Chiefs meeting which was to open in Suva in the morning. That night Sir John Falvey stuck his head into the room where I was working and said, '*dum spiro spero* - while I breathe I hope.'

MONGOOSE ON THE LAWN

MAY 20 DAWNED and the Great Council of Chiefs was gathering in Suva. Ratu Penaia's speech was written, the briefings were done and it was time to go. Two police motorcycle outriders were stationed in front of the governor general's black Daimler, and police cars before and aft completed the formation. Pulses quickened as their motors roared into life and last minute instructions were being given over the noise. In the excitement of the moment it was only as we moved towards the cars that I remembered I wasn't going. I wished Ratu Penaia good luck, he told me to hold the fort, and then the cavalcade was off down the palm-lined sweep of Government House drive. I watched as the bikes and then the cars passed through the gates 400 metres below me and followed their progression along the waterfront past the Grand Pacific Hotel. The governor general was being driven to the Civic Centre, where a big crowd had gathered outside the Council's meeting place.

It vexed me that I had been left behind and it hurt to know the reason why. The outcome of the meeting was crucial to the establishment of the governor general's authority over the army, the Taukei movement and the chiefs themselves. I wanted to attend the meeting in order to observe and learn. But it was not my right to be there; I was not an indigenous Fijian.

I wandered along the lawn in front of Government House, looking up at its imposing bulk and thinking of the six generations of my family that had passed respectfully through its doors, or indeed those of its wooden predecessor. On the driveway in front of me, purple and mauve bougainvillea flowers were caught in a little whirlwind which swirled the flashing petals across the hot tarmac and flung them onto the green of the Thurston grass lawn. Spooked by the petals, a turtle dove took off from the lawn and flew off in the direction of the royal palms by the drive below, leaving a slapping sound of wings on feathered flanks in its wake. A mongoose crossing the lawn had made an over-ambitious leap at the dove, which was well beyond its reach. It looked around furtively to see whether its mongoose theatrics had been observed, spotted me and slunk off towards a drain. The dove rose up above the African tulip trees and glided down through the palms into the cool shadows of the Botanical Gardens.

For all the beauty and familiarity of this scene, looking at it then I felt a creeping sense of delusion at being part of a country which, because of my European forbears, was now pointing a finger at me and saying 'foreigner'. The bougainvillea, the turtle dove, the mongoose, the tulip tree, the royal palms, the Botanical Gardens, Government House, these were all now an inseparable part of Fiji and yet had been brought here by us non-indigenes. Indigenous soil absorbed non-indigenous roots, but above ground people were making other plans.

I lifted my gaze across the harbour to Lovonilase cemetery where my great great grandfather, my great grandparents and my grandparents were buried and remembered the musty smell of the earth pit when we lowered the body of my grandmother down into its place of rest. Her grave looked out towards Mount Korobaba and the volcanic plug of Joske's Thumb, just as the Nasese house in which she was born in the last century had done. I surveyed the outline of those harbour-fringing mountains, Korobaba's bulk and next to it the double summit like the head of a giant manta ray. How would my grandmother console me now if I could lean on her shoulder once more and confide in her? Perhaps she would take back all those tales which had fed my youthful imagination, of adventure and misadventure, of family and friends, of places and times past, in order to unweave the spell of attachment to this place that was our home.

She was a loving grandmother, but hard times had bred her tough, and I was satisfied she would have wanted me to box on. Her mother had died young and her widowed grandmother, Grannie Petrie, had brought up the grandchildren frugally at their Knolly Street home. It was not an easy life for those early Suva women. My grandmother's aunt, Emma Meredith, lived in the same street and was usually alone, as her husband was the captain of the trading schooner *Meg Merrilees*. When a ship had been sighted from the lookout on the spine of Suva's peninsula at Flagstaff, youths would run down to the harbour past their houses yelling, 'Ship ahoy!' Aunt Emma would don her bonnet and go down to the pier, where she would call up to the master of the arriving vessel, 'Do you know the whereabouts of Captain John Meredith of the *Meg Merrilees*?' And news might be given that the ship had been seen riding at anchor in Apia or Sydney not three weeks before; until the time came that no news of the *Meg Merrilees* could be garnered, and weeks and months crawled by, and finally the dreaded fourth-hand news arrived that she had gone down with all hands, somewhere amongst the reef-strewn waters of the Torres Strait.

But still we were *vulagi*, and on this May day the continuation of our status as citizens was an implicit part of the debate at the Great Council of Chiefs. Who would speak for us at that gathering, other than the governor general?

It was inconceivable to me that there were people in Fiji, or indeed the world, who wished ill of the indigenous Fijian people. The beauty of our island environment aside, our chief pride as citizens of Fiji was in our people, and in this regard the indigenous people were our leaders and our foundation. They were the essential point of difference between us and other countries. As a descendant of white colonial society I had a heritage to deal with in relation to the arrogant attitudes of our race in times gone by, but I had long learned to get on with life in my own way in the post-colonial era in which I lived. After the experiences of the Second World War, paternalism was on the same death bed as colonialism, and both were dead and buried when I came out of university in 1972 and joined the Fiji civil service as an administrative officer. The only bosses I had in my career all had brown faces.

Indigenous Fijian society is famous for the warmth of its welcome to visitors, *vulagi*, as long as they show respectfulness to their hosts. The Fiji tourist industry bears this out to this day, for tourist survey results repeatedly rank interaction with the Fijian people as the best feature of a Fiji holiday. But our central problem of nationhood was that most Fijians still regarded the non-indigenous citizens, who made up about half of our population, as *vulagi*.

As hosts they had provided us with land to farm and live upon and had governed the nation in a manner which was the envy of most of the developing world. In the meantime we prospered in a modest sort of way. And then the bowl got tipped. The way the Fijians saw it, the 1987 general elections had shown gross disrespect to them as hosts, because for the first time since Independence the Fijian-dominated government had been voted out of office and a *vulagi*-dominated government was installed in its place.

As warm and welcoming as it is, there is an exclusivity about Fijian culture that allows one to go only so far. The closed shop is probably based on its communal nature and the wish of the Fijian people that their culture lives on in their minds and deeds, not just in the genes of its people. Even intermarriage does not necessarily bring one's children into Fijian society, for if the mother is Fijian and the father a *vulagi*, the offspring cannot be registered as Fijians without great difficulty. Our family had come about as close as *vulagi* get to Fijian society without being part of it, respecting its customs, serving its people, speaking its language, fighting in its regiments, playing in its rugby teams, but always as *vulagi*.

And what has this society produced? There are no fine pyramids or paintings to point at. Again it is the Fijian people that are the source of Fiji's pride. A people with flowing physical prowess, wild humour, and thoughtful comradeship. How often visitors leaving Fiji would remark on Fijians as the salt of the earth, and how often they draw from that society feelings of goodwill and faith in the enriching diversity of humanity. The earth would be a far poorer place if Fijian society were to go the way of the Ainu in Japan or the Cornish in England, off to that graveyard of cultures visited by none but students of history and prehistory.

But what of us, the *vulagi*? Butadroka and other would-be ethnic cleansers in the Taukei movement were down in the streets shouting that we should be shipped off to where we came from. It is true that most of their ire was aimed at the Indian community, but all non-indigenes were basically in the same boat. It's not for me, as someone of Scottish descent, to comment on what the Indian people felt about all the vilification that was coming their way, but it must have been a bitter experience. All the Fijian doubts about Indians were being brought to the fore – mistrust of their motives and fear of a new national order run by Indians – while the provocateurs played heavily on Fijian prejudices that Indians were greedy, inconsiderate and dismissive of Fijians as lazy and undependable 'jungalis'.

The finger has been pointed correctly at white colonial society for creating the situation that pitted Fijian against Indian, but the assumption that this was exacerbated by a deliberate policy of divide and rule misses the point. Fijian and Indian society were like oil and water, neither society wanted to integrate with the other and neither made any great effort of their own volition to do so. Intermarriage between a Fijian and Indian was rare. Indians did not play rugby, the national sport. Indians excelled academically and looked with disdain on the preferential scholarships given to Fijian students.

In my father's book *Fiji in the Forties and Fifties* he addresses the charge that colonial administrators of the time should have done more to quicken the pace of racial integration. He admits that the melding together of the disparate racial communities in Fiji was still in its infancy in those two decades, but points out that such a quickening was against the wishes of the communities at that time. 'The promotion of English as the sole medium of education in all schools, to the exclusion of the Fijian or Hindustani languages, might have speeded up integration, but such an edict would have provoked an uproar.'

After Independence, encouraged by the espoused multiracialism ethos of Ratu Mara's leadership, many of us young non-indigenes saw ourselves as a new breed of Fiji Islander. Freed from the oppressive introspection of the issues of our elders – colonialism, the scars of indenture, the Pacific War experience – we saw ourselves as Fiji Islanders first and only subsequently as Fiji Indian, European or whatever. We had so much more in common with each other than with expatriates or people who were still bound within the narrow definitions of their race.

During the seventeen years between Independence and the coup d'état most of us had come to believe in the national ethos of multiracial harmony. In our national anthem we sang 'Stand united, we of Fiji'. Pope John Paul called us 'a symbol of hope for the world'. If you believed in this ethos and put it into practice, living in Fiji was an uplifting and fulfilling experience. But for every person that did, around the next coconut tree was someone who didn't. If you call the latter people cynics, then the coup d'état was cynical. If you call them realists, then the coup was a reality check.

For all this, unless one lived in more isolated communities in the islands or the mountainous interior, it would be a poor Fiji citizen indeed who did not count among his personal friends people of other races. But while cross-cultural social and workplace harmony was the norm, it was at an individual level, while at a communal level the two main races kept their distance.

31

Here is a story not told to denigrate anyone but to demonstrate the exclusivity of the Fijian social unit. Some might take it the wrong way, but it is a true and soul-searching story so it's worth telling. In the early 1970s I was swimming with some friends in a pool above the waterfall which is inland from the Bay of Islands in Suva Harbour. The waterfall is about four storeys high, falling over a vertical soapstone cliff. One of our number wandered off in the direction of the waterfall. I became concerned when he hadn't returned after about five minutes and I went off to look for him.

Peering cautiously over the brink of the waterfall I was horrified to see his motionless body prone on a ledge half way down the falls, water cascading on him, his arm at a crazy angle. I yelled for the others to come, and clambering down the edge of the falls through rain forest, slipping on mud and wet roots, we made our way to the ledge that had stopped his fall. He was in shock, his right arm was badly broken and it seemed when we tried to move him that his hip was broken. We wrapped him in towels and our shirts and then I bolted through the bush to the nearest telephone which was located on the foreshore of the Bay of Islands at the Tradewinds Hotel. His father was a high-ranking police officer, so I rang him for help.

Twenty minutes later his father was with us on the waterfall ledge. An ambulance arrived and then a squad of policemen. They strapped my friend tightly to a stretcher, cut a passage through the bush and lowered him by ropes and safe arms to the base of the waterfall. He was then carried to the ambulance and borne off to the CWM hospital.

There was a moment in this drama when my injured friend's father was standing on the ledge with us, and the Landrover containing the police squad careered to a halt below us. The policemen bundled out of it with ropes and machetes. My friend's father had been formulating a plan for the rescue and shouted down at them, 'How many of you are there, sergeant?'

The burly Fijian sergeant looked up and bellowed, 'Six men and one Indian, sir!'

In the heat of the crisis the import of this retort was skimmed over, and perhaps only a perverse mind would now retain the memory of it. What was important at the time was that the six Fijians were a unit, they knew that they could do this well, in their hands everyone would be safe. Their confidence and other's confidence in them was understood. The Indian constable did not appear to take any offence, he was happy to let the

Fijians do the physical stuff while he looked after the vehicles. But thinking back on it now, who but he can judge how he felt? And what did that exclusion, welcomed or otherwise, signify for the future integrity of our security forces?

The exclusion could occur in more subtle ways. After work one day at Government House, Ratu Penaia asked me to stay for a whisky or two. We were discussing the ambivalent Fijian attitude towards democracy and the lack of experience that the Fijian people had with the ups and downs of the democratic process. He contrasted this with what he called 'your country', where there had been centuries of experience with parliamentary democracy.

The country he was referring to was Scotland, the land of my forbears, for which I felt a romantic admiration but no immediate sense of belonging. I was quietly stunned. If this man who had cradled me in his arms when I was an infant in Vanua Levu and had watched over the last thirty-eight years of my life in Fiji thought of 'my country' as Scotland, what hope did I have of an ordinary Fijian seeing me as anything but a *vulagi*? The exclusion was made quite innocently, but it was there and, ardent Fiji nationalist that I was in those days, it hurt. The cracks in the foundations of my implicit belief in my Fiji nationality were opening, and I thought wistfully of that mongoose on the lawn.

GREAT COUNCIL OF CHIEFS

THE GREAT COUNCIL of Chiefs was an advisory body which had outlived the colonial government that created it. To some Fijians it was an anachronism, but to most its very survival expressed the special status of the indigenous Fijian nation within the overall nation of Fiji. During the colonial years Fijian representatives had been present in the colony's Legislative Council, and after Independence in 1970 Fijians had dominated the seats of government in Parliament. However, to many Fijians the Great Council of Chiefs had always been and continued to be the true voice of Fijian opinion.

Fijian chiefs had, of course, gathered together before Fiji was ceded by them to Queen Victoria in 1874, and one of the early acts of the colonial government, in line with its policy of governing 'in accordance with native usage and customs', was to give legal status to the gathering to be known as the Great Council of Chiefs. Over the next 100 years the Council preserved for itself the right to address the monarch, through the governor, on matters of concern to the Fijian people, and the linkage between the royal family in Britain and the chiefs of Fiji became a special relationship based on mutual respect and loyalty. In 1982 Queen Elizabeth II came to Fiji at the request of the Great Council of Chiefs to open the Council's session being held that year on the island home of the famed paramount chief of old, Cakobau Rex, who had presided over the cession of Fiji to Queen Victoria.

After Independence the Council had become something of a side-show and its importance was overlooked by many of the Suva academics, journalists and bureaucrats whose words tended to be those heard and seen in the media. The same comment can be made of many of Fiji's elected politicians, including some of the Fijian politicians of chiefly rank. The Council of Chief's debates were closed to outsiders, as a result of which non-Fijians tended to pay little attention to their meetings, other than to look with surprise at the sometimes reactionary and sometimes radical nominees put forward by the Council to be their representatives in the

Senate, the upper house of Fiji's Parliament. The Council was chaired by the minister of Fijian affairs thus providing a link between the Council and the government of the day.

I had been taught to respect the Great Council of Chiefs, and this had had its impact on me when, after the fateful general elections, I was summoned to the first meeting of the Bavadra government's cabinet on April 15, 1987. The prime minister wanted me present to answer some questions and take a directive on a press statement. I knew most of the ministers present, including Navin Maharaj, the minister of trade, industry and tourism. I had already met with Maharaj in preparation for my assumption, scheduled to take place on May 18, of the role of permanent secretary of the newly-created Ministry of Trade, Industry and Tourism. This was a government not daunted by the acronym.

I have one clear memory from the moment I walked into the cabinet room that day and observed the new ministers seated around their long table. The Indian members of the cabinet were seasoned, competent troopers who had either sat on the opposition benches of Parliament for many years or had pegged their way up through the gruelling ways of city councils and trade unions. But the Fijians present, admirable academics, idealists and activists that they were, in terms of the body politic of the Fijian nation were decidedly light-weight. The ominous conclusion that I made as I stood by their table was, 'there is no-one present who has the *mana* to chair the upcoming meeting of the Great Council of Chiefs', and then the accompanying thought that this government would not last long in its present form.

Such was the august body which Ratu Penaia drove down from Government House to address at the Suva Civic Centre where the Great Council of Chiefs had gathered on the morning of May 20, 1987. He trusted in his status as a former chairman of the Council, his pre-eminence as a Fijian chief and leader, and above all his vice-regal status, to carry the day. In his address to the gathered chiefs and representatives of the Fijian people he plainly stated his legal position as governor general and the need for him to act within the Constitution of Fiji. He told them that he would be appointing a council of advisers to assist him in his new role as sole executive authority of the nation and that he did not recognise the legality of Rabuka's Council of Ministers.

He did not carry the day. In fact he was rebuked in the strongest terms available within the respectful confines of *vakaturaga* debate. The dominant mood of the Council was that Fijians should finish the job that Rabuka had begun and produce a new constitution for Fiji which would irrevocably entrench political power in the hands of indigenous Fijians.

In the course of this dark day a crowd of Indians had gathered near Government Buildings for a prayer meeting. This was interpreted by some as an anti-Rabuka political protest in the guise of a prayer meeting. The Indian assembly was attacked by an ugly mob of Fijians who punched and kicked their way through the Indians as they dispersed in panic. The mob then rampaged through the centre of Suva smashing cars, shops and any unfortunate Indians they came upon. The clammy spectre of inter-ethnic violence which had haunted us for some weeks now had briefly but unmistakably exhaled its foulness into the streets of Suva. Spontaneous street violence spread to Nausori and Suva's suburbs, where mobs looted, assaulted and stoned people and property.

That day's rioting was another confirmation that we were at the edge of a precipice of awful consequence. Up at Government House the security briefings conveyed a message of incipient racial retribution, and the reality of this threat and our duty to combat it underlaid all our efforts. For the duration of my time at Government House, the containment of the forces pushing Fiji towards that precipice assumed priority over all other issues and crises. I am happy for those who conclude the threat was overstated. I don't believe it was, and it was the chief reason that, in spite of all he put awry in 1987, I recognise the willpower of Sitiveni Rabuka and the stop that he put to overt communal violence in Fiji.

When writing recently about *The Crucible* and Senator Joseph McCarthy's reign of terror in the USA in the 1950s, Arthur Miller remarked how he had lost the dead weight of fear he had back in the time of the play's conception. 'Fear doesn't travel well; just as it can warp judgement, its absence can diminish truth. What terrifies one generation is likely to bring a puzzled smile to the next.' And so, thank God, it is with Fiji today; not yet at the puzzled smile stage, but well back from the precipice. Only when concentrating on writing about that time am I able to dredge up the dead weight and remember the sourness of the fear at our backs in Suva in 1987.

Before leaving the Council of Chiefs meeting, Ratu Penaia agreed not to name his council of advisers until the Great Council of Chiefs had made its resolutions. Rabuka announced that he might continue running the government with his Council of Ministers if the Great Council of Chiefs disapproved the governor general's plans. Back at Government House we were acutely aware that decisive action was required.

We put out a statement for the evening news that the governor general was meeting with the chairman of the Great Council of Chiefs, Ratu William Toganivalu, and Lt. Col. Rabuka to discuss the views of the Council. It was announced that Ratu Penaia would address the Council again in the morning. We also put out a radio message in which citizens were warned, 'in the interests of peace', against unlawful assemblies.

Qoriniasi Bale, a former attorney-general, was given the task of writing the governor general's next address to the Council, and he worked through the night to produce the Fijian words of respect and compromise which were necessary to win the Council over to support of the governor general's position.

The following morning the large crowd of Fijians assembled outside the Civic Centre booed as the governor general's car bore him to the Council meeting. In Fijian cultural history this sign of disrespect for one of the highest chiefs of the land was unprecedented. It graphically demonstrated the extent to which the dogs of anarchy had been let loose in our midst.

The Great Council of Chiefs listened to the more accommodating tones of the governor general's address, the main message of which was that while he was confined to act within the confines of the Constitution, he would not 'undermine or adversely affect the best interests of our people, the indigenous Fijians, which have been so aptly described throughout this meeting of the Great Council of Chiefs'.

This time the day was won by the governor general, and when night fell Ratu Sir Kamisese Mara and Rabuka came up to Government House to drink kava with him and hammer out the compromise that the Great Council of Chiefs would agree to in the morning. The three agreed to the dissolution of Rabuka's Council of Ministers, but Ratu Penaia was made to concede that the Great Council of Chiefs would be able to add the names of eight of its nominees to the membership of his council of advisers. In the months ahead the effect of this unfortunate concession was to bear heavily on affairs at Government House.

Vaturekuka Hill

MY ATTACHMENT TO Ratu Sir Penaia Ganilau went back to the time of my infancy in Fiji's most northern town, Labasa. This dusty sugar-milling centre is set on the long leeward coast of Vanua Levu. It is separated from the sea by many kilometres of mangrove swamps and the surrounding sun-scorched hills send waves of heat down onto the narrow coastal plain on which the town is situated. About three kilometres out of Labasa is a hill called Vaturekuka where the government station was built during colonial times. The hill sits marooned in a wide sea of rustling sugar cane, through which the main road approaches Vaturekuka, curves around its base and then runs along the banks of the Qawa River, still navigable at this point below the rambling Indian settlement at Bulileka.

For some reason in the past, the summit of the hill was taken up by the prison, while the bungalows of the divisional commissioner, district officer and other government officials were nestled under flamboyant trees and a teak grove along the flanks of the hill or out on the spurs that ran down from the summit of Vaturekuka hill. The prisoners kept the station's gardens well trimmed and maintained the grass tennis court and the pound for strayed horses and cattle.

From 1929 to 1930 my grandparents, William and Constance Kearsley, with their five daughters and one son, lived on Vaturekuka hill. My mother showed me the house that they were living in when the monster hurricane of 1929 hit Labasa, ripping the corrugated iron roof from their house. The family had run through the storm, whipped by flying foliage, to another bungalow near the prison. My great grandfather Ambler had been an avid stamp collector, and Connie had inherited his prized collection. In the Kearsley's abandoned house the stamp collection had exploded in a philatelic tornado, and in the eerie calm after the hurricane had passed, my mother recalled wandering around Vaturekuka and seeing the Ambler stamp collection plastered over tree trunks and rocks and over the metallic mosquito gauze which had been blasted from the windows of their house.

Lost stamps were the least of their worries in the aftermath of the storm. It was Christmas holidays and the children who had been at boarding school in Suva were returning to Vanua Levu on the CSR motor vessel, the *Rani*. One of the Kearsley girls, fourteen-year-old Dorothy, was on board. The *Rani* had lost radio contact during the hurricane and it was two tortured days before it was established that the ship had run aground on the west coast of Ovalau and all on board were safe.

By the 1940s, when my mother returned to Vaturekuka as the wife of the district officer, not a lot had changed. My mother took the four-day trip by boat down to Suva for my birth. My father was attending to official duties down on the Bua coast on the trading vessel *Adi Rewa* when he heard a radio announcement that I had arrived in the world. There was no electricity and most transportation in the district was by coastal vessel or on horseback.

Before we left Labasa in 1950, my brother John had been born there, my nurse had died of galloping consumption and Tasman Empire Airways Limited had introduced a weekly Solent flying boat service which cut the four-day boat trip to Suva down to a one-and-a-half-hour flight.

By 1976, when I turned up again at Vaturekuka as the district officer, things in Labasa hadn't changed much. Fiji had become an independent nation, and we had electricity and an airport at Labasa with daily flights to Suva. But the town was still hot and dusty, the road from town to Vaturekuka was still unsealed and the prisoners were still weeding away on Vaturekuka hill.

My office in Labasa was a modern one, an ugly cement box squeezed between the market place and the muddy Labasa river. The road in front of it was a pot-holed gravel mess impregnated with discarded corn kernels and mandarin skins. On wet days passing trucks splashed mud onto our veranda; on dry days the dust came through the glass louvres and spread itself evenly over our linoleum floors and plastic furniture.

At my back door was a recking public toilet and next to that was the corner of the market reserved for goat sales. Large bearded goats brought up from Nasarawaqa were tied to my back veranda rail. They fetched high prices in the Labasa market, and while they waited to be sold they filled the air with the acrid aroma of goat's urine. And when leaving the front door you had to be careful not to slip on duck's droppings. The duck lady was positioned there. Wearing silver amulets, gold nose-studs and purple sari, she stood on a bundle of strings to which were attached dozens of black and white muscovy ducks, quacking around and lifting their waggly tails to spurt over our entrance way.

As a diversion I used to smoke *suluka*, which were roll-your-own cigars filled with rough local tobacco wrapped in dried banana or pandanus leaves. We would buy the *suluka* ingredients in the market and smoke them while we drank kava and listened to cane farmers who came to seek settlement of feeder road disputes. We drank kava down at the fire station, with its one fire engine and volunteer brigade. And over at the Grand Eastern Hotel run by old Mrs Gibson, we sat in cane chairs drinking Fiji Bitter and watching the tidal river in its ebb and flow.

At Vaturekuka Hill, parties held to celebrate a special occasion warranted the preparation of Labasa's speciality, goat curry. There were three Indian men who were considered to be the masters of goat curry preparation in Labasa at that time. Of these we preferred to engage the man who worked at the sugar mill, and we had to arrange for his release from work to prepare the curry. First he would select the goat from the collection at the back of my office, a sturdy billy goat was required. The goat would be taken to our residence and slaughtered by pinning its horns into the ground and cutting its up-turned throat. Our curry maestro would collect the blood from the gaping throat in a flat tray.

When the blood had coagulated in the tray, it was cut into cubes and, together with the testicles and selected organs, was set aside for a searingly hot fried curry which men would nibble as a 'chaser' with their beer and whisky in the evening. The head and entrails of the goat were the share of the curry maker who took them home to prepare some special concoction for his family. The rest of the goat was butchered and cooked with turmeric, birds-eye chillies, cumin, cardamom, mustard seed, garlic, ginger, onion, masala and curry leaf into a strong dish which was served to guests in the evening with pilau rice.

The dominant culture of Labasa was Hindu and goat curry was just one of the many advantages which we shared in as a result. There were many Hindu temples around Labasa, and one to the east was built over a rock formation that had emanated from the ground in the form of a giant hooded cobra which was reputed to be growing in size.

One day I was working in my vegetable garden at Vaturekuka when I came across a smooth stone just over a metre long shaped like an elongated egg. On a whim I spent about half an hour rolling it up to the end of our driveway and setting it upright in the ground as an entry feature. The next day an old Indian lady had daubed it with ash and garlanded it with marigolds. It was a *lingam* emerging from the ground and it continued to receive such treatment from Siva's devotees for as long as we lived in that house. I used to sit on my veranda looking across at the decorated *lingam* and try to fathom whether I was a reluctant confidence trickster or indeed a guileless servant of Siva.

On the other side of our driveway was the site of the house that my parents had lived in when I was an infant. During his time at Vaturekuka, my father forged two close friendships which were to last throughout his adult life. One was the divisional commissioner, Archie Reid, a fellow Scot, Cambridge-educated and much respected for his knowledge of Fijian language and custom. The second was my father's fellow district officer, Ratu Penaia Ganilau, the future governor general of Fiji. When Ratu Penaia married Adi Laisa in 1949, my father was his best man and Archie Reid hosted the reception at his residence at Vaturekuka. Throughout my childhood our families spent much time together and Archie Reid and Ratu Penaia were like warm but highly respected uncles to us Thomson boys.

Ratu Penaia had made his mark soon after graduating from school when he was selected to play for the Fiji national rugby team. The team was judged strong enough to tour the high temple of rugby, New Zealand, where it was undefeated. The manager and coach of the team, J.B.K. Taylor, was to become the commanding officer of the 1st Battalion of the Fiji Infantry Regiment when the Pacific War began in 1941. Taylor thought very highly of the young Ganilau whose abilities soon saw him serving as a platoon commander. After the war, as a government officer, Ratu Penaia's innate leadership qualities were recognised and he was sent to Oxford University from 1946 to 1947 for training in development leadership.

And so it was that in 1948 he was posted to Vaturekuka and became my father's fellow district officer, neighbour and friend. They were often away together on extended field trips tending to community matters in the villages of the Northern Division to which they travelled by boat, horse or on foot. Life at Vaturekuka was pretty spartan and neither of them could afford a car, so on Saturdays when there was the weekly market at the Labasa sugar mill, the two of them would take the dusty walk to the mill to buy weekly supplies for their families. I have heard each of them say in reminiscence that the privations of the life at Vaturekuka were amply compensated by the good fellowship shared.

Ratu Penaia was of one of the great chiefly families of Fiji from amongst whose number the Tui Cakau, 'Lord of the Reefs', was selected to rank over all others of northern and eastern Fiji. Towards the end of his life Ratu Penaia became the Tui Cakau, but as a district officer in Labasa in the late 1940s he was making a conscious effort not to take advantage of chiefly status or indeed to be burdened with customary obligations. He had the self-discipline, reinforced by military and academic training, to do so. He was also making a determined effort at this time to understand and be understood by non-Fijians and was for the first time working closely with the Indian community.

From 1953 to 1956 Ratu Penaia was in Malaya as a company commander and then as the commanding officer of the Fiji Battalion, which proved itself second to none in the jungle warfare of the Malayan Emergency. On his return to Fiji, influenced by what he had seen in Malaya, he recognised the inherent threat to the atmosphere of goodwill in Fiji if the indigenous Fijians were not able to keep up with the rest of the country's development. His prime concern had become lifting the economic standards of the Fijian, as he clearly perceived these as falling behind the other races. He was posted to his home province of Cakaudrove where he put his heart and mind into his new preoccupation, winning further recognition from the Fijian people for the exceptional leadership qualities he possessed.

As Fiji's Independence approached, he emerged as one of the four chiefly Fijian leaders who would shepherd Fiji from colonial to independent status, becoming in due course deputy prime minister of the country. This had involved him resigning from the civil service, and becoming a politician and running for elections. To the end he was a reluctant politician, having an aversion to self promotion and reservations about the tyranny of the majority.

He also believed that politics would be divisive to Fiji society, since

Westminster-style political parties pushed their own barrows and were confrontational by nature. Politicians understandably looked after the interests of those that had voted them to power, and in Fiji these interests would usually be racially motivated. He lost to racial voting in the 1972 general election in the Indian-dominated Macuata electorate and the point was clearly made. This defeat left no scars on his heart, and I know that it would please him immensely to know that today in Safdarjang Road, New Delhi, in the Indira Gandhi Memorial Museum, there is a photo of him and Mrs Gandhi shaking hands and smiling warmly at each other.

His cultural roots and leadership experience in times of war and peace, made him an exceptional leader of his own Fijian people, but his instincts and training were to protect the interests of all. He was a man for all the people of Fiji to follow with trust, and it was to their great fortune that in May 1987, at the time of Fiji's most ominous crisis, he was the governor general.

HE KNOWS WHAT TO DO

FOLLOWING THE COUP and his stand against the illegality of what was being perpetrated, the governor general, Ratu Sir Penaia Ganilau, was regarded by the deposed Bavadra government and the international community as Fiji's saviour and hope for the future. Bavadra had been released from detention and he wrote to Ratu Penaia on May 21: 'Let me say once more how much I appreciate and admire your actions in the last week and all you have done to heal our country and to protect Fiji's sacred democratic institutions and the rule of law. I have told the nation of my complete trust in you and my sincere belief that you, as the Chief Executive of our nation in this time, will do what is right to restore peace to Fiji. I have urged the people of Fiji to share that trust.'

The newspapers had resumed publishing on May 21 and they were strongly in support of the governor general's position. At the meeting between Ratu Penaia and Rabuka, seated around the *tanoa* at Government House on the night of May 19, Rabuka agreed to withdraw his soldiers from the newspapers' premises at 8am the following morning. It was also agreed that there would be no further censorship but that I should meet with the general managers of the newspapers on May 20 to 'give them good advice off the record'. I remember the passion of that advice and the message that the governor general's path was the only practical way back to a peaceful, morally acceptable Fiji.

Then two things emerged which were to hobble the governor general's progress along the path he had chosen. The first was the compromise that he had been forced to make with the Great Council of Chiefs over the Council of Advisers. The original make-up of the Council of Advisers was a racially and politically balanced group that co-opted a couple of leaders from the deposed government and opposition including prime minister Bavadra, deputy prime minister Sharma and former prime minister Ratu Mara. In creating the roll call for the council, we were diligent to ensure that it would reflect the integrity of the governor general's position. Most of the council membership was recognised talent from outside Parliament, such as the governor of the Reserve Bank, Savenaca Siwatibau, and the chairman of the Fiji Trade and Investment Board, Mumtaz Ali. Lt. Col. Rabuka was also part of the original make-up of the council.

When, as conceded, the Great Council of Chiefs' nominees were added to the council, not only was it heavily overloaded with Fijian membership, but it yawed in favour of the radical activists of the Taukei movement. Ratu Penaia could see the public relations disaster that this represented. He had been dealt a rough hand, but he was not to be put off his course. In his radio address to the nation on the evening of May 22 he said: 'I know that not all of these appointments will meet with the approval of every member of our nation, but I am confident that in the short period of their service ahead, they will give their best to our nation.' He emphasised that all the members of the Council of Advisers would come under his command in the performance of their duties.

The Fiji media was on side and called upon everyone to support the governor general's efforts. They emphasised that Ratu Penaia had stood firm as the representative of the Crown and the defender of the Constitution throughout the crisis and the Great Council of Chiefs and the RFMF had recognised his authority. But the distortion of the Council of Advisers' membership was a huge and bitter pill for the ousted government to swallow. For Dr Bavadra and Harish Sharma, who had initially advised Ratu Penaia of their willingness to serve on the council, it was just too hard to accept and, while the invitation remained open for the life of the council, they were never to take up their membership.

The second hobbler was the arrival of legal challenges: first on Rabuka and then on the governor general. The first was a *habeus corpus* writ served on Rabuka to secure the release of Bavadra and his colleagues. The timing of this writ was unfortunate. The decision to release the parliamentarians had already been made when the governor general had asserted his authority and Rabuka had drunk kava with him at Government House on the evening of May 19.

I remember the depth of satisfaction which was evident in Rabuka's demeanour when he left Government House that evening, confident in the leadership which Ratu Penaia would provide. But this mood was shattered when, up at Queen Elizabeth Barracks, he was served with the writ and suddenly feared for his vulnerability before the law.

In order to return Rabuka and the army to submission to the governor general's authority we needed to act fast. Rabuka returned to Government House later that night in an agitated state. He was phoning Taukei movement members to get their advice on his next move. We assured him that amnesty would be granted to him and his men. The director of public prosecutions subsequently signed an order granting immunity of prosecution to Rabuka and 'all other persons who may have been in any way implicated in the unlawful seizure of the power of State' and the governor general proclaimed a grant of amnesty in the *Fiji Royal Gazette*. The alternatives to this course of action had been assessed and they were bleak.

The second legal challenge was mounted by the deposed government, disputing the legality of the governor general's dissolution of Parliament which it was argued could only be constitutionally done upon receiving the advice of the prime minister. This was all very well, but the governor general was the one who had put his hand into the fire and doused the flames when Fiji was on the brink, and Bavadra had said when he was released from military captivity, 'We must all stand united behind the governor general. He knows what to do.'

The writ against the governor general's actions was to be heard in the Supreme Court and if successful would have taken the country back to the chasm opened by the coup d'état. The governor general could not ignore the challenge, for it was he that was upholding the laws of Fiji. The situation demanded that he respond to the challenge in the Supreme Court. He hired George Newman, an English QC, to defend his position and went through all the necessary legal preparations.

Owing to later developments, the case was never heard in court, but for several months it hung around Government House like a dead fish. The deposed government had brought the case as a legal defence of their position as the elected government of the country, but it was in reality more of a bargaining chip for them. It was not a victory which they wanted to win in court. What was the point? Everyone knew they were legally elected and if the governor general was ruled to have acted illegally, where would this leave them and the nation? They were surprised when, later in the fray, they went for an adjournment only to discover Government House's stance was that the case should be heard as scheduled or be struck off.

Unfortunately the case provided fuel for the Taukei movement to play on the Fijian fears of litigious revenge from the Indian leaders and it mounted a hurdle of distrust between Bavadra's deposed government and the governor general. Many Fijian opinion-leaders erroneously held out the case as a sign from Bavadra and his political colleagues of their lack of respect for Ratu Penaia and all he had stood for. For his part Ratu Penaia had been at pains to avoid any loss of trust or communication between himself, the deposed government and the Indian community that it represented. He worked at bringing down this barrier throughout the rest of his term as governor general.

On the night of May 27, I was driven around the island to Viseisei village where I was to have a meeting with Dr Bavadra. He had taken up residence back in his modest home within the village. I arrived at the village at 7pm and found him to be quite understandably upset at the indignities that had been heaped upon him over the last two weeks. I sat in silence while he railed away. Having spent most of my time since the coup up at Government House, it astounded me to hear the level of suspicion that Dr Bavadra expressed in relation to the governor general's motives, and how he was becoming convinced that Ratu Penaia was acting in cahoots with Rabuka. I did my best to dissuade him of this opinion and he appeared cautiously satisfied with my account. At least I sensed his wish to believe what I was saying.

I had been sent to persuade him to join the Council of Advisers, in spite of the changes that had occurred to its composition. My main argument was that the governor general was the sole executive authority and, regardless of the council's weighting, he would make the rulings. This can hardly have been music to the ears of a recently deposed prime minister. I pressed on with the point that what was important to the governor general was the voice of Dr Bavadra's political supporters being represented and heard at the council meetings.

This set him off again and he made it vociferously clear that he and his political colleagues had grave doubts about the legality of the governor general's proclamations since the coup. How could the governor general dissolve Parliament and declare vacant the offices of the prime minister and his cabinet without the advice of the prime minister himself? I could take it from him that they weren't going to compromise this position by joining the governor general's illegal Council of Advisers.

His combative spirit was certainly alive and well. For good measure I received some further ear bashing on the subject of the perfidy of Eastern Fijians. Then he calmed down a bit and kava was brought for us to drink.

His sons and wife were present, together with a few villagers, some of whom I knew personally. While many found Dr Bavadra politically naive, he was undoubtedly a very likeable man, intelligent, over-flowing with humanity and had the common touch. He also had a gorgeous chuckle and spoke with a slight speech impediment. When he was prime minister I had had to write a speech for him and he had asked that I not use the letter 's' too often because of his sigmatic lisp.

Dr Bavadra's storm had now abated and we sat cross-legged on the floor of his house, drinking kava and conversing quietly in the tranquil lull. Then the time came for me to step back into the night and return to Suva. But as I was driven past the avenue of mango trees that bordered the village and turned towards Nadi, I was aware that my night's mission had been a failure and the storm was far from over.

On the advice of his colleagues Bavadra was to take his struggle for restoration overseas, putting himself out of contact with the governor general's efforts to begin the process of national reconciliation.

Meanwhile up at Government House we got down to the business of national administration, our priorities being the safeguarding of a tattered national economy, maintaining the peace, explaining our situation to the world, and achieving a solution to Fiji's constitutional crisis.

Suva Rain

In Suva you have to learn to love the rain. The southeast trades bring endless flotillas of cumulus clouds in from the humid Pacific. Like towering battleships they float in over the reefs, across the harbour and bank up on the mountain ranges behind the capital. When enough of them are assembled to commence action the first lightning bolt is fired, followed immediately by a sharp crack and crash of thunder, and then down comes the rain. '*Sa tau mai na uca!*'

And when it really rains it's like living under a waterfall. Parks become lakes, drains become rivers. While birds seek refuge and sit with hunched shoulders and glum looks, toads emerge from holes and leap about in the puddles in their thousands. Women hitch up their skirts, take off their shoes and squeeze together under shared umbrellas. They shriek with laughter, dodging the bow-wave splashes of cars with fogged-up windows cruising the flooded streets. Wet cotton clothes cling seductively to bodies. From under shop verandas and porticoes, faces with far-away looks stare out through the sheets of water cascading off roofs and are mesmerised by the magnitude of it all.

For those indoors the heartbeat slows during these downpours. Conversation subsides and work gives way to reflection, for the rumbling thunder and the power of the rain belittles all else. In these private moments there is a sense of comfort and security, evoked perhaps by childhood memories of lying in bed while the sheltering tin roof roared overhead. Cuddled in a dry cocoon under the drenching night sky you would lie there praying that the rain would never stop. And after the rain, how desultory the intermittent splats of water dripping onto the sand-papery leaves under the breadfruit trees.

When we were young we used to wait with mounting excitement when an afternoon downpour was on its way. As soon as the first drops began falling someone would shout 'rain bath!' and out into the rain we'd go, bony-bodied boys in khaki shorts gathering a pack of neighbourhood brats as we ran. There was a long steep slope near our house in the Domain and at the top of it were royal palms from which we pulled fronds. The stocks of the fronds were leathery and boat-like and one or two boys could fit into these vessels for a slide down the slope at an impressive rate.

Drain-sliding was another rain bath activity. From the top of the Domain, concrete inverted drains ran for about one-and-a-half kilometres down to Nasese. The inverts were just wide enough for a boy's rump and they lay in the bottom of soapstone ditches as deep and broad as the height of a man. The concrete was lined with a slippery green algae which minimised friction and lengthened the life of khaki shorts. During a standard downpour there was enough water to sluice us along at speed and culvert pipes could be shot through with little risk. In a big storm the ditches turned into raging torrents and the skill lay in leaping out of them before you got sucked into a flooded culvert.

The drains in the Domain empty into Nasese Creek, which flows through the mangroves out to Turners Bridge on the foreshore of Suva Harbour. Residential reclamation has since greatly diminished the scale of Nasese Creek and its surrounding mangrove forest, but in our drain-sliding days it was as full of mystery and adventure as the Amazon itself. So when we reached the point where drain tributaries met the creek we hopped out and retreated, padding back up alongside the banks of the flooded drains through the warm rain and the *teitei*, where wet banana leaves would pat our skin as we passed.

Voyaging down Nasese Creek was a dry weather pursuit. These ventures were undertaken around high tide in tin boats. To make our tin boats we would first have to raid a Public Works Department building site to liberate some half-sheets of old corrugated iron. The iron was placed on concrete and we'd belt it with a hammer to take some of the corrugation out of it and to fold over its sharp edges. The bow and stern were then created by bending the iron around a short wooden plank and nailing it in place. Melted tar was scooped off the road where the heat of the tropical sun had made it blister and run, and the tar was applied to nail holes in the tin and to any gaps in the joinery of the bow or stern. If any leaks occurred after launching, heavy black mangrove mud was used to plug up the problem area.

Our little flotilla of tin boats was usually launched under the trees at the foot of the Falvey's hill at the headwaters of Nasese Creek. The boats were powered by paddles or the palms of our hands. The edge of civilisation was Nasese Bridge next to Draiba School and thereafter, until we reached Turners Bridge on the seashore, as we paddled through those dripping mangroves we were in our minds venturing through a forbidden unmapped quarter. The mangroves were full of echoing sounds, clicking crab claws, ominous plops and the slithering splashes of fish that ran across the top of the water and clambered up the lower branches of the mangroves to stare at our passage with bulbous blinking eyes.

Snake-eyed *belo*, the grey mangrove heron, would fly off at our approach, and there was a theory about him bringing good luck, depending on whether he crossed your bows from left to right or vice versa. *Kikau*, the wattled honeyeater, shrieked his derision, and the red, blue and green *kula* flashed overhead, the sound of their shrill chattering receding rapidly as they flew over the treetops at reckless speed.

Diversions up small tributaries would lead to the back of a squatter's house, where mangy mongrels yapped and howled until we withdrew. Another tributary led to a taro garden, where the sound of a chopping cane-knife was heard. Through the undergrowth a broad heavily-muscled Fijian back could be seen and the flash of a wide knife going up and down. Its owner straightened up from his weeding and smiled broadly at us. I see his face looking down at me in the creek, calling out '*Bula* Captain Bligh'.

Eventually Turners Bridge would appear around the bend, with the sea beyond it. As we paddled under the bridge curious onlookers bent over its railings to take in all the details of our little fleet. And in the sea we would engage in naval manoeuvres or races close to the seawall, returning calls and waves from the people in the open-windowed buses driving along the waterfront.

Near one of the sources of Nasese Creek, at the Allardyce Road end of the Domain, is the big old wooden house that our family lived in from 1950 to 1954. After the Thomsons vacated it, the house became the home of Ratu Penaia and Adi Laisa, and the Ganilau children were brought up there when their parents returned from the Malayan Emergency.

My earliest memory comes from this house. I was only three-and-a-bit years old and I'm told you aren't able to remember that far back, but I have a picture in my mind's eye that is like a faded Polaroid. There was never a photo taken of that scene from which I might have derived my picture, so I have only my three-year-old eyes to attribute it to. It was January 1952 and a monster hurricane had cut a swathe over Suva. At Laucala Bay a gust of 212 kilometres an hour was recorded just prior to the moment the anemometer was blown down. Leading up to our house was a steep gravel drive about 100 metres long lined on one side by a row of tall eucalyptus trees, and in the hurricane most of these trees came down and many ended up lying across the road. My mother's parents were staying with us that year, and my father and Grandpa Kearsley took to the trees with axes to clear the road. In the ensuing weeks the two men spent a good deal of time chopping up these trees, because eucalyptus made good fuel for the wood-burning stove which was the main means of cooking in our kitchen. At some stage during all this chopping, I stood at the top of the drive and imprinted the earliest lasting memory in my brain, that of these two men lifting their axes and chopping down into the creamy trunks of the eucalyptus amongst all those leaves and branches.

One of my younger brother John's earliest memories is also of the forces of nature. In 1953 an earthquake, centred just beyond the entrance to Suva Harbour, caused a tsunami to crash through the harbour and flood the low-lying city streets. Our mother was driving the station wagon past Albert Park towards our Domain home with the harbour directly behind her. Wee John was the only passenger. As the car started up the foot of Cakobau Hill she was trying to calm John down with some soothing chat, unaware of the reason for John's alarm. He was trying to make her aware of the giant wave that had smashed over the seawall and was following them up the road.

At dusk or dawn, I'm not sure which, I used to lie in my bed at that house and peer sleepily through our bedroom window into the canopy of a huge rain tree, picking out imagined shapes of animals and such in the patches of pale sky that were silhouetted by the darkened branches and leaves. Every now and then, throughout my life, in moments between waking and sleep, I see that view into the tree and the little sky-shapes.

I most clearly remember the kitchen of the Domain house It bustled with jovial activity. There would be bundles of root crops on the floor, and big red fish lying on boards and being scaled with a metal spoon; the black wood-stove with its little cavern of orange flames would be covered with steaming pots; and I would sit amongst tottering piles of emerald *rourou* leaves at the sour-smelling wooden table, where you could stay as long as you liked, as long as you were good. '*Raici Pita, sa gone vinaka.*' 'Look at Peter, what a good boy.' The kitchen screen-door was on a creaking spring hinge and it let out onto a wooden landing which hung out over the ground floor. From the landing, a rickety flight of steps led down the side of the house to the driveway. By the door, inside the kitchen, was an iron bird-cage as tall as a man. I vaguely recall the red, green and blue Kadavu parrot that lived and died in it, but its next occupant made a big impression.

Uncle Peter was driving near Navua one night and came upon a *lulu* sitting in the middle of the road. The *lulu*, a white barn owl, was dazzled by his headlamps and just sat there blinking. So he captured it and brought it to the house of his nephews to take the place of the recently deceased parrot. I sat at the kitchen table staring at the round impassive face of the *lulu*, hoping in vain that I would catch it opening its eyes. I'm not sure how long it was with us, but it didn't take to captivity and the decision was made to release it. The cage was manoeuvred through the kitchen door out onto the landing, into the bright daylight, and someone managed to extricate the sleepy owl from the cage. And then the moment that I can pull right out of the river of time, as if I were experiencing it again and again, observed from between the legs of the adults who released the bird. The white owl takes flight in one long swooping glide across the wide space of green lawn, heading for the row of dark trees beyond. And as it does so, all the Domain's diurnal birds, the *kikau*, the mynahs, kingfishers and bulbuls, set up a raucous chorus of alarm.

COLD COMFORT KAVA

IN THE VERANDA-shaded offices of Government House, where he was coping with day-by-day crisis conditions on the domestic front in the aftermath of the coup, foreign relations were a secondary priority for the governor general. His primary challenge was to produce a Fiji solution to a Fiji problem, for he was fully aware that the day had passed when the Fijian element of the population would be prepared to accept a foreign solution. His international accountability was safeguarded in his own thinking by his need to satisfy the Queen, the head of state of Fiji and the head of the Commonwealth, as to his ultimate solution of the crisis.

In terms of the Commonwealth, the position of India was of course critical. The Indian high commissioner, in his first post-coup call on the governor general, made it clear that the government of India remained alive to the interests and welfare of people of Indian origin overseas regardless of their nationality. The high commissioner reinforced this point by later giving me an Indian government white paper entitled 'Indians Overseas'.

But short of sending the powerful Indian fleet to the South Pacific, what could the Indian government do to exert its influence? The main thrust of their response was to the Commonwealth and to the British government to whom they emphasised that Fiji's 1970 Constitution had been painstakingly negotiated 'between political parties representing Fijians and Indians in Fiji and the British government' and should thus not be altered. Their expectation that the United Kingdom would intervene in some way was understandable in a British-Indian-Fijian historical context, but was sadly misplaced in 1987, as the British government had long since jettisoned any real involvement in South Pacific affairs.

India's position was critical, however, in the involuntary 'lapsing' of Fiji's Commonwealth membership at the Commonwealth Heads of Government meeting in Vancouver in October 1987. The loss of Commonwealth status was of no real consequence to Fiji in an economic or strategic sense, but there was a general feeling in Fiji that family ties had been cut. Around the kava bowls, popular belief had it that, like the prodigal son, Fiji would one day return to the Commonwealth fold.

Buckingham Palace was satisfied that the governor general was loyally serving the Queen of Fiji, indeed the Queen was later to express 'her admiration for his courageous efforts to avert changes to the form of government in Fiji by force.' It is therefore not surprising that when Natwar-Singh, the Indian minister of state for external affairs, visited London as Prime Minister Rajiv Gandhi's special emissary to discuss the situation in Fiji, the British government told him they were giving the governor general 'every support in his efforts to resolve the crisis'.

But British support for the governor general's efforts was lip service only. In reality the British government had washed its hands of the consequences of its colonial policies in Fiji, and a sympathetic ear was the extent of its contribution to the resolution of the crisis. For us at Government House the penny dropped fairly early on in the light of the response we got to our request for British assistance in filling the critical position of Fiji's commissioner of police.

In the last week of May we had resolved that the appointment of an expatriate commissioner of police was urgently required and a formal request was put to the British government to provide an appropriate officer. The Royal Fiji Military Forces were overwhelmingly Fijian in racial composition and were clearly dedicated to Rabuka's cause. However, the Royal Fiji Police Force was racially well-balanced and given non-political leadership could be crucial to an upholding of the governor general's will.

On the day of the coup, Rabuka had sacked P.U. Raman, the commissioner of police, along with the deputy commissioner, and had appointed the assistant commissioner, Joe Lewaicei, as the new commissioner. Lewaicei was a good man but, given the nature of his appointment, was in an invidious position.

Since Fiji's Independence there had been several commissioners of police who were on secondment from the ranks of Britain's police force and their professionalism had been of good service to the integrity of the Royal Fiji Police Force. The initial response from London to our request was favourable, and some work was done in Britain by John Kelland, a former Fiji commissioner of police, in identifying the right person for the job. London's main concern was that the commissioner would report directly to the governor general, and we gave them explicit assurances that this would be so.

Then the British government started dithering. I suspected the reasons for this were that they were worried about offending India, that they did not want to assume a significant role in the Fiji crisis and, mostly, the consequences of a failure of the commissioner's mission were unpalatable to them. By July it was clear they were backing away from providing us with a commissioner, and by then the damage was already being well and truly done. This lack of nerve in the British government was a bitter pill to swallow and Ratu Sir Penaia often remarked on it ruefully to me as we endeavoured to control the overzealous actions of the militant Fijian elements of the Royal Fiji Police Force.

Since the glory days of the Pacific War when the Americans swept all-powerful through the South Pacific, their contribution to the welfare of the Pacific Islands had been desultory. In Washington's eyes their ANZUS surrogates in Canberra and Wellington were responsible for security of the region, an arrangement that had worked reasonably well until 1987. Washington's main concern after the coup was to deny the charges of the politically paranoid that it had given Rabuka its backing in the execution of the coup. I was pretty close to the action and I am satisfied that Rabuka's plans and their execution were his own and to the extent that he got direct encouragement it was domestic and from Fijian political activists.

The US Embassy in Suva released two brief statements: one on May 15 saying their government was profoundly disturbed whenever a democratically elected government was removed by force and saying that their ambassador had affirmed to Rabuka the importance of respect for democratic traditions and processes. They added to this brief statement the qualifier 'we are gratified there has been no bloodshed'. Some took the latter as a veiled indication of approval, but I have no reason to believe it was intended as other than a positive humanitarian statement for the good of Fiji.

The embassy's second statement was released on May 20. It said that they considered it a positive step that persons held in detention had been released and that it hoped the people of Fiji would heed the governor general's call for calm. It said the US government welcomed the actions of the governor general 'who represents the constitutional authority in Fiji, to find a solution to the current crisis in keeping with Fiji's tradition of democratic constitutional government. We hope all parties will co-operate with the governor general in finding a peaceful solution.'

The Fiji crisis came at a time when rumours of Libyan destabilisation games in the South Pacific had been rife and the US State Department was digesting the implications of the election of a left-wing, Indian-dominated, trade union-backed, coalition government in Fiji. In spite of its championing of democracy in Asia, New Delhi's role in the Cold War had as a rule been far too cosy with Moscow for Washington's liking, and now suppositions would be made about the linkages between New Delhi and Fiji. Regardless of their scruples on the overthrow of democratically elected governments, one can surmise that Washington was far from devastated by the news from Fiji.

This was not so in Canberra and Wellington, where the Fiji crisis was the dominant foreign news item from May to October 1987, until it was supplanted by the crash of the New York Stock Exchange. The level of dismay which the Fiji crisis brought to these two governments was caused by a number of factors, not the least being that in both Canberra and Wellington there sat Labour governments at the height of domestic power and confidence. They had recently welcomed to the Australasian political scene the new government in Fiji, which for the first time in the political history of the South Pacific Islands saw a Labour party in power. As an ironical aside, at the time of the coup leading representatives of the Australasian centre-right political parties (Australia's Liberals, New Zealand's Nationals and Fiji's Alliance, at that time all in opposition) were gathered at a Pacific Democratic Union meeting at the Fijian hotel on Viti Levu's southwest coast.

At the forefront of the distress of the Australian and New Zealand governments was the overthrow by military force of a democratically elected government in Fiji. This struck at the heart of their own long adherence to the principles of parliamentary democracy and their former comfort in having Fiji as a firm regional partner in this tradition.

In addition the new Fijian argument of the primacy of indigenous rights over the democratic rights of non-indigenes was anathema to the governments of Australia and New Zealand, particularly at a time when a resurgence of indigenous rights activism was underway in both these countries. The prime ministers of Australia and New Zealand, Bob Hawke and David Lange, protested long and hard, but in the end had little effect on the situation in Fiji other than to harden Fijian attitudes. While they might think differently today, it is fair to say that amongst the Fijian establishment at the time, the prevailing view of the Hawke-Lange side-show was that it was bluster and buffoonery.

For Ratu Mara, the architect of Fiji's multiracial entry to the community of nations in 1970 and the trusted leader of regionalism in the South Pacific for seventeen years or more, it was more personal. He felt that he had been insulted by his former colleagues, Hawke and Lange, by their berating him in public without first contacting him to hear his side of the story. Lange went so far as to accuse Ratu Mara of 'treachery'. This injected a rather bitter personal note into his role as adviser on foreign affairs when dealing with the Australians and New Zealanders. He contrasted this with the understanding shown by the leaders of the Pacific Island countries and those of East Asia.

When asked by a journalist on May 27 what his priorities were as adviser on foreign affairs, Ratu Mara answered, 'to get in touch with as many countries as possible, particularly the people of the eastern side of the Pacific, from Japan, China, South Korea, Malaysia, which have been very supportive to us, and see whether they will be able to substitute the goods that will not be coming from Australia and New Zealand. That is our first priority.' This was a natural reaction, especially since the trade unions of Australia and New Zealand, at the request of Fiji's ousted government, had imposed bans on exports to Fiji.

The attempt to forge closer economic links with Asia was nothing new, it had been government policy for at least a decade and was in tune with similar efforts by most of the South Pacific countries. However, the idea that this should be done as a rebuke to Australia and New Zealand was something new. The governor general's preferred line of approach, as he outlined in his letter to Buckingham Palace on May 27, was to put pressure on the Australian and New Zealand governments to retract their advice to their citizens not to travel to Fiji and to get the trade union bans on shipments to Fiji lifted. His endeavours in this regard soon met with success.

Meanwhile the Asian trade rationale was extended by people with various motives into something of a political doctrine, and its lack of economic success has not dented its political attractiveness. In April 1994 an article in the *New Zealand Herald*, supposedly written by Prime Minister Rabuka stated:

> ... the chances of us developing a relationship on more equal terms with Asian countries are better than with Australia and New Zealand. I say that because of the cultural similarities between the Pacific Island nations and the Asian countries. The major similarity is that the Asian countries are run by the indigenous people of those nations and we in the Pacific run our little indigenous governments in our own little island countries. We see each other as being in similar situations.

Now I have worked as a Fiji diplomat in Tokyo and in Sydney and I have worked as a businessman in Auckland, Singapore and Hong Kong, and I can say with equanimity that it is baloney that the Asian giants will ever treat the Pacific Island minnows on equal terms. There is some truth in the cultural similarity statement, but only in its application to South East Asia, and this statement is decreasingly true with the steady growth in New Zealand's Polynesian population. In terms of the indigenous political similarities, I doubt that Tibetans, Timorese, West Irians or, for that matter, the indigenes of Bougainville would agree. The fact is that the South Pacific is an isolated geographic region within which, thanks in part to the large gaps of water between them, the community of nations had got along pretty well up to 1987. The apple cart was upset then, and has been since with the Bougainville crisis and the French nuclear tests, but on the whole, even allowing for the endemic Australian ability to thoroughly peeve its neighbours from time to time, there is no reason to suppose any dramatic shift in the way countries get along in the South Pacific.

Be that as it may, there is no doubt that 1987 was the lowest ebb in Fiji's relations with Australia and New Zealand. The respected role that these two nations had as givers of good advice and assistance would never be quite the same after the South Pacific Forum Heads of Government meeting in Samoa at the end of May 1987. Lange and Hawke had approached this meeting with declaratory statements on Fiji and were primed for a regional interventionist solution to the Fiji problem. On May 25 Krishna Datt, the Foreign Minister of the ousted coalition government, had had a positive meeting with Lange in Wellington and had asked that New Zealand take part in an 'independent regional peace-keeping force' to be despatched immediately to Fiji. Krishna Datt also asked the New Zealand government and trade unions to impose economic sanctions on Fiji until its constitutional government was restored. He told reporters later that day that his ousted government 'anticipated some violence' in Fiji.

The request for a regional interventionist force was a shift in call from the overthrown government, which had initially asked for direct military intervention by either Australia or New Zealand to restore them to power. This had led to a state of siege mentality in Fiji, and for a few days it seemed in Suva that New Zealand military intervention was imminent. I had the task of writing a letter to the New Zealand high commissioner on May 23 giving the government of Fiji's instructions that HMNZS *Wellington* should 'leave the port of Suva at first light and proceed directly out of Fiji waters'. As a further indication of mistrust, the letter also declined the high commissioner's request that some New Zealand naval ratings be retained to provide protection for the high commissioner's residence in Suva.

At the South Pacific Forum the message was loud and clear. The Australian and New Zealand prime ministers took a cold shower, while the Pacific Island leaders were sympathetic with Fiji's troubles and were adamant that it was for Fiji to call the shots. They sent a message to the governor general asking him if there was anything the forum could do 'to help in sorting out the difficult problems Fiji was grappling with'. I drafted the governor general's response, which said that the most useful assistance the forum could give Fiji at that time would be to use what influence it had to get trade, tourism and aid bans against Fiji lifted. 'These bans will cause long term hardships in Fiji and will make my job of quickly restoring parliamentary democracy in Fiji all the more difficult.' As a face-saver for Lange and Hawke, the Forum suggested the despatch to Fiji of an eminent persons mission headed by Hawke, but this was politely declined by the governor general.

Contrary to his declaration of support for the governor general's efforts on May 21, Dr Bavadra and his colleagues in the deposed government moved to a position of non-cooperation and distrust which dominated their thinking and actions in the month of June. This shift was exasperating for the governor general as it was going to make his task of reconciliation all the harder, and he was personally saddened by their lack of trust in the integrity of his purpose. I was at his side for much of this period and an inspection of our written minutes to each other will verify that between the two coups of 1987 he never wavered from his duty to look after the best interests of all the people of Fiji.

My assessment of the uncooperative stance the representatives of the deposed coalition government initially took, is they believed that as the legitimately elected government they could be restored to power if international assistance was obtained. They needed time to test whether such assistance was available. The governor general had dissolved Parliament, so to support him was to deny themselves the opportunity of external intervention for their cause. The governor general had been forced to agree with the Great Council of Chiefs that the 1970 Constitution would be reviewed to see how indigenous rights could be strengthened and this presented another major problem for the coalition in spite of Ratu Penaia's publicly broadcast assurance that 'no changes will be made to the Constitution in an unlawful manner'. They also adopted a strong attitude of distrust after the governor general's acceptance of the Great Council of Chief's demand that the Council of Advisers take on their eight nominees, thus heavily slewing the political and racial balance of the Council of Advisers. The governor general offered to provide the coalition with another two seats in addition to the two already allocated to Dr Bavadra and former deputy prime minister, Harish Sharma, but this offer was not accepted.

The deposed government's stance probably led to the ambivalence of the New Zealand and Australian governments towards the governor general's efforts in the critical months immediately after the coup. It distressed me that at the very time when forces of goodwill for Fiji should have been giving him every support, Ratu Penaia was being hamstrung in this way. There were many from the ranks of the Fiji Indian community, and from Australia and New Zealand, who contacted him to give him encouragement. There were also many of the opportunistic jackals of this world who came offering support for their own nefarious reasons. Happily for Fiji, Ratu Penaia was a man of sufficient judgement and principle to distinguish good from bad, and he was prepared to take on the burden of responsibility with or without the support of those whose welfare he had protected in their hour of need.

By early June a strategic plan entitled 'The Governor General's Path to Return Fiji to Parliamentary Democracy' had been set upon. Ratu Penaia's speech explaining this path was broadcast over radio on June 11 and the following day it was received by the daily newspapers with high praise. In order to gain international understanding and support for the governor general's position, it fell to me to put together an 'overseas emissaries programme'. The emissaries were provided with a detailed brief on the important steps that Ratu Penaia had taken since the coup and a full picture of what was to be achieved in the 'Governor General's Path.' Emissaries were selected on the basis of their special ability to get the message across; for example, a former deputy prime minister, Mosese Qionibaravi, undertook the New Zealand assignment, for in their university days Mosese and David Lange had shared student accommodation in Auckland.

There were some interesting responses from the emissaries programme. Joe Clark, Canada's minister of foreign affairs, said he was very pleased to have been briefed directly by Fiji, as the Australian reports he had been receiving had been so negative. Sonny Ramphal, the Commonwealth secretary general, sent a strong message of support and said that he had advised Bavadra in no uncertain terms to work with the governor general in restoring parliamentary democracy. But strongest of all were the Pacific Island governments who made it crystal clear that Ratu Penaia had their full support and some of them added that they saw nothing wrong with the Fijian's call for greater indigenous rights.

In the first week of June, Dr Bavadra, accompanied by the former attorney-general, Jai Ram Reddy, and two other deposed ministers, set off to London to see the Queen. Buckingham Palace was informed of this visit by a telegram sent by the 'secretary to Bavadra delegation' from Haberfield, New South Wales. There was no return address to reply to so the Queen's private secretary, Sir William Heseltine, could not get hold of Dr Bavadra prior to his hurried departure from the Antipodes to advise him that it would not be possible for him to meet Her Majesty during his London visit.

On June 8 at Brent Hall in London, Dr Bavadra addressed a large gathering of supporters and called for the Queen to instruct the governor general 'to declare the illegality and unconstitutionality of the military coup d'état, so that the duly elected representatives of the Fijian people can resume their rightful role. This action is bound to succeed since the allegiance and loyalty of citizens of Fiji to Her Majesty the Queen is unquestioned.' The naivety was breathtaking. There was ample evidence in Fiji at that time that such a course would have resulted in either military dictatorship or fearful racial violence. In the same address Dr Bavadra said it is quite clear from the governor general's latest speech that 'no real attempt is being made to achieve national reconciliation'. This statement was particularly galling for the governor general since it blithely ignored the fact that such reconciliation was made doubly difficult by the fact that the leaders of the ousted government were incommunicado on the other side of the world.

Dr Bavadra met with Sonny Ramphal and Heseltine, both of whom advised him to go directly back to Fiji and support the governor general in his efforts to find a solution. Heseltine put it in writing to Bavadra that 'Her Majesty feels that in lending her support to the governor general in the actions which he has taken so far, not only is she following the only course open to her, but also taking the course which is best calculated to serve the long term interests of Fiji and all its people.'

From London Dr Bavadra went to Washington, where we contacted him with a request that he return to Fiji as quickly as possible to assist in matters of national reconciliation. We particularly needed his list of names for the Constitutional Review Committee. Dr Bavadra replied on June 17 that he had 'a string of most important appointments' with people in Washington and it would be 'churlish and impolite' of him to cancel these. He asked for and was given assurances on his safety and freedom of movement and speech on his return to Fiji. One of his senior aides told me they were deeply concerned that the army would 'do an Aquino on him' when he disembarked from his plane at Nadi.

Jai Ram Reddy had returned to Fiji via New Delhi, where he had met with prime minister Gandhi and briefed him on the situation in Fiji and the results of their trip to London. Gandhi had expressed the usual concern at the overthrow of constitutional governments and emphasised India's concern at efforts to change significant portions of the 1970 Constitution.

Meanwhile in Washington Dr Bavadra unwisely allowed James Anthony, a former Fiji trade union activist then living in the USA, to take a prominent role in his itinerary. At a press conference in Washington, those present said that Anthony high-jacked the conference from a rather embarrassed Dr Bavadra. Among points made by Bavadra and Anthony at the conference were a call for a US congressional investigation into possible American involvement in the coup; that arms dealer Adnan Kashoggi had allegedly financed the coup; that William Paupe of the US Embassy in Suva, the so-called 'barefoot Ollie North', was the link man between the CIA and the coup; and, most bizarrely, that six of the masked soldiers who raided the Fiji Parliament with Rabuka at the time of the coup were Americans and two were South African mercenaries.

Bavadra was not only seriously damaging his reputation in the USA, the word was getting around internationally. He had planned to see Hawke in Australia, but the latter found an excuse not to see him. And a cartoon in the *New Zealand Herald* of June 24 summed up the mood of his former friends there. A disconsolate Dr Bavadra is pictured sitting on suitcases with travel tags labelled London, USA and NZ. In the background, New Zealanders in grass skirts are shown pouring a bucket of 'cold water' into a large *tanoa* where it is being mixed with the contents of a sack of 'dust and ashes'. In parody of a kava ceremony, a po-faced David Lange, also dressed in a grass skirt, is offering Dr Bavadra this mixture in a coconut shell. The cartoon is titled 'Cold Comfort Kava'.

IN PRAISE OF KAVA

I'VE NEVER READ a particularly positive description of our national drink, kava, or *yaqona* as we call it in Fiji, and it is time to set that right. Kava in our islands is the *wai ni vanua*, the beverage that comes from the very land under our feet. The Scots have malt whisky, their 'water of life', and the French drink their 'vin du pays'. Think of the soaring profusion of effusive remarks that have tumbled forth on the subject of those alcoholic beverages. But were they not responsible for the drugging of the human mind would they inspire the same devotion? Yes, it is true the same can be asked of kava's devoted throngs, but in the restrained nature of their response you would identify one of the finer points of kava's qualities, especially when compared with the raucous riposte of alcohol's legions.

But don't mistake my intentions; I write not to undermine the place of these alcoholic beverages, merely to put kava in its rightful seat alongside them. Alcohol has been lauded from the heights of Omar Khayyam to the depths of Bukowski, opium through Maugham and Shelley, and Mark Twain champions tobacco, rightly saying that a taste for it is 'a matter of superstition'. It is time that kava's truth was out.

I present myself in kava's tribute as one who has known it in most of its guises. I was once a kava farmer, planting it on the upper slopes of Taveuni and selling it in the markets of Viti Levu. I drank an average of some ten bowls of kava per working day in my sixteen years in the Fiji civil service. I drank it in hill villages, *sosoko* from deep coconut *bilo*; I drank it watered-down from enamelled tin *pyala* in the rear of Gugerati shops; I accepted and presented it as ceremonial *sevusevu* countless times; I dispensed it to curious Japanese at Fiji trade missions in Tokyo; I drank it dried and I drank it green, I did everything with it but inject it into my veins.

Kava is in my blood, and after a lifetime of usage I stand before you the jury, a middle-aged man of passably sound health and mind, as proof of its compatibility with the human coil. In explaining this fact I believe my healthy condition, let me pause here to touch the wood of the *tanoa* beside me, may well be related to the beneficial diuretic effects of kava drinking on my kidneys. This information I have from the late Dr Ifireimi Buaserau, who so advised me with words of encouragement as we were making our way through a particularly kava-swamped tour of Namosi villages. I respected his sage advice, for in his life as a Namosi chief and rural doctor he not only consumed great reservoirs of kava, he had a wide range of medical knowledge. Evidence of this knowledge was on display when we hiked out of the villages in question. As the people of the villages waved their farewells to us, some would be holding their swollen jaws from which the good doctor had just manually, and without anaesthetic, extracted errant molars. Meanwhile the village boys stood in a chastened group, their little brown bodies clad only in white cotton bandages tied to the ends of the batch of penises Buaserau had circumcised earlier that day.

In Fiji virtually everyone drinks kava. This is not because the government gains in any way from encouraging its populace to partake. In fact the Fiji government gains not a penny of revenue from kava, while alcohol and tobacco are excised to the hilt. No, kava is drunk in profusion because people enjoy it. This is startling news when you think of all the bad press it has received over the years. Yes, people enjoy its fresh, slightly peppery taste, and it is a welcome thirst-quencher in the sometimes debilitating tropical air.

Most importantly, kava is a drink which has as its essence the ritual of sharing fellowship with other humans. This is no brew for pouring into a martini glass and moping over in a lonely bar. It would be aberrant behaviour indeed for you to mix some kava and drink it by yourself, for the preparation and serving of kava is a process of social interaction, of story-telling, of shared laughter, of communal solemnity, of inclusion and of understanding.

Kava is an indigenous plant of Melanesia, of which island region Fiji is the most eastern member. There is a common theme in both Melanesia and Polynesia which gives kava's origins as being a gift from the gods, with the first plant growing from the grave of a legendary hero. A fascinating fact is that the kava plant is sterile, meaning it can only propagate with human intervention. Thus the plant's dependence on humanity assists the body of knowledge surrounding the great Polynesian migrations, for the plant was carried as far as Hawaii, the Marquesas and Tahiti by the Polynesian canoes. Incidentally, J.G.A. Forster, one of the botanists on Captain Cook's second voyage (1771–1775), gave kava its scientific name *piper methysticum*, which means 'intoxicating pepper'.

If you know where to look in Fiji, kava drinking is everywhere. In all the years I worked on the austere top level of Government Buildings in Suva, where Prime Minister Ratu Sir Kamisese Mara had his office, there was always one *tanoa* of kava on the go, either in the Ministry of Foreign Affairs' registry, or at the other end of the floor in the PM's secretariat. Around the *tanoa* was where the good oil was to be had, and fifteen minutes of kava swilling and chat usually got you more pertinent information than you could get from a day of memoranda and telephone calls.

Don't let them fool you, everyone's into it in Fiji. Unless they're culturally impregnable, it doesn't take long for expatriates to get into the habit. An Australian insurance executive will have a morning break for a few rounds of kava with some of his local staff in their air-conditioned Suva office. Meanwhile out on the road a Public Works Department road maintenance gang will down tools for a swig when the *pani-wallah* comes round with a bucket dispensing not water, but kava as a liquid refreshment. The Indian community is probably its biggest consumer and kava exports to Fiji Indian immigrants around the Pacific Rim now earn Fiji significant levels of foreign exchange.

When kava is served to and drunk by the Queen, as it has been on many occasions, or by Pope John Paul, as it was in 1986, or by visiting heads of government and other VIPs, it assumes its ancient status and becomes the medium for conveying high ceremonial welcome and sharing the fruits of the land. Kava then appears as part of a series of presentations: first of whales' teeth, then of a kava plant, followed by kava prepared for drinking, then cooked food, fine mats and bark cloth, and finally a performance of traditional dance. All of these presentations are accompanied by ritualised speeches and solemn ceremony, the performers of which rarely fail to impress visitors with their dignity and deep cultural pride. To describe the detail and significance of these ceremonies is not my purpose herein, but any visitor to Fiji should at least be aware that kava drinking is imbued with greater cultural value than just an idle swig.

Ceremonies for the installation of Fijian chiefs, for instance, vary from place to place in Fiji, but they all have in common the serving of a bowl of kava, the *vagunuvi*, which upon consumption by the chief seals the ceremony. My father's great friend Archie Reid once wrote of the importance of kava in this context and illustrated it with a story involving the British royal family. In 1881 Queen Victoria's grandsons, the Duke of Clarence and the Duke of York, visited Fiji as midshipmen on HMS *Bacchante*. A ceremony of welcome was held for them at Levuka and the first bowl of kava went to the Duke of Clarence, who was the elder of the two brothers and was in direct line to the throne after his father the Prince of Wales. But Clarence refused the bowl of kava, and York drank it in his stead. This was taken in Fiji as an omen, and sure enough Clarence never arrived at his kingship. He died in 1892, predeceasing his father, and it was the kava quaffing Duke of York who went on to assume the throne as King George V.

Elements of the high ceremonial use of kava filter down to the etiquette of our everyday drinking. The *cobo*, a crosswise clapping of cupped palms three times, signifies entry into ceremonial territory, and it is normal for it to be heard before kava is drunk, even in an informal setting. A few ritual words will usually be said at the beginning and ending of a drinking session. Drinkers defer to the most senior people present, or to visitors, when the coconut shell *bilo* of kava is being served around. Soft hand-claps precede and follow each individual's draining of the *bilo*. People do not cross in front of the *tanoa*, the bowl of *vesi* wood in which the kava is mixed, without respectfully touching its rim. Tobacco goes very well with kava, but cigarettes are not lit until after the first round of kava has been served. A *tanoa* is rarely untended while it still has kava in it. All these little reverences for the beverage, the *wai ni vanua*, serve to socially bind the participants in its consumption.

The link between the ritual and the mundane drinking of kava is best described by Ratu Sir Lala Sukuna, the man who was more influential than any other person in shaping the character of twentieth century Fiji. His words bring you close to the essence of our national drink.

Kava only came into general use through the change of religion and the decay of local political institutions. Originally it was a solemn rite confined to the chiefs and elders, having a definite place in the political and religious life of the tribes. Its connection with religion lent it an air of solemnity, its relation to politics gave it the characteristic of permanency, the immutability of its ritual sealed it with dignity – all tending to make it the symbol of order and respectability. With the advent, however, of a new Church and the rise of a new State its religious and political importance rapidly waned, leaving its symbolical significance and its ritual to grip the imagination.

And gripped we were. In the 1970s when I lived in rural Fiji, kava was the most remunerative cash crop around. No matter how much you grew, the market was insatiable. I decided to get into a bit of kava production myself when I lived on Taveuni and went looking for opportunities to buy a kava plantation. An Indian man was selling his farm up at Delaiwelagi. It was freehold land and could thus be freely traded, and it had several thousand kava plants on it, so the opportunity sounded like it was worth investigating. I drove up to Delaiwelagi, some 300 metres up the side of Taveuni's fertile flanks, looking down onto the waters of the Somosomo Strait iridescent with tidal currents. I met the vendor and we walked over the land inspecting the health of the kava plants. Then I climbed down alone to a tumbling stream that ran through the middle of the land.

The stream lay in a steep-sided valley and its route was strewn with boulders as big as small houses, between and under which the water splashed and echoed. On the stream's opposite bank was the dark, dank, primeval rain forest. I was sitting by this stream weighing up what I had seen, mulling over the purchase price, wondering if I could afford the time and dollars, when a flash of neon colour passed rapidly before my eyes. On a sloping tree trunk covered in emerald green moss nearby, a *bunedamu*, an orange dove, had alighted. It was the first time I had ever seen one and its identity was unmistakable with its vivid orange plumage and yellow head. Sitting on its emerald perch, that bird gave off the most intense display of orangeness I have ever experienced. It opened its beak and said 'tock-tock!'

I mistakenly took the bird's message as a good omen and decided to buy the land and name it Bunedamu Farm. Two years later, after persistent pilfering of the kava crop, disease hitting some of the plants and the interest bill at the Fiji Development Bank rising, I rued the day I met that feathered fraud.

With my government duties taking precedence, I could only work the farm on weekends or holidays. I would hire men from the nearby settlement of Naqilai to weed the crop, but my ability to do so was hampered by the low pay of Fiji civil servants. In 1977 when I brought the farm, my salary was the equivalent of about US$2000 per annum before tax. Kava should be left in the ground for at least five years to get it to maturity, but I made the decision to harvest some of the crop prematurely to pay for the maintenance of the rest.

My brother Mark, back from university in England, was staying with us when we undertook the harvest. The plants were uprooted and transported in trucks down to the swimming pool at the back of our Waiyevo house. The stems were detached and sold to other farmers as planting material. Then the roots were sliced off and washed in the pool prior to drying. The roots are called *waka* and are consumed by those who prefer a more peppery kava product. The next job was to laboriously peel the fibrous, knotty stem-bases of the plants. The operation was led by Mark who sat down by the pool for a couple of days with some hired hands and sharp knives, peeling and peeling and peeling.

The skinned stem-bases, called *lewena*, were then sliced into chunks half the size of apples and laid out with the *waka* for sun-drying on sheets of corrugated iron lined across our back lawn. They made an impressive sight drying out there in the sun as we wandered happily amongst them inhaling the kava's sharp aroma – until the weather deteriorated. A low pressure zone hung around Fiji for the next two weeks and while it dumped its torrential rain on Taveuni, our half-dried kava began developing mould and rot. We brought it indoors and spread it all through the house, leaving narrow tracks through the kava carpets from the bedrooms to the kitchen. It continued to rot, so we took it in batches over to the Waitavala copra drier where we laid it around the shed that housed the big oil dryers, careful not to let it get too close to the copra dryers as they would turn the kava into worthless brittle biscuits.

Finally we bundled the *waka* into big bales secured with sack and rope, stuffed the *lewena* into copra sacks, and shipped it all off on an inter-island trading vessel to Suva. I took some leave, went to Suva to meet the boat at Princes Wharf and sold the *lewena* in minutes to a vendor from the nearby Suva Market. The *waka* I loaded into my father-in-law's Valiant. The boot was so full of kava roots I had to secure it with string and the car's kava-crammed interior left only a small driving space for me to squeeze into. I was heading for the markets of the Western Division with the *waka* because it fetched a higher price over there.

The kava buyers at the Sigatoka Market had never seen a sight like it when I pulled up in my kava-mobile, but their prices didn't impress me so I continued up to the markets at Nadi, Lautoka and Ba. I ended up selling the whole car-load to an Indian middleman up in the hills behind Navo. To pay me, he pulled wads of money from a tin that he had extricated from under his bed in a ramshackle shed on his family's cane farm. The payment equalled my annual salary, but sadly it was all destined for the Fiji Development Bank.

After I was posted to Suva I sold Bunedamu Farm to Ratu Jone Radrodro who was the divisional commissioner in Labasa. By birth he was the Tui Taveuni and his ancestral home was on the coast of the Somosomo Strait below Delaiwelagi, so the freehold land was a good buy for him. His Tongan wife Lua owned a kava saloon in Labasa and by their owning a kava farm she could supply their own kava to the saloon. A kava saloon? Again Ratu Sukuna, in a 1925 memorandum, gives the best description of them:

> In themselves there is nothing attractive about kava saloons. The dismalness and dinginess of their exterior are matched by the gloom and dullness of their interior. Composed of large bare rooms suspiciously dirty, or of cubicles with dark and speckled walls, they are furnished with nothing more than cheap wooden tables and forms. The surroundings are reminiscent of the Chinese bars in Papeete without the characters that haunt those places.

It is true that most people drinking kava for the first time don't wax lyrical about its taste. They tend to expend too much effort on analysing its effects on them and can be heard muttering that they don't feel a thing, while the experienced practitioners, with relaxed looks on their faces, are listening contentedly to a story being told by one of their number. The drug relaxes the muscles slightly and tranquillises the mind without impairing logic. It makes for good monologues and sympathetic ears. Where alcohol produces stimulation and then havoc in human gatherings, the effect of kava is quite the opposite. Even when it is drunk to excess, the worst symptoms will be lethargy and the necessity of frequent trips outside to have a pee. People who do nothing with their days and nights but incessantly drink kava can be afflicted with *kanikani*, a scaling of the skin which gives them a reptilian look; but this condition is easily corrected with oils and abstinence. All in all the plant is one of Nature's gifts to humankind, to be enjoyed and respected.

There is a Fijian expression '*Maca na wai, ka boko na buka*' which translates directly as 'the water has gone and the fire is out'. It means 'we're out of kava and tobacco'. What makes this expression so full of pathos is that the dearth of kava implies no gathering together around the *tanoa* to listen to the stories which, through their humour, irony and ritual, serve the social values of sharing and togetherness which bring harmony to the community.

Having convinced you of kava's merits, it is galling for me to have to report that the governments of the United States and Australia have in the recent past banned, and to some extent continue to restrict, the importation and enjoyment of kava by the supposedly free citizens of those countries. The government leaders and diplomatic representatives of both nations have besported themselves around the kava bowl on countless occasions in Fiji, and while President Clinton may not have inhaled his marijuana, you can be sure he would swill down his kava if he was to visit Fiji. I am at a loss to explain the slighting of our national drink by these government restrictions, surely their powerful liquor lobbies are not fearful of kava saloons nudging aside their bars and pubs.

I would suggest that part of the problem is the limited knowledge the legislators of these countries have about kava's properties. By way of example, when I was Fiji's consul general in Sydney in the mid-1980s, a Fijian missionary was working with the Aboriginal communities in Northern Australia. He was distressed at what alcohol abuse was doing to many of the people of these communities, so he decided to introduce kava and its associated rituals to them. The effect was marked. Relieved of alcohol's divisive and degrading influence, under kava's gentle rhythm the communities enjoyed evenings of socialising in a spirit of togetherness.

Unfortunately, when the Fijian missionary was not around, some people took to mixing kava with the rough liquor they were previously partaking in and, while the taste may have been thereby improved, alcohol's wild reign resumed. Arising from this, kava was then unfairly accused by the less-than-intellectually-rigorous senators from these areas as being a pernicious new drug, and it was not long before the Australian Senate slapped the first of its bans on kava importation.

The Australians would have done better to look to Europe, where it is estimated over a million people are currently using kava pills as a herbal, medically-prescribed remedy for nervous anxiety, stress and restlessness. While benzodiazepines like valium tend to promote lethargy and sedation, kava has been shown to improve concentration and memory for people suffering from anxiety.

The stringent pharmacological standards of the Europeans have given scientific recognition to the gentle, natural benefits of kava's pharmaceutical powers, so beware the wowsers and look, for example, to what they did to America with Prohibition. Just as Prohibition proved untenable and against the grain of human spirit, so too will kava be freed from prejudice, its peaceful properties properly perceived, and in the words of the Dane himself, 'We'll teach you to drink deep ere you depart.'

TAUKEI MOVERS

THE TAUKEI MOVEMENT came to life shortly after the defeat of the Alliance party in the general elections of April 1987. It has been described as a spontaneous grassroots political movement that arose from the dismay and anger that was widespread in the Fijian community in the election's aftermath. From my vantage it seemed to be more in the nature of a loosely-coordinated group of opportunists exploiting that angry dismay. People have called the Taukei movement a front for the Alliance party, but this too misses the mark as the Alliance, whilst undoubtedly Fijian-dominated, had democracy and multiracialism as its central principles. The Taukei movers dismissed democracy and had as their central rallying point the cry 'Fiji for the Fijians'.

That the Taukei movement played a short decisive role of great importance in Fiji's history is indisputable. Their protest marches and gatherings gave visible focus to Fijian discontent and their plans to disrupt the functioning of government and initiate racial strife were a crucial element in Rabuka's decision to stage his coup. Amongst the cabal that initiated the movement there was a heavy leavening of Bible-thumpers and an air of irascibility. This petulance was aimed not just at the perceived enemies of Fijian hegemony, but at elements within the movement who deviated from their hagiocracy of hate. The more moderate members of the movement, like Gonelevu and Bole, withdrew from it not long after the first coup, leaving the spotlight to the more demagogically inclined.

When the latter took over, it was tempting to take refuge in the Fijian proverb *kava ga e lala, e rogo levu*, empty vessels make the loudest noise. But it is truer to the time to admit that those Taukei movers took us close to that revolting pit of humanity wherein the bloodied corpses of Bosnia and Rwanda are revealed. I read and listened to sufficient reports at that time to convince me that elements of the Taukei movement were ready to take up the club of retribution and bring it down on the heads of innocents. That this fate did not befall us is due largely to the forbearance and reservoirs of goodwill amongst the general populace of Fiji. I also firmly believe that many lives were saved by the will and restraint of Lt. Col. Sitiveni Rabuka, and will always recognise this, even though he later exploited the by-then-receding threat of this violence as a tool for the political aims of Fijian nationalism.

The Taukei movement mob were the bogey men of 1987, even after they became marginalised by the obvious grip that Fijians had on power in the form of both Rabuka's army and the governor general's administration. I remember having a drink with Bharat Jamnadas and a few of my other friends down at Gary Apted's bar on Victoria Parade on the night of September 12, when we were called outside to look at the red sky over Toorak. Someone said, '*Isa lei*, the bastards are burning Suva.' Anyone listening knew who those being referred to were: the Taukei movement. The fire was up on Marks Street. It was arson, and luckily the wind conditions were such that the Suva Fire Brigade was able to bring the blaze under control before it turned into a general Suva conflagration.

The Taukei movement blamed the Marks Street arson on a splinter group called the Taukei Liberation Front, but the dynamics were plain. The ambivalence of some elements of the security forces, and more particularly the encouragement given by Taukei movement leaders, gave the criminally inclined the view they had the nod to carry out violent antisocial acts. Fire bombings and personal intimidation were rife and on September 23, Naboro Prison was set on fire and over 100 prisoners escaped. Later in the day they made a deal with the security forces and were allowed to march through Suva to meet the governor general to express their opposition to Dr Bavadra's coalition.

The wilder Taukei movement leaders were typical of the type that comes to the fore when society has lost its discipline and messianism, mob rule and the politics of malice are set upon us. This type has been in evidence throughout history, from the French Revolution to the streets of Kabul. Ever since 1987, wherever I am in the world, I chastise those who, like a broken record, persistently deride the elected representatives of parliamentary democracies. For these deriders, 'politician' is a dirty word. Talk-back media hosts are champions of this populist line and are notable mainly for their lack of suggestion of an alternative means of government, though government by opinion poll would no doubt have them salivating.

To them I would say get ready for the mad dogs and warlords that await you when parliamentary democracy has gone.

One day at Government House my work was interrupted by a monologue of shouts coming from the orderly's room between the governor general's office and the administration building. I went downstairs to investigate and was told not to worry, it was Taniela Veitata and the governor general would be seeing him shortly. Veitata sounded inebriated, but probably only from the heady tonic of his recent ascendancy to the position of chairman of the Taukei movement. It was very unusual for anyone to speak in a loud voice at Government House, particularly in the nearby presence of the *turaga*, but Veitata was delivering a sermon to the cowering orderly at a volume that was making the glass louvres of his room rattle.

After his meeting with Ratu Penaia, I was minuted a copy of the paper which Veitata had written to represent the Taukei movement's position. It is worth quoting part of the paper verbatim to record the tone and logic that was prevalent in the movement at that time.

> Most of the people in the world today have outlawed the Western concept of Democracy, branding it as the crazy demon who goes around the world imposing its will of greed, corruption and debauchery in the form of constitutionalism and legality as means of insidiously consigning an entire race of people and all their inheritance into the dreaded custody and care of the Devil himself and other foreign interests.
>
> History, of course, also relates to the case of the British people who were once at the acme of world power and domination. With their Bible and their Constitution imposed on countries like India, Uganda and such other places, guaranteeing them, the right to stay in those countries, the British were also bold to say that the land in those countries, belonged to God and not to the natives. The British were also successful in the fields of education, business, trade and in other professions.
>
> If after all the sacrifice and the hard work which the British had injected into the overall development of those countries and yet the people in those countries still saw fit to grant the British a constitutional

divorce and told them to pack up and go home, then surely, the claim that the land in those countries belonged to God and not to the natives did not hold much water and was pretty weak and unreliable.

The British soon found out too late and with much misgivings, that God Jehovah, the Omnipotent ONE, possessing that enormous and unlimited power was of course responsible for creation.

But by the event which subsequently took place at the tower of Babylon, by God Himself making the people to speak in different tongues and languages and sending them away to various parts of the world, really places our world today in perspectives exclusively in terms of human values and experiences.

As was the experiences of Indian and other countries, that the customs and characteristics of their people had been nurtured through age-long adaptation and so naturally, that the process of evolution had acquired for their people exclusive rights and claims of ownership to their respective parts of the world.

Based on that, Fiji belongs to the Fijians and the same can also be said about India, as belonging to its indigenous people.

So, to that crazy demon, Democracy and his cronies in the Labour/Federation Coalition camp, yes, the choice is really yours, to recognise and accept the present political situation, as the legitimate and natural consequence of our most earnest desire to redress the existing anomalies, so that, ultimate and absolute political power should again be surrendered back into the hands of the Fijians, the choice is really yours, Dr Bavadra, to decide between the two evils, Democracy or the Chiefly Fijian leadership and should you be requiring guidance, always remember, that, it's better to be with the devil you know, than the devil you don't.

The Fijians have always had spontaneous love and respect for their Chiefs and with consanguinity also providing the main binding factors in Fijian Society that, the Chiefs were able to coerce their people into unity and discipline and so, with such cohesiveness providing the main support pillars to our traditional system of administration, that Fiji had been enjoying a long reign of peace and stability.

The present political crisis, however, an unfortunate incidence of history, has really been brought about by Dr Bavadra's obsessions over some political illusions, that he and his Coalition party were destined to change the course of history.

As the victims of such political pigmentations, caused by the evil refractions of that crazy demon, Democracy, to deflect the Fijians away from their traditional sanctuaries and havens, that Dr Bavadra had succeeded, not in mapping out a new course of history, but in foundering the ship of state on the rocks of chaos and disunity.

Old customs die hard and he who is not proud of his race has no need to live and should go scurrying with that crazy demon, Democracy, to bloody hell!

Another leading light in the Taukei movement was my old colleague, Jone Veisamasama. Jone had been the secretary general of the Alliance party prior to its defeat in the 1987 general elections and was reputed to be a member of Rabuka's 'kitchen cabinet', a group of Taukei movers who were Rabuka's sounding board prior to and after the coup.

Veisamasama was from Macuata province, with which I had many connections. He was a contemporary of mine, we both served in the Ministry of Fijian Affairs and Rural Development in the 1970s and used to enjoy each other's company on the occasions that we got together around the *tanoa*. I think we both fancied our chances of advancement in the ministry and we shared a common passion for getting more resources into rural development.

Jone was always a bit of an eccentric. He had good-looking Melanesian features and embellished these with a severe centre parting of his straightened hair, heavily oiled to keep its immaculate crinkly look. His thick moustache was unique, but in saying that, it should be remembered that in the 1970s many of us had facial hair features we would now prefer had never been recorded by photography. He brushed his moustache vertically from his upper lip over the tip of his nose and up his cheeks toward his eyes. This gave the impression of a man hiding behind a hairy thicket. When Jone was given a scholarship to the University of the South Pacific by our ministry, I was present at the little party that was put on to farewell him. The going-away present was a tortoiseshell comb for his moustache which, in spite of the touchy seriousness with which he took himself, he accepted in good humour.

After the coup d'état, Veisamasama found his way into the governor general's Council of Advisers when the Great Council of Chiefs imposed a number of Taukei movement names on the governor general as their price for backing his leadership. His inclusion in the Council of Advisers was a point of dismay for many, as he had shown himself to be unreliably radical in his political views by this time, and had resigned from his government post of controller of transport the previous year under a cloud of investigations of improper practices.

He was not daunted by the seniority of the other members of the Council of Advisers and strongly represented the Taukei movement line in council debates. One day the council was discussing an issue which was divergent from the movement's aim of disenfranchising the Indian people. I will never forget Jone's retort, 'If that is done we will have to start killing them.' The movement's threat to visit bloodshed on the Indian population was often mooted or referred to third-hand by people, but here was my former colleague letting the words fall from his lips in a forceful but matter of fact way, as if we were discussing the fate of straying cattle.

The council meetings always broke for morning tea, when the staff from Government House would serve mountains of cakes and sandwiches with pots of tea and coffee on silver trays. The morning tea was served in my offices, and as people broke into little conversational groups, there was always the chance for a bit of steam to be released and some background gossip to pass around. A few of us would drink kava rather than taking tea and cake, but during the morning tea following Jone's 'start killing them' remarks, he and I were the only ones around the *tanoa*.

The pendulum had swung for the Taukei movement, and former government ministers and officials that had been in boots and all with the movement leading up to and shortly after the coup were now distancing themselves from it. The movement was seen as too much of a loose cannon, and for them it had now served its purpose. This was apparent to Jone as he and I were served kava and others kept their distance. I was hoping he would say something like, 'Hey, I was just kidding in there.' Instead he turned to look out over the harbour and, leaning close to me, muttered, 'Look at all those Taukei movement bastards. They've said the same things as me when we've had our own meetings, but none of them support me when I speak out here at the council.'

Within a year Jone Veisamasama was dead. He was at his house on a small farm ten miles from Suva and was fitting a pen-pistol into his shirt pocket. Apparently a few such surreptitious weapons had been brought back from the Lebanon by Fijian UNIFIL soldiers. As he put the pen-pistol into his pocket it discharged and shot him in his groin. By the time they got him to hospital, Jone had bled to death, for the bullet had severed his femoral artery. I think of that ugly moment of explosion and the pain and shock, the exasperation at the foolishness of the accident, the panic of the unstoppable blood flow, the rush to the hospital and the waves of unconsciousness, and hope that in those last moments there was a chance for reflection and a reconciliation.

Another of the Taukei movement activists was an old friend of mine. Senator Jona Qio was the same age as me, and in our teens we used to sail together in the Yasawa Islands. My father was the commissioner Western in Lautoka and Jona's father was the captain of the commissioner's launch, the *Cagi mai Ra*. In 1965 Jona was the fastest schoolboy runner in Fiji. He was at Queen Victoria School and I was at Natabua High School. By then we were sixth formers and we both got into the 100 metres finals of the 1965 Fiji School Athletics Championship. Here the similarities cease, for as I was bringing up the rear of the field, Jona's heels were flashing ahead of me as he collected the winner's tape across his chest.

By the time I returned from Auckland University and joined the Fiji government as a district officer, Jona had got himself into trouble with the law and was serving a jail sentence. I think it was related to embezzlement. We carried out a correspondence relationship while he was inside, with me egging him on to fulfil his potential and he affirming that he was going to make a better go of it when he got out.

He got out and made a better go, and before too long Jona Qio was running the Young Alliance, the youth wing of the ruling Alliance party. He did a good job. He was pretty hyperactive, usually in a positive way, and he had this cheesecake smile that was still as naive and winning as it was that day he won the 100 metres trophy. Even so, I was staggered when some time in the 1980s the Great Council of Chiefs selected Jona as one of its nominees to the Senate, the upper house of Fiji's Parliament. I guess they wanted to put up a young face, and he was from the Western Division which tended to be overshadowed in national politics. When he came for kava and *talanoa* at my office in the Ministry of Information, we would have him on by addressing him as 'Senator' and would draw out the larrikin in him by getting him to tell funny stories about the goings-on of the elderly senators.

When the Alliance party lost the general elections in 1987, Senator Jona Qio did not sit back. Even though he was related by birth to the newly elected prime minister Bavadra, he was determined to bring down the new government and restore the reins of political power to the traditional Fijian leadership. On May 14, the day of the coup, the banner headline of the *Fiji Sun* was 'Jona Qio in court on arson charge'. He was charged with fire-bombing the offices of the Indian leader Jai Ram Reddy and throwing molotov cocktails at other Indian business premises in Lautoka. Senators throwing firebombs around was new territory; in terms of mood, this was one of the benchmarks in Fiji's political decline. The coup saved Jona from another spell in gaol, but a year later he too was dead, killed in a car smash near Nadi airport.

FIELDS OF VUNIDAWA

MY MOTHER'S BROTHER, Peter Kearsley, had a love of horses from the days as a boy when he would clamber over the back fence of the Suva Point racecourse to watch the horses run. As a young man he spent some time as a jackaroo in outback Australia and then as a police officer in Northern Fiji where many of his duties were performed on horseback. Back in Suva as a lawyer, then a parliamentarian, he kept horses with his old friend Hankar Singh not far from what had been the old racecourse. As a horseman he was keen that his nephews should know how to ride, and he would take us to stay on the Edwards's farm.

Oliver Edwards had a farm at the confluence of the Wainibuka and Wainimala rivers up in the hinterlands of Viti Levu, just south of the government station at Vunidawa. The Wainibuka sparkled crystalline over rapids of rocks and gravel while the deep Wainimala flowed powerfully into view. Together they form the Rewa which curves through the farm then sets off southwards, past the tribute of a three-tiered waterfall, to the lowlands of Tebara and the mangrove forests of the Rewa delta.

On the gravel riverbank of Oliver's farm was a packing station for bananas. Up-river, Fijian farmers would make *bilibili* – rafts of bamboo tied together with vines – load their banana harvests onto the *bilibili* and then pole them downstream to Vunidawa. At the packing station, the green bananas were weighed and crammed into small wooden crates, and the buyers from the New Zealand company that managed this trade paid the farmers in cash. Trucks were loaded up with the banana crates and set off across the farm for the long dusty trip down to Suva for shipment on the SS *Matua* or the SS *Tofua* bound for Auckland.

At the packing station the hill country farmers mixed kava on the river bank and caught up with friends and relatives. Some took a ride on the trucks as far as Nausori in order to buy a few treats, like loaves of bread from the Chinese bakery, or lengths of cotton print for the family back in the hills. Others would leave the packing station crammed into river taxis, long wooden punts driven by Evinrude or Johnson outboard engines, to make the upstream return voyage. The *bilibili* were called 'HMS Nocomeback' because they were abandoned once they had completed their one-way banana-bearing voyage.

Between the ages of nine and twelve I spent many holidays on Oliver's farm with my brothers, Andrew and John, and the Falvey boys. We spent most of our time there on horseback and were allowed the use of a .22 rifle which accompanied us on our unsupervised expeditions. The farm was struggling to survive and life there was pretty basic, but it was a heroic time and place in our childhood.

Oliver's son Rodney lived in New Zealand and would visit the farm during holidays. Rodney was to become well-known in New Zealand for his elegant etchings and woodcuts, but when he was eleven years old his artistic medium was his marionettes. With his long puppeteering fingers he would artfully weave new dreams for us as those strangely-jointed wooden people danced in the glow of kerosene lamps. The Vunidawa farmhouse filled in the night with Fijian children from the nearby village. Some of them might have seen a picture book, and perhaps one or two had, like us, seen two or three movies in Suva; but in that lamp-lit, television-free world the marionettes were a startling new kind of entertainment for us.

We couldn't get enough of the puppet performances, and whenever one of the marionettes gave the cut-throat '*kua ni kana*' sign to another, 'I love you so much I will never eat again,' there would be shrieking laughter and crowd hugging, and we would tumble around on our backs in delirious delight, slapping the wooden floor-boards.

The only time I can recall us having any form of adult supervision at the farm was during the mounted 'parades'. Oliver was from an old Fiji family and had been an officer in the Fiji Military Forces. His horsemanship was widely recognised and, as a symbolic representative of the colonies, he had ridden as one of the escorts to Elizabeth Windsor as she was driven through London on her way to and from her coronation in 1952.

Six years later he stood on the rickety steps of the Vunidawa farmhouse overlooking the Rewa river, taking the salute at our parades. At our request he had taught us how to salute with sword from horseback. He still had his military sword, but we had cut ours from gnarled guava trees. Our horses were harnessed with rope bridles and saddled with old sacks, our uniforms were khaki shorts spattered with red clay. On command our horses were trotted wheeling into line for the parade, over the uneven muddy yard, guava swords lifted, hilts passed across chest, held in front of the chin and then slashed down to the right as we filed past Oliver acknowledging our salutes with his own.

Skinny brown bodies on big bay horses with guava swords in hand, we galloped off over the fields of Vunidawa preparing ourselves for service in an empire whose sun, though it had not yet dawned upon us, had already set well below the western horizon.

At the time of which I write, my family lived at a house called Raicakau, so called because it was at the end of a ridge in Suva's Government Domain with views of the main sea reef. We lived at Raicakau from 1956 to 1962 in what for me were the golden years of childhood when all was well in the world. The single-storied, rambling wooden house sat well back from the road behind flamboyant trees and clumps of bamboo, approached by a drive which was lined on one side by bamboo and on the other by a lawn which was used for our neighbourhood's version of a rugby game.

Occasionally huge RNZAF Sunderland flying boats would lumber over the top of Raicakau on their way to landing in the waters off the Laucala Bay breakwater. Sometimes they were so low you could see the rivets on their big white flanks, the sculptured lines of the keel contrasting with the brutish bulk of the wings and fuselage. Spotting the rear-gunner's glass dome under the aircraft's tail we'd set up a racket of artillery noise as we fired our imaginary ack-ack guns at the descending seaplane.

At the entrance to the Raicakau drive was a broad-leafed *dilo* tree, and its shade provided a popular loitering spot for the Thomson boys and our friends. The entrance was at the bend of a long, sparsely-housed crescent, so its views commanded the neighbourhood and from it we could spot the approach of friend and foe. Our gang sometimes got into stone fights with rivals; the name 'Tony Moray's Gang' comes to mind, though who he and they were, and why they were our enemies, I couldn't say. A stone-fight involved picking stones from the gravel road and hurling them at your opponents. Injuries were rare but quite severe when they occurred.

From the shade of the rain tree we could see our cubby house perched high in a neighbour's backyard banyan tree. Up there we planned campaigns and made ourselves blood brothers by cutting our palms with rusty nails and pressing them against another's palm, just like we'd seen in a Red Indian movie.

Underneath the *dilo* tree there was a soapstone bank which must have been exposed when the driveway was originally cut into the house. In our early days at Raicakau we cut roads and tunnels into this soapstone with knives, creating a cliff-front network on which to drive our Dinky Toy cars. As the older boys grew out of playing with toy cars, the younger boys inherited the soapstone legacy and I would sit up in our tree surveying the neighbourhood while they would while away the hours below me acting out vehicular fantasies with soft 'brrmm brrmm' noises.

If one of the boys had the requisite funds, sixpence would do it, we might take a hike down to the Chinese store at Nasese to buy some Chinese lollies. These lollies were dried, salted plums from which you nibbled very salty, tart morsels. If the funds stretched a bit further you could purchase an ice-block. The latter came in two flavours, milk or sweet orange, and were made on the premises in what must have been rusty ice trays because there was always a slight sedimentation of brown metallic substance on the top of the ice block. Strangely enough the sediment was part of their appeal.

What a shop that was. The Cantonese family who owned it and served behind the counter were so rude and unfriendly to their customers, but we all kept coming back for more purchases, and the verbal abuse and surly service were taken for granted. The grey-haired proprietor sat on a stool in his khaki shorts and white sleeveless singlet, watching his family trading with the customers across the broad wooden counter. On the counter, which was chin level for us, a grimy, wire-gauze cabinet contained shelves of long loaves of white bread with burnt black tops, sweet buns and squares of dense yellow cake.

You could order 'one roll' and the proprietor would take a cigarette from an open packet and sell you the cigarette with a dismissive air. There was a candle burning in a tin on the counter with which customers, or passers-by, lit their cigarettes.

The shelves of the store were crammed with bolts of floral-motif cotton print, jars of milk biscuits, Double Rabbit mosquito coils, pink sachets of powdered aspirin, dusty bundles of kava roots swaddled in newspaper and secured with twine, packets of Guards and Crown cigarettes, red-labelled tins of Japanese mackerel, and dusty stacks of chipped enamel basins and thick china soup-bowls. From its ceiling hung paper kites, woven Fijian baskets, bundled mosquito nets and wispy *sasa* brooms. The floors were worn wooden boards blackened by countless bare feet. The walls were lined with sacks of rice, raw sugar, New Zealand onions and Australian potatoes and slightly off-centre of the store was a long glass case, the sliding doors of which rattled when opened because of the thinness of the glass.

Many of the other customers were the families from the nearby Nasova police barracks; big Fijian women with casual gaits, Indian women in saris with jingling bracelets, and lots of kids loitering around the front of the shop. Nibbling our Chinese lollies we would linger a while inside the store to check out the contents of the glass case: spangled bangles, jars of glass marbles, hair slides, a marvellously cheap array of cosmetics, scented pomade with the picture of a Bombay matinee idol on its label, little red tins of Tiger Balm, talcum powder, pink plastic picture frames and Made-in-Taiwan tinplate toys with wind-up keys sticking out of their brightly painted sides.

The smell of fresh bread mingled with the rancour of dried fish, and the pungent cooking aromas from the family quarters at the rear of the store wafted through to us. An ancient lady in a faded cotton dress, with a back as bent as a boomerang, could sometimes been seen through the doorway to the family quarters, and gruff Cantonese utterances could be heard in there. I can still clearly hear the squeaking sound of the frail tin pump being primed to transfer kerosene from a drum to the customers' bottles, and the grumpy tone of the proprietor as he demanded payment, and the slapping scuff of his rubber thongs as he returned to his vigil on the stool. When you'd had your fill of all this, out the front door you'd go, usually in the company of a cockroach or two.

A dominant element of Fiji childhood is the presence of 'housegirls', the Fiji expression for live-in domestic help. Most Suva houses are equipped with housegirls' quarters and, as the term implies, the people involved were usually young women, although it was, and remains, common for a woman to perform such a role into old age. Depending on circumstance and personality, some housegirls became integral parts of their host families – confidantes, elder sisters and surrogate mothers, in addition to their handling of the domestic chores of cooking, cleaning and childcare. Some graduated from housegirlship with English language or cooking skills that took them into commercial careers, and others returned to the villages from which they had come to marry and raise children of their own.

We had a special relationship with Visama village, from whence many of our housegirls came. From this village, women like Wati and Salome came to Raicakau to accompany us through our childhood and fill our heads with much of our early way of looking at the world. We were raised in the laps of such women, and the smell of perfumed coconut oil, distinctive Fijian body odour and smooth brown skin have continued to evoke feelings of well-being and happiness when encountered in adulthood.

No doubt in the interests of discipline, they taught us about the evil spirits lurking in the night outside. They taught us to respect the communal interest and be responsible for each other's welfare. After one of the housegirls had been downtown to see a movie, she would recount the story to the rest of us from beginning to end, in a manner often more moving than the original film. Following one of these oral movie sessions, a particularly graphic account of a Dracula movie, I spent the next year going to sleep each night with my arms in the shape of a protective cross across my chest.

On weekends we would sometimes be taken back to their village, Visama, where we walked, canoed and swam around the Nakelo district with the village boys our age, Mika and his crew. Up the road at Vunivaivai bridge was a 'rubbish hall' with walls made of palm fronds where fund-raising dances were held. We'd pad up the road from Visama to Vunivaivai in the dark and sit on the bridge listening to the band, watching the goings-on and learning how to smoke Cina cigarettes.

We were taught many of the meatier matters of life, such as sexual attitudes and racial prejudices, by our housegirls rather than our parents, and of course these were drawn heavily from Fijian village culture. Respect for the achievements and authority of your betters was impressed on us and this would be reinforced when my father's Fijian friends came to the house. We grew up in as much awe of these men as our housegirl mentors so manifestly were.

The men concerned were the Fijian chiefs that had by then emerged as the leaders of their generation. Ratu George Cakobau had shared a tent with my father when they were young officers in the Fiji Military Forces. Ratu Penaia Ganilau had been a close friend since the days when they were neighbours and fellow district officers on Vaturekuka hill. Ratu Edward Cakobau and my father had spent many months together in small boats sailing around the Lau Islands as native lands commissioners. These men had been star players in the Fiji rugby team; they had been decorated for outstanding leadership in warfare; they were big, handsome men full of laughter and wisdom. There was no way we could hope to emulate them but, encouraged to do so by our housegirls, we could aspire to behave according to their code of *i tovo vakaturaga*.

Vakaturaga means 'in the manner of chiefs' and refers to a code of behaviour that chiefs and those that follow them are supposed to live by. Briefly, this code inculcated responsibility for the welfare of others, careful consideration of the best way ahead for the communal good, and respect for such ideals as service, deference, honour and loyalty. The code was best exemplified in the life of my father's boss at the Native Lands Commission, the courtly, Oxford-educated Ratu Sir Lala Sukuna, whose name was mentioned around Raicakau in terms of reverence. We would catch glimpses of Ratu Sukuna's grey head in the back of his car when he would drop our father home after they had returned from a long tour of the outer islands or the inland hill country. But in truth, I mainly remember the car concerned, which was a green Vanguard, and its khaki-uniformed driver, a poker-faced Indian named Hansraj. The latter would brook no nonsense from the Thomson boys, but he kept an avuncular eye on us.

It was a short walk from Raicakau to Albert Park where we would go to watch rugby games or slosh around in the mud at the annual Hibiscus Festival. Invariably the festival was subjected to deluges of Suva rain, but the crowds were not deterred by this and would churn the surface of the park to chocolate mud which squished up between your toes as you moved around the stalls. Some stalls would be selling aromatic parcels of curry and roti, others steaming *lovo* food, huge big brown wedges of *purini* cake, pink candy floss and sticky yellow Indian pastries. The rattle of spinning wheels of fortune and cries of 'place your bets' competed with the sound of string bands in the kava saloons. We preferred to gamble our limited supply of Fiji pennies, big and round with a hole in the middle, on the over-and-under-seven boards, where the odds were easier to judge if you stood for long enough around the naïf-painted boards.

During the Hibiscus Festival our neighbourhood gang competed without honour in the Soap Box Derby in our 'shot-shot' home-made carts. The derby was raced down the rough tarseal of Cakobau Hill, and only about fifty percent of the starters ever made it to the bottom. Wheel-collapse was the most common fault. As I write these words my hand moves to the brown scar on my left hip, caused from a wound when I spilled out of my box-cart at speed while trying to dodge a pot-hole during a training session on the back road to Government House.

One Hibiscus Festival, a boxing ring was erected on Albert Park in front of the small grandstand. The warship *HMS Cook* was in port, and its boxing sailors were to be pitted against the local boxers from Charman's All Races Club. As curtain-raisers on the night, the junior fighters from Charman's were to take part in three-round bouts. As one of the latter, I remember climbing into the ring in my light-blue silk boxing shorts; and the breathlessness of the fight, hiding behind the leather boxing gloves, and occasionally wind-milling into my opponent. My brother John and I both won our fights that night and were presented with minuscule silver trophies which sat in pride of place at Raicakau. My trophy went out of existence when one of my younger brothers took it out onto the driveway as an experiment to see how flat a car's wheel could squash it.

Our family grew to its final number at Raicakau: seven boys and our little sister Sally. At meals we were usually joined by other children from the neighbourhood. There was always plenty of wholesome food on the table, and not a scrap ever went back to the kitchen. The staple diet was beef stew, boiled taro and *rourou* for main course, with banana custard or fruit salad for dessert. A child from a small family who spent time at our table told his mother that every meal the Thomson kids had was a party. It was a bit like that. We were all very compatible, happy in our own company and welcoming to those that wanted to go with our flow. I guess we knew the pecking order, and our parents and the housegirls wouldn't have tolerated any unfairness between us. The eldest three boys, of whom I was the second, were known as the 'big kids' and were expected to take responsibility for the welfare of the 'little kids'.

On Sundays we'd do our best to get out of going to church. My father was an elder at St Andrews Presbyterian Church and an hour before the morning service he would round up as many of us as he could lay his hands on. My mother would be bustling our reluctant bodies into short-sleeved white shirts, ties, white shorts and sandals. The cuts and grazes on our knees and elbows were gaily painted with antiseptic tinctures: the crimson of mercurochrome, the gold of iodine and the purple of gentian violet. We would pile into the family car, and the flower arrangements of red anthiriums and poinsettias for decorating the church would have to be protected from all the jiggling juvenile legs; one of us would usually be in a bad humour by the time we pulled up at St Andrews.

On arrival at church the big kids would help with the handing out of Bibles and hymn books at the front door, while the rest of the family took their place on one of the creaking pews, filling a whole row and spilling into a second if Dad had been successful in his morning round-up. The big kids would join them on the family pew when the droning organ ceased its warm-up music and the minister took to the pulpit.

I would sit there bored out of my brain, staring up at the stained glass windows, the grainy silver paint on the organ pipes and the electric fans whirling slowly in the tropical heat overhead, while words like 'Galilee and Pharisee, Zechariah and Zebekiah, Shadrach, Meshach and Abednego' swirled round the little timber building and spilled out the wide-open side-doors, through the green palm fronds, to fall upon the maroon croton leaves which fringed the church.

St Andrews is one of Suva's oldest buildings, built in 1883 by Scottish settlers and government officials with names like MacGregor, Duncan and Thomson. Six generations of our family have sat on those same pews, and four of my siblings were married in St Andrews. It was a huge part of our lives, but I must be a hedonist because when I think of all those Sundays at St Andrews my chief memory is of the ritual drive after church to C.C. David's Café down on Victoria Parade where my father would buy us choc-bombs – delicious home-made vanilla ice-creams dipped in chocolate sauce. We'd still be finishing off these treats as we arrived home at Raicakau, and those that had escaped the morning round-up would ruefully weigh up whether the avoidance of the mind-numbing boredom of the church service had been worth the foregoing of the weekly choc-bomb.

At the beginning of 1961 the eldest of the Thomson boys, Andrew, went off to boarding school. Andrew had always been the most independent of us and we had a sense that he would return as nothing less than a conquering hero. We were doomed to go to St Kentigern College in New Zealand, an 'independent Presbyterian school', because the school's redoubtable headmaster, Reverend Adam MacFarlan, had been in the same Master of Arts class as my father at Glasgow University. Andrew was away for the whole of the 1961 academic year, spending term holidays in New Zealand with school friends on their parents' sheep farms in the King Country and the Bay of Plenty.

Finally the end of year came around. My father picked Andrew up from Nadi Airport and Hansraj drove them around the island in the green Vanguard, eight hours of rumbling along on the dusty Queens Road. Back at Raicakau I had been hatching a plan with my other brothers and the neighbourhood gang. We would give Andrew the sort of welcome home that a warrior chief would expect. We'd dress up as Red Indians, we tended to prefer them to cowboys, and would whoop it up big-time.

The great day came and we put on our war-paint and collected our spears, bows and arrows made from fiddlewood saplings. Brother number five, Richard, was our scout out at the white gates at the top of Cakobau Hill. On sighting the Vanguard he was to wave his spear at brother number four, David, who was stationed at the corner of Berkley Crescent next to Uncle Charles's house. David would then pass on the signal to the rest of the tribe who were sitting around the gates of Raicakau having a pow-wow. Richard and David were to jog back as an escort to the Vanguard.

The car was spotted coming up Cakobau Hill and the signals were given. Poor little Richard ran out of puff and had to be let into the front seat next to Hansraj. They rounded the corner at Uncle Charles's and saw David high-tailing it up the middle of the road in his Cherokee rig. As they approached our driveway the welcoming ambush was let loose. I swung out across the road on a rope from an overhanging tree. Arrows were fired and spears thrown. A dozen pre-pubescent boys whooped and war-danced around the car. On my return swing I crash-landed into the tree trunk and the oleander bushes below and as I extricated myself from the oleander all I could see in the car was Hansraj's beaming grin behind the driver's wheel.

The Vanguard drove slowly up the driveway and we ran alongside with our hands to our mouths tapping out our war-cries and leaping about like crazy horses. The car came to a stop under the porte-cochere and out stepped my father with a delighted expression on his face. And then Andrew emerged, still in his St Kentigern greys, newly-sprouted black hair on his muscular legs, a grown-up quiff in his Brylcreamed hair. He coolly surveyed us suddenly-silent striplings and then said in a deep adult voice, with a Kiwi accent as thick as that of any back-blocks farmer, 'G'day'.

He had changed. God had he changed. There was something fearful, foreign and foreboding about this change. It was a moment of time-shift. The end of a golden era – perhaps, in retrospect, a too beloved an era. I was due for boarding school at the beginning of the next school year, and I saw in the much altered shape of my brother my Fiji childhood slipping away and all the unwelcome challenges of puberty, boarding school and exile looming ahead.

DEATH THREATS

SHORTLY AFTER I had taken up office as the governor general's permanent secretary, I needed Rabuka's signature on an important document and, rather than entrust it to someone else, I took the document down to Government Buildings myself. In spite of his status now being that of the governor general's adviser for home affairs, Rabuka was still ensconced in the prime minister's office, so I sat in the ante-room with a bunch of plain-clothes security officers eyeing me coldly until Rabuka was free to see me. Out of the prime minister's office came Reverend Inoke Kubuabola, who with an officious air said, 'Colonel Rabuka wants to see you'.

I had never met Kubuabola before, but I counted his father and brother as friends of mine. He was head of the Bible Society and had recently gained a reputation as a radical member of the Taukei movement. The Kubuabola family is a highly respected one within the *Ai Sokula*, the chiefly families that surround the Tui Cakau, the paramount chief of Northern Fiji. When I lived in Taveuni his uncle, Ratu Kitione Kubuabola, was probably the most respected chief actually resident on the island. Interestingly, on May 14 I had spotted Ratu Kitione in the crowd at Government Buildings quietly observing the coup d'état in progress.

Now Inoke Kubuabola entered the prime minister's office with me, wherein I found Colonel Rabuka standing in front of the prime minister's desk. He took the document I handed him, signed it and gave it back to me. Standing about a metre away from me and looking me straight in the eyes, Rabuka said, 'It has been reported to me that you have been overheard giving secret information from Government House in a phone call to Sir Vijay Singh. What have you to say to this charge?'

Kubuabola's face was about sixty centimetres to the left of mine. I glanced at him and saw he was tense with the look of an over-eager prefect. That zealot's expression really got to me, it angered me and scared me too. I felt like I was back at boarding school, about to get a caning. I said that the report was a lie, at which point Kubuabola declared that I was the liar and that a Fijian telephonist at the Sugar Growers Council had overheard our telephone conversation. So this was my accuser. I did my best to ignore Kubuabola, and addressing Rabuka, stated that my loyalty to the governor general was total and that he should place more credibility in that than a hearsay exposé from a telephonist who had never met me.

Rabuka said that it was a commander's job to decide what was and was not true from the intelligence reports that were submitted to him and that in this case he believed me. But he warned me that I was being watched. I left Government Buildings nursing what I imagine are the usual emotions of frustrated anger and humiliation of any innocent who has been falsely accused and threatened.

On my return to Government House wheels were set in motion for the adviser for home affairs, and his advisers, to be moved out of the prime minister's office and into the Ministry of Home Affairs downstairs. The move was symbolic, but important to the reinforcement of the governor general's position. Thus in his first address to the Council of Advisers he said, 'I have issued instructions that the prime minister's office and the cabinet conference room in Government Buildings are to be locked up today and are to remain closed until a duly elected prime minister is ready to once again enter those offices.'

At the governor general's office there was a clear distinction between those people that were working solely for the governor general and those whose first loyalties lay with Rabuka. Loyalty was one quality which Ratu Sir Penaia of all men had a right to expect from his secretariat at that time of his onerous duties; but those with loyalties to Rabuka outnumbered the rest of us. Upstairs I had a hand-picked group who were steadfast to their duty throughout the time I was at Government House. Downstairs it was a different matter. I suppose it was to be expected that those on the Government House staff like the ADC and our legal adviser, Captain Isikeli Mataitoga, as commissioned army officers would be reporting our every move to the army. While I filled the role of permanent secretary to the governor general they behaved towards me in a distrustful and dismissive manner, an experience quite foreign to me in my sixteen years of relationships working within the Fiji Civil Service.

Two remarks made to me by Ratu Sir Penaia illustrate how this situation hurt him. One was after the army boys had manoeuvred to have two of their number located in an adjacent office to the governor general. Shortly after that I was giving him a briefing in his office when he motioned me outside. We walked across the lawn and he said that we should talk about confidential matters outside of his office on the lawn in future because he thought our conversations were being monitored from the adjoining office. The second remark was made when I paid him what was to be my farewell call. In the tone of one betrayed he said, 'Those people downstairs weren't working for me you know. All along they were reporting to the army camp.'

As the governor general's progress towards achieving an internationally acceptable solution to Fiji's crisis gathered momentum, there were inevitably those who saw their own goals and positions of influence diminishing. They were uneasy about attacking the governor general because of his *mana*, so for want of any other target at Government House they would have a go at me instead. I had tried to keep a low profile, and my news releases were as depersonalised as possible, usually referring to a 'Government House spokesman'. I did this because I was not a politically accountable figure and I had no interest in enhancing my personal profile.

Ratu Meli Vesikula, at that time a Taukei movement firebrand with a penchant for the microphone down at Sukuna Park, was forever denouncing me. In the *Fiji Sun* on August 31 under a headline of 'Sack Thomson', the Taukei movement were reported as calling for my ousting, stating I was not being fair, that I was acting against the interests of the nation and 'there were a lot of Fijians in the civil service who could do a better job than Mr Thomson'. Ratu Meli was quoted as saying that he had evidence that I had been helping the coalition and that if I denied this claim he would release the evidence. Not caring to play silly newspaper games, I chose not deny his claim.

Reverend Raikivi was another of my Taukei movement detractors. The governor general once said to me that we had made a big blunder in appointing Raikivi to the post of adviser for information. He was one of the Great Council of Chiefs' extra nominees that we had had to find a place for on the Council of Advisers. Raikivi was of absolutely no use to the governor general in his role at the Ministry of Information as we could not put anything through him without it coming out with a Taukei movement slant. This led to the situation wherein press releases had to be prepared at Government House and made in the name of the governor general or a Government House spokesman. When he figured out what was going on Raikivi was enraged, and I was warned by my old colleagues at the Ministry of Information that he was openly resentful of me.

In the Council of Advisers meetings I sat behind the governor general's chair, from whence I was able to see the faces of all the advisers except Mumtaz Ali and Ratu Josua Toganivalu, who sat next to Ratu Sir Penaia with their backs to me. During one council meeting there was a worried discussion over the fact that a sensitive matter, which was supposedly only privy to the council, had made its way into the public arena. How this could have happened was being sensitively debated. Raikivi sat next to Rabuka, his friend since school days, and at one point in the debate could contain himself no longer; eyes bulging and moustache flapping he blurted 'there's the leak' and pointed rudely at me. There was an embarrassed silence and then the debate continued on another tack.

If you stuck your head above the trenches you could expect to be shot at. The editor of the *Fiji Sun* received a letter with a live bullet in it; the implication was clear. Bavadra's spin doctor Richard Naidu approached a Taukei movement demonstration and ended up in hospital after the demonstrators chased him inside the Travelodge lobby and beat him up. I guess everybody in Fiji at that time has some degree of intimidation to recount, and Indian leaders like Jai Ram Reddy no doubt bore a disproportionate brunt of this dark side of humanity. I don't want to give the impression that one was unaffected by these personal threats, but at the end of the day you couldn't let them get you down.

Ratu Penaia received written death threats, copies of which I still have, and he put them behind him. One such letter, posted from Australia, reads:

Dear Governor,

If you change Fiji's Constitution you are in my red book. I will assassinate you. I'm coming to Fiji soon. Three men on my list. I am your killer.

Abou Abas

The main point made to me in the threatening messages I received was that if the governor general's plans did not hold together, there were people that had a score to settle with me and settle they would. These threats were made by anonymous phone calls or were passed through neutral or friendly parties. You had to brush them off as gossip or crank calls, or you would have become fixated with them. We had no way at Government House of tracing phone calls to their source, and it was difficult to vet all the incoming calls. Ratu Penaia for instance was conned into a long telephone call with a man claiming to be Sir Geoffrey Howe, the British Foreign secretary.

Unlike the governor general or the members of the Council of Advisers, I didn't have personal security provided for me or my home, and I never requested any. I didn't see much value in being protected by people who might not fulfil their duty. One evening during a particularly tense time in Suva, I returned to my home in a normally quiet part of the Domain, to find a crowd of Fijians and some trucks blocking the road outside my house. People were sitting in the dusk under the bamboo up my driveway. I cursed my lack of concern for my family's safety and, jumping out of my car, demanded to know what was happening. My fears were quickly allayed when it was explained to me that the crowd had come down by truck from the Province of Ra with the purpose of escorting Ratu Jo Nacola back to his home there. Ratu Jo was our next-door neighbour and had been minister of agriculture in the deposed government. Up on our lawn my son James and his friend Meli, Ratu Jo's red-haired son, had pith helmets on and with white hurricane-shutter battens over their shoulders were pretending to be military guards for our residence.

The Public Emergency Regulations, which came into force on May 14 when the governor general declared a public emergency after the coup, were in force throughout the remaining term of the governor generalship. These gave the army and police emergency powers of search, arrest and detention, and presented Government House with a struggle to keep the security forces from being over zealous in their use of these powers. As in any such forces there were those in the Fiji police and army who got their kicks from bullying and oppression. Happily they were in a minority, and the majority carried out their duties with discipline throughout what must have been a trying time for them. The governor general, with his background of service in the Malayan Emergency, had a great deal of sympathy and respect for Fiji's security forces and the job they were doing. However, the excesses of the minority often gave the public the impression that the security forces were a law unto themselves and were by no means politically neutral.

My efforts to temper this trend, and presumably suspicions of my motives in doing so, resulted in an official request by the security forces for my absence from their briefings for the governor general at Government House. Ratu Penaia advised me privately of this and, in his acceding to their request, said that I should not be personally offended. That was fine with me, but in response to continuing bad publicity and calls for assistance from the relatives of people being detained, I arranged a meeting on July 10 of the relevant security force personnel at which the governor general bluntly told them that there were too many arrests on flimsy evidence and that more discretion was required. He said that wrong-headed arrests, such as the recent one of James Raman, were making the governor general look foolish and lacking in control. The solicitor-general was also present and he said that while 'reasonable suspicion' was still the criteria of the criminal procedure code, the security forces should err on the side of caution in making arrests.

After the confiscation of his passport on June 18 at Nadi Airport, a former government minister, Sir Vijay Singh, described Fiji as a police state under the control of the army. He wasn't too far wrong at the time. Rabuka was nominally in an advisory role to the governor general, but his public and private signals made it clear that he was keeping his options open. The governor general was being continually frustrated in his attempts to create confidence and goodwill by the latest press reports of a meeting being closed down or summary arrests being made by the security forces. I continued with my meetings with army and police representatives to get them to exercise restraint. It was a cat and mouse game, and on more days than not I would be on the phone to the police headquarters, the army HQ or the Ministry of Home Affairs asking for, in the governor general's name, the release of the latest detainee.

After Dr Bavadra's unfortunate overseas tour, he called at Government House on June 26 to meet with the governor general. It was important that the meeting went well if our bridge-building exercise with the coalition was to proceed smoothly. But the army had other wishes and from my upstairs office I could see the governor general's ADC and some other army personnel giving Bavadra and his aides thorough body searches as they came through the back gates of Government House. Then they searched the boot and interior of Bavadra's maroon sedan. The back gates were out of sight of Government House and the governor general's office, but I could see the goings-on there from the veranda of my office, where I had positioned a *tanoa*. I rushed downstairs to ameliorate the humiliating welcome, but by the time I got out onto the road, Bavadra was storming down it. He saw me and blurted, 'Is this how you treat me?', and was still spitting tacks as he entered the governor general's office. The governor general was also angry when he later discovered the reason for Bavadra's discontent, but by then the damage had been done.

I had briefed the ADC, a commissioned army officer, on the importance of the visit going smoothly, and when I remonstrated with him over his treatment of Bavadra I was met with the sardonic look of one who knew better. As I have said, the ADC and the senior staff on the ground floor of the governor general's secretariat held me in no esteem; they served other masters, and my presence was tolerated by them only because I was the governor general's personal choice as permanent secretary.

In August the security forces somehow obtained a copy of a minute from Bavadra's spokesman, Richard Naidu, to Dr Bavadra recommending a certain course of action in relation to the court case which Bavadra was bringing against the governor general. The court case was purportedly to challenge the governor general's dissolution of Parliament. The minute clearly demonstrated the feeling in their camp that the case had become no more than a tool for political leverage and that there would be a point soon when it would be dropped.

In the content of the minute it refers to my views on the case, supposedly gleaned by Naidu in discussions with me, to the effect that I was 'considering the possibility seriously' that Bavadra would win the case and that I thought the case was damaging Bavadra's support amongst Fijians. This was meat for those in the army/police/Taukei movement ranks who believed that I was betraying the governor general's confidence.

After the governor general was given the minute he asked me to comment on its content. In my written response after analysing its main content, I turned to its reference to my views on the court case. I corrected what I had been reported as saying in order to bring it into line with what I had actually been trying to get across, which was in accordance with the thinking on this issue at Government House at the time.

Ratu Penaia wanted me to keep channels of communication open to the full political spectrum, and the carrying out of this directive was putting me increasingly in a position of suspicion. The army and police had their paranoid theories about my motives. Some of Bavadra's supporters painted me as a reactionary coup collaborator. Public statements by the Taukei movement demonstrated that to them I was a troublesome *vulagi* who was undoing their advice to the governor general, and then there were those in the Alliance establishment who were resentful of the independence which I had to exercise in conformity with the governor general's new status. In my response to the Naidu minute, I said that if these external suspicions were making Ratu Penaia's burden as governor general any heavier, I would stand aside to let a less contentiously-viewed permanent secretary take my place.

On August 18 Ratu Penaia sent my response back to me with his own comments:

> The suspicions you mentioned in this minute are already known to me and I have told the people who expressed them to me that I don't believe the allegations and I don't want to hear anymore of it. I don't want you to take to heart what they have said to you. I want you to know I have no doubt whatsoever about your loyalty, integrity and ability to carry out your duties as a permanent secretary to my entire satisfaction. I don't want another permanent secretary and you will remain with me until we have together found an acceptable solution to our Constitutional problems.

Oh yes, he was the kind of man who you could stand up and march to the end of the world with, and I was proud, and am proud, that when he called my name I stood by him faithfully when many of his countrymen said '*Io, saka*' and made other plans.

On August 25 the *Fiji Times* front page story under a banner headline of 'Bavadra case ploy exposed' gave full details of the Naidu minute, which it described as 'a secret document leaked to the *Fiji Times* yesterday'. Presumably unhappy with the unperturbed way it had been received at Government House, some bright sparks in possession of copies of the minute felt it too good to waste and had passed it to a *Fiji Times* reporter. Its publication produced more howls for my resignation, but the issue was well behind me, we were by then hard on the scent of victory in getting the leaders of the opposing political parties into national unity talks.

LAUTOKA CANE FIRES

IN MY LIFE there have been few moments of pure joy to equal the first morning of school holidays when I would be woken by a familiar bird call and realise that I was back in Fiji. The fullness of this joy is quite moving for me now as I remember its power. I would have spent the previous nine-and-a-half months in the Calvinistic confines of a New Zealand boarding school listening to conversations on the relative butterfat merits of Jerseys or Fresians, and repeatedly being caned for such heinous crimes as reading books by torchlight under my bed-covers after 'lights-out'. In later life I met David Attenborough, whose zoological books were amongst those I got caned for reading, and thanked him for the escape that his words gave me from the grinding homesickness which afflicted me during those long boarding school nights.

At that time my father was the commissioner for the Western Division of Fiji and we lived in Lautoka. We flew up from New Zealand in TEAL's Electra turbo-props, and when the doors of the plane were opened at Nadi airport and you stepped out onto the platform at the top of the gangway, the mixture of aviation fuel and tropical air was a harbinger of the joys that lay ahead: a mother's outstretched arms, the quizzical grinning faces of younger siblings, bundling into a Landrover in a hurricane of hugs and stories, all in a mood of sublime happiness.

I remember arriving at Nadi one night in August 1963, and as I was crossing the tarmac from the plane to the terminal I stopped to take in the moment. Moonshine highlighted the black cliff face of the Sabeto hills above the stone quarry near Lomolomo, and the horizon glowed from a cane-fire off in the direction of Viseisei. I was fourteen years old and with my feet back on Fiji soil I felt whole again, sure of my place in this world and deeply in love with my country. I have in later years on arrival at Nadi airport searched my senses for the intensity of that moment of commitment, stirring the ashes of adult disillusionment for the spark of that which was so precious to me.

Our family lived the first years of our Lautoka period out at the old government station at Natabua which is about seven kilometres out of town. The settlement was collected around a hill on the summit of which sat the commissioner's residence. Today the main remnant of the station is the Lautoka Prison and the Teachers College which are still located down the mango tree avenue at Natabua. These were the years leading up to Fiji's Independence and in the sugar-growing areas centred around Lautoka there was political unrest and industrial action. A year before my father's appointment, the incumbent commissioner had been shot in the belly by an assassin as he mounted the steps leading up to our Natabua house, so for the duration of the time that we lived there we had an armed guard of six policemen in the grounds at night.

How necessary this guard was I don't know. My father had been chosen for the role of commissioner because people from all walks of life in Fiji respected him as someone who was fair and understanding. However, I do remember one night when an intruder entered the house, crept through my bedroom and was bending over my father's sleeping body when my mother awoke with a scream that caused the intruder to flee, me to awake and the guards to come running. As we stood at the top of the drive watching the fleeing figure receding down it, one of the guards, with rifle in hand, bent down, picked a stone off the road and threw it with all his strength and a curse in the direction of the man. At breakfast, the main interest in the event was the humorous retelling of the guard's stone-throwing reaction.

The sugar industry dominated our lives in the Western Division and we learnt to recognise the different sugarcanes in their dense rows: Ragnar and Yasawa for fertile land and Mali and Mana for poor soils. At dinner, in an effort to impart some of his economics training onto his offspring, our father might paint us a picture of the complexities of the world sugar market.

The tempo of life in the sugar belt rose during the harvesting season when the mills at Lautoka, Rarawai and Penang fired up in preparation for the crushing of two million tonnes of cane. Growers were predominantly smallholder Indian farmers, who ploughed their fields with massive bullocks and banded together in 'gangs' to harvest their cane under the direction of an elected *sirdar*. As these gangs slashed their way through a canefield, some of their number would load the cut cane onto little railway trucks, which would be hauled on temporary tracks by the bullocks to the nearest railway line. When the time was right, the trash in the field would be burnt off in a controlled burn to allow the ratoons to come through for the next crop. But after the day's work, the bullocks were allowed to stand in the harvested fields knee-deep in the discarded cane-tops, with eyes closed and waggling lower jaws as they munched away at the cane leaves.

The cane-filled railway trucks would be linked up with those from other farms, and an engine would come from the mill to haul them back in a rickety line-up sometimes 800 metres long. In the 1960s diesel locomotives were replacing the steam engines, but some of the latter were still in service, valves hissing steam and fat brass funnels chuffing smoke as they trundled around the Fiji countryside.

When the cane-laden trains approached a road crossing they would slow down, for there were no level-crossing signals or gates, and this was the time for an adventurous youth to run alongside the train and pull off a couple of juicy-looking cane stalks. The hard purple skin of the cane was removed by a combination of biting and peeling, leaving the white fibre exposed. This you bit at, sucking and masticating the fibres, while the refreshing sweet juice dribbled down your throat.

At night during the harvesting season, perched up on the summit of our hill at Natabua, we would look over the black sea of cane fields that stretched out on all sides and were lit up here and there by cane fires. Long lines of orange flames advanced dancing upwards high in the night. And the crackling sound of burning cane trash and the whiff of ash, tinged with an imagined odour of caramel, rose to us on our veranda. Later, lying in bed, you would hear a cane train rounding the point that jutted out into the mangroves near Lauwaki and the rattling progress of its cane-laden carriages and the hum of its engine as it made its laborious way past the Natabua turn-off would last for about twenty luscious minutes, the sound of it drifting away as it entered Lautoka with a distant low moan of its horn.

After three years of weekly letters filled with the miseries of boarding school, I managed to win my parents over to my not returning to New Zealand and I spent my sixth form year at Natabua High School in Lautoka. Entry to this school was by academic merit and in 1965, when I attended it, the school roll was ninety-five percent Indian. With the exception of the year that I spent at Cambridge University, I have never attended class with fellow students amongst whom were some who could be described as geniuses. There were half a dozen of them in our year at Natabua High who hit close to 100 percent in their New Zealand University Entrance exams in Mathematics, Physics and Chemistry. However, a mark of over 30 percent in the English exam was a prerequisite for the attainment of the NZUE certificate, and some of these intellects, like my friend Bhagwat Lal, were struggling to get by. I was able to help them out a bit in English, and in return was taught how to write in Sanskrit script, my grasp of which today is limited to the writing of my name.

Amongst all those brain-boxes there was still time for things other than study. Vincent Aiyappan lead us in the school sports of soccer, cricket and hockey. Shalendra made sure we were well supplied with cigarettes when we nipped around the back of the school. We formed a band which did Beatles and Rolling Stones covers and performed at the school dance and the Sugar Festival. Max Foon and an English VSO teacher were on electric guitars, George Konrote was on drums and, oh yes, I was on microphone. I wonder how bad we really were. George Konrote, a Rotuman, stuck with the drums through cadets, got into the army and rose to the rank of lieutenant colonel. After the coup d'état, George and I would sometimes sit down to a table together at Government House for security meetings, but, given the seriousness of these occasions, I refrained from reminding him of our musical past and the rather appropriate name of our band, The Sadists.

Salvaging the Economy

IN THE MONTH of June, 1987 the main preoccupation at Government House was the salvaging of Fiji's economy, in particular ensuring the harvesting and milling of the sugar cane crop, the restoration of the tourist industry and the lifting of post-coup economic sanctions against Fiji. In this regard the governor general was ably supported by, among others, Savenaca Siwatibau, the governor of the Reserve Bank, who served as his adviser for finance and economic planning, and by Mumtaz Ali, the chairman of the Fiji Trade and Investment Board, who served as his adviser for trade, industry and tourism. While some politicians of both sides appeared ready to ride rough-shod over the economy in order to score their political goals, the steady minds and hands of these two men were of special assistance to the governor general in his fulfilling of the first duty of a leader: to ensure the people would continue to have food in their bellies.

At a time when some of the Taukei movement representatives on the Advisory Council were advocating that the Indian workforce should be replaced by Chinese, Ratu Sir Kamisese Mara was off in Indonesia trying to teach the Australians and New Zealanders a lesson by opening up new trading relationships, and the security forces were being suggested as a labour source for cane harvesting, it was like a blessing from above to hear the voice of Siwatibau rationally and calmly explaining to the council why certain economic measures were unavoidable and why others were just not on.

Foreign reserves had to be preserved; they had fallen from F$195 million before the coup to F$107 million just two months later. On Siwatibau's advice there was a 17.5 percent devaluation of the Fiji dollar at the end of June, interest rate ceilings were removed and capital exports stopped. Hard decisions were necessary and taken with regard to the deficit in the public sector: the army and the civil service were lined up for big pay cuts, and government departments and statutory bodies were instructed to cut their costs by twenty percent. We were in damage control mode, and on the economic front the Advisory Council meetings and operations took on the atmosphere of a war cabinet.

Sugar is by far the dominant export of Fiji – the life-blood of its economy – and for most of the twentieth century the lead-up to the annual harvesting season has provided a combative arena for Fiji politicians. This was traditionally a time of industrial action and political argy-bargy involving the government, the opposition, the millers and the various trade unions representing the farmers, the transporters, the mill workers, the engineers and so on, demanding better this and more of that. The mills, dormant during the off season, have to be painstakingly prepared for the crushing season, and getting the mills ready is like prodding a sleeping dragon into activity: once he's breathing fire he's got to have something to blow it at or everyone can get burnt. The dates set for the commencement of crushing are thus critical dates in the Fiji calendar, and politicians and trade unionists love a deadline when it comes to extracting concessions.

As a result of our early June visit to the Western Division, home of Fiji's sugar industry, the governor general learnt that the farmers were not averse to harvesting if they could be assured that full payments would be made to them in the normal manner. A well-orchestrated political campaign was sowing doubts in the farmers' minds as to whether payment would be made. The spreading rumour was that the rising costs of the military would be met by deductions from the farmers' cane proceeds.

There was also the question of whether the sugar mills could be relied upon to accept and crush the cane. The mill owners, the Fiji Sugar Corporation, were on side, but the mill workers were highly unionised and, as supporters of the ousted government, some of them could not be relied upon not to sabotage the mills if crushing began before they were politically ready to cooperate. Mill sabotage was relatively easy to accomplish, and millions of dollars of damage and indefinite stoppage of mill operations could be achieved through allowing a boiler to blow or wrecking the cane crushers by throwing solid metal objects or rocks in with the cane.

On our return from the Western Division, Ratu Penaia made an address to the nation over Radio Fiji on June 7. In it he reassured the sugar industry that our traditional buyers overseas had reaffirmed their commitments to purchase the sugar and molasses from the 1987 crop. He said that the farmers would definitely be paid the proceeds from their cane in accordance with the terms of their contracts with the millers. 'I give you this assurance categorically and anyone who gives you advice to the contrary is either misguided or mischievous.

The farmers were keen to start the harvesting, but their political bosses in the NFP/Labour coalition choked back the reins, aware that the commencement of the cane harvest was one of their key points of leverage. Ratu Penaia held meetings with representatives of all parties in the sugar industry and by mid-June he thought he had their backing. On June 18, broadcasting over Fiji's radios, he made a speech specifically to the Fiji sugar industry in which he announced that he had given directions for the army to restrict its presence in the cane areas. He said that permits were to be issued to cane harvesting gangs and trade unions to meet in harvest preparation (public meetings had been restricted under the Emergency Regulations), and that an interim payment to farmers for cane proceeds would be bought forward to June 30. He then said that the sugar mills would commence crushing at the end of June.

After the June 18 speech the governor general received a letter signed by six Indians purporting to represent 'ninety-nine percent of Indians here in Fiji'. In this letter their retort to Ratu Penaia's call for the cane harvest to get underway was: 'We now regard you as an uncouth, downgraded and rascal person. The God will never forgive you for what you are now doing. You will decay in hell! Thousands of Indians curse is upon you …'

Arson in the cane fields was increasing. With the mills not working, a field of burnt cane could not be harvested and had to just lie there and rot. Something had to be done to kick-start the harvesting season. So the governor general went along with a plan to start the crush at Labasa; there the millers had large estates of their own cane, which would be the initial crop to be harvested. We flew up to Labasa on the morning of June 22 and set up camp out at the divisional commissioner's residence on Vaturckuka Hill where a *vakatunuloa* had been built for the governor general's meetings on the lawn in front of the residence overlooking the valley of the Labasa River and the rocky Three Sisters hill range beyond. This was the same lawn on which Ratu Penaia and Adi Laisa's wedding reception had been held some forty years earlier.

An army of cane-cutters had been bussed up from the Fijian stronghold of Cakaudrove, and together with the people of the nearby Fijian village of Nasekula they set to harvesting work in the mill's estate canefields. Observing the long lines of cane-cutters in action, Ratu Penaia was hugely encouraged by the industriousness and enthusiasm of it all, and as we walked around the hymn-singing harvesters, shaking hands and taking swigs of kava from plastic buckets, the air was one of almost revolutionary fervour. Labasa is basically an Indian town and unfortunately while all this was going on there was considerable nervousness about the presence of that machete-wielding army of hyped-up Fijian cane-cutters on the outskirts of town.

On the morning of June 24 the Labasa mill was ready to start the crush and at 10.30am Ratu Penaia was on hand to tip the first cane trolley into the crusher. The newspapers reported with relief that the harvest was underway; but by July 3 the mills were closed again. The reality was that, without political and trade union support, the risks to the mills of serious sabotage were too great, as was proved by some incidents in the interim at the mills. It was made clear to me by a leading Indian member of the ousted government that it was in their constituents' interests that harvesting get underway, but only after we had resolved some of the political blockages that were still to be dealt with. And so it wasn't until the end of July, after intensive negotiations between the millers, the farmers, the unions and Government House, and when progress was being achieved on the political impasse, that the choke-hold was released and the sugar crush got underway in full.

The sugar industry is a perfect example of the economic interdependence of the Fijians and Indians. Most of the land is supplied by the Fijians for the growth of the cane, for which they get a rental. In the main the farmers are Indians who grow the cane and supply it to the mills, for which they get a contracted cane price. The mills are largely owned by the government of Fiji, and the export of the raw sugar and molasses provides Fiji's economy with a great part of its foreign exchange. All this should be a recipe, not for shaping up for a fight, but for holding one anothers' hands in cooperative effort; and so it would probably be if the politicians and provocateurs could be kept out of the picture.

Observing the attitudes of some of the Council of Advisers when the harvest was being delayed was an interesting diversion. Apart from calls for the army to undertake the harvesting, and comments that Indians should be replaced with Chinese (an incredible viewpoint when there were so many unemployed Fijian school-leavers), someone in the council gave a warning, probably incorrect, that if Fijian people were not able to buy sugar in the shops there would be a violent reaction, such had become their dependence on sugar as a cheap energy supply.

It is instructive to appreciate that in the very area in which the Indian population was centred, the Western Division, where the majority of the supporters of the ousted government hailed from, most of Fiji's productive wealth was also based. Western Fiji, with its cane industry, gold mines, the main hotels of the tourist industry, and the man-made pine forests, was thus of great strategic importance in the safeguarding of Fiji's economy after the coup. The difficulty of doing this was exemplified by frequent arson attacks on the Fiji Pine Commission's man-made forests. It was tragic to fly over these forests and look down on thousands of hectares of blackened hill-sides where the lines of charred and smouldering stumps of countless destroyed pine trees were graphic demonstration of the destruction of the nation's investment wealth.

After the post-coup cessation of tourist arrivals, Fiji's international airline, Air Pacific, was fighting for its survival, and we were well aware that its collapse would have had far-reaching negative effects on the Fiji tourist industry and the wider Fiji economy. In solidarity with Fiji's trade unions, the Australian Council of Trade Unions and its New Zealand counterpart imposed post-coup bans on marine shipping and categories of aviation connections with Fiji. With Australia and New Zealand the chief source of tourists for Fiji, the bans were a crippling blow for Air Pacific. The airline wasn't being helped by the Air Pacific Employees Association either, who appeared ready to sacrifice the existence of their members' jobs to the grinding of the political mill.

The bans had to be lifted, and we used every channel open to us to get the message across that they were a negative force likely to cause long term economic damage to Fiji, a hardening of attitudes within Fiji, and extended souring of relations between Fiji and its big brothers to the south. It is generally agreed that the governments of New Zealand and Australia played their hands poorly after the coup, and they were slow to come round in support of the governor general's efforts to save the situation. Even after they had come around to a far-from-vigorous support, the trade bans were still there, and the emissaries of these governments had to weakly inform Ratu Penaia that their governments were doing everything possible to have the bans lifted.

Basically, by early July everyone wanted the bans to go away, but a face-saver was needed for the unions. James Raman, the general secretary of the Fiji Trade Unions Council, took the bit between his teeth and asked for and received a letter from the governor general confirming that trade unions in Fiji had lost none of their rights since the assertion of the governor general's authority. Raman went with this letter to Australia and negotiated with his counterparts for a lifting of the bans.

Still a face-saver was needed, and the Australian union leader, Simon Crean, and a representative of the New Zealand Federation of Labour were received at Government House by the governor general for a short meeting. This achieved nothing, but it provided an opportunity for these leaders to then return to their countries to make some hollow claims about their effectiveness and announce the lifting of the bans. This sounds cynical, but it is about what happened.

While all this was going on, the tourism industry had been doing its best to throw itself a life-belt as it wallowed out in the middle of the Pacific Ocean. To assist the governor general to resuscitate the tourism industry, Rory Scott was approached in Hong Kong to head up a tourism action group in Fiji. Tourism had come to exceed sugar as Fiji's main foreign exchange earner, and it was vital the industry got back on its feet. Rory had served as a district officer in Nadi in the 1960s before becoming the head of the Fiji Visitors Bureau in the 1970s, and he was a personal friend of Ratu Penaia. He agreed to leave Hong Kong to take on the onerous challenge. It was indeed a tough call for Rory, as the flow of tourists to Fiji had all but dried up, and I noted him saying in July that tourism grossed only F$750,000 for Fiji in the two months after the coup, compared with the F$32,000,000 that Fiji earned from it in a normal two months.

The June devaluation of the Fiji dollar was a big help to the tourist industry, and the tourism action group put in place a programme of bargain airfares and hotel rates which capitalised on these incentives and turned the tourism tap back on. True we were getting a type of tourist who only dropped $20 a day rather than the $200 a day we were used to, but at least the beds were being filled and the industry was starting to function again.

The salvaging of the tourist industry was operating within a precarious environment. Rory and I had several meetings with the security forces to discuss the industry's concerns that the military were overbearing with their presence at airports and at road-blocks along tourist routes. Their guns and officiousness were a turn-off for tourists. It was a delicate balance because sabotage of the airports or hotels was an easy option for destabilisation of the country. We already had evidence of this and were wary of further incidents that could destroy the recovery. In Australia, Krishna Datt, the former foreign minister of the deposed government, continued to make scaremongering press statements which were body blows to the Fiji tourist industry. The governments of USA, Australia and New Zealand had all issued advice to their citizens not to travel to Fiji after the coup and even when they had withdrawn this advice, potential tourists had an understandably cautious attitude.

The owners and operators of Fiji's hotels had been through hardships before, especially in the aftermaths of the hurricanes that had wrought destruction on them in the early 1970s and early 1980s, and they took on the challenges of 1987 tenaciously. They kept to the June 8 schedule for the Fiji Tourism Convention and the governor general lent his support by opening the convention at the Fijian Hotel's Cuvu venue. To the assembled hoteliers, tour operators and overseas travel agents, Ratu Penaia announced a raft of economic measures he was putting in place to rehabilitate economic activity in Fiji. For the tourism industry he said that for the rest of 1987 the airport departure tax and hotel turnover tax would be suspended and $500,000 of extra marketing was immediately allocated to the Fiji Visitors Bureau. He called for an end to the deluge of negative publicity about Fiji and said that the great mission before us was threatened by those who had shown they wanted to wreck Fiji's economy and stir up ill-will.

As a result of its pull-yourselves-up-by-your-own-bootstraps attitude, the tourist industry was soon in recovery. It almost seemed that whatever Fiji at large did to complicate matters for the tourist industry, the basic fact always remained that Fiji was a great place to holiday, thanks to its climate, environment, and its population of currently-distracted-but-fun-to-be-with people.

An Air New Zealand flight engineer did his bit for protection of the industry when on May 19 an Air New Zealand jet full of tourists was hijacked by an Indian man who demanded the release of Dr Bavadra and his colleagues from detainment, and then said he wanted to be flown to Libya. The first demand was fair enough, but Libya! Had he said Auckland he might have been accommodated. The flight engineer chose his moment and rendered the hijacker unconscious with a bottle of whisky – on the back of the head, that is.

TAVEUNI

TO CAPTURE THE essence of an island you must approach it for the first time by sea; only then will you appreciate the bulk of it rising out of the ocean, the surf-encircled haven, the mystery and sensory delight of incipient maiden landfall. When an island offers as much as Taveuni, this is doubly so. Approached from the southeast the island presents a massive flank of primordial rainforest slashed with frothing cascades and glimpses of maroon and green parrots. There is no coral reef on this uninhabited windward coast; the ocean's surf storms onto the rocky foreshore, where it mingles with the torrents of fresh water falling from streams above.

Taveuni is usually approached from the southwest, where the leeward coast and the deep waters of the Somosomo Strait offer safer access. The island looms to starboard in a monolithic ridge rising over 1200 metres. No peaks or craggy outcrops from this perspective, just a great slab of some of the most fertile ground in the Pacific Islands leaning upwards.

At this south end of Taveuni, the land slopes away like a dove's fanned tail into the sea. On these southern slopes are thousands of hectares of coconut plantations and, in the days when copra was king, the European families that established these plantations were swaggering at the zenith of colonial society.

The Somosomo Strait is over 500 metres deep and is run with strong tidal currents that well up and surge along, rich in nutrients and marine life. Pods of whales are common in the strait, and when you take them unawares you can lean out over your boat's gunwale and watch them fall effortlessly away down into diaphanous depths. Big sharks are common too; and under Korolevu, the islet in the middle of the strait, is a cave in which the shark god Dakuwaqa lives. Throughout the Fiji Islands, sailors have traditionally poured a bowl of kava overboard, or more recently a tot of rum, as a libation to Dakuwaqa in recognition of his lordship over Fiji seas.

Halfway up the leeward coast is the government station of Waiyevo, where I was posted from 1976 to 1978 as the district officer. From the sea,

Waiyevo looks like little more than a few structures strung along the beach, for most of the settlement's buildings are out of site behind the trees on a narrow flat sward on the hillside above. Far more conspicuous is the neighbouring Catholic mission of Wairiki, with its red-roofed buildings, towered church and huge white cross erected on a hill some hundred metres above the mission.

Between Waiyevo and Wairiki the road runs along the seashore past a sign pointing on one side to 'Yesterday' and on the other to 'Today'. It marks the 180 degree meridian, and in the days before the International Dateline did its dog-leg around Fiji, there was reputedly a store at this spot that was able to trade seven days a week by choosing whether to be in Saturday or Monday while others were observing Sunday.

Landfall on the beach at Waiyevo was sometimes shared with the Polynesian fishermen of Kioa Island who had crossed the Somosomo Strait in their tiny outrigger canoes; paddling with the currents and fishing on the way, they would then sell their catch under the trees on the foreshore at Waiyevo. They would buy a few essentials from the Burns Philp (South Seas) Ltd store and then paddle back to their island when the tide changed and currents ran in their favour.

On the waterfront were the Burns Philp store, Kondaiya's shop and bowser, a hotel and the public bar, from whence a road wound up some 200 metres to the hillside shelf on which the government station sat. In my days as a district officer, the government station was made up of a courthouse, police station, hospital, post office, rest house, assorted government offices and residences for *na i vaka-i-lesilesi ni Matanitu*, as those of us who worked for the government were known. My office was tagged onto the end of the old wooden courthouse, and from my veranda I could look out across the Somosomo Strait to a wide vista of the Vanua Levu coastline stretching off to the western horizon. From the roof beams of the courthouse hung a *punkah*; this was mobilised, when court was in session, by the repeated arm movements of a prisoner hauling on its long piece of string.

At the back of Waiyevo station, descending from the rain forests of the mountains above, runs a stream from which a fern-edged water-race diverts a flow of fresh cold water along the side of the valley to a rock-lined swimming pool which had been created some time earlier at the back of the district officer's residence. While I was living in Waiyevo I refurbished the pool, and built a bamboo fence for privacy and a small *bure* next to it as a sun shelter. From the pool, the water flowed out through irrigated terraces of watercress and taro to a bathing pool at the back of the police quarters. Along the path up to the back of our residence, our milking cow grazed amongst citrus, avocado, mango and soursop trees; we also kept a fowl yard in which strutted *toa ni veikau*, the native jungle roosters.

The residence was arch-colonial. You could play indoor cricket down either the back veranda or the front hall, and the kitchen annex could have serviced a small army. Our bedroom was in another annex that had once been the courthouse, and from our bed, through what was once the public entrance to the court, we had a view that took in the whole sweeping progression of land up the northward coast. The view from the front porch of the residence was framed by two immense rain trees that were home to a profusion of birds, ferns and daydreams, and within this leafy frame was a picture of the blue ocean currents swirling through the Somosomo Strait below us and the squat hills of Vanua Levu beyond.

We were aware when we were there that we would probably never dwell within such an idyll again, so we lived its beauty day by day, and where decay and neglect had occurred I set about restoration. I was assisted in these endeavours by a platoon of prisoners. Fiji had a prison programme whereby if a gaol sentence was of six months or less, the sentence could be served 'extramurally'. If a local official was prepared to take on the responsibility of supervising these extramural prisoners, the alternative of a prisoner being shipped off to fester in an urban gaol was avoided. I would put the prisoners under the charge of the most responsible one of their number, and they would work with me on rural development projects on the island, collecting rations at the end of the day and sleeping in their own homes.

I fully admit to a touch of sentimentality in my attachment to Waiyevo. I had asked to be posted there and my choice had been more aesthetic and soul-searching than career-oriented. Apart from the beauty of the place, my mother had lived there for six years as a girl and I was curious to see if I would feel a sense of belonging if I lived on the island. Her family home was on the other side of the sports field from my office at Waiyevo and, from all the stories she had told us as children, it was easy for me to picture her there as a Taveuni youth. She and her sisters would put on their party dresses and sail with their mother down the coast to Waimaqera for an overnight party, to meet the men who would have ridden down on horses. Music at the party would be provided by a band shipped up from Suva, and the girls would watch from the verandas as the adults danced late into the night.

The glory days of Taveuni copra plantations were already fading fast when my mother was a girl, and they were long gone by my time on the island. However, some vestiges remained. One such was the cinema at Waimaqera, a tin-walled hall with wooden benches for the patrons and a raised, armchair-covered platform at the back of the hall for the grandees. There we sat with our elderly host J.V. Tarte, the owner of Waimaqera plantation, and watched the movies. If the film action intensified or slapstick was involved, the level of shrieking and laughter would rise to a crescendo which reverberated off the tin walls. When this happened, J.V. would press a button next to his chair and a small red light would come on just below the screen, at which signal the audience quickly resumed silence.

As district officer Taveuni I had a dilapidated long-wheel-base Landrover at my disposal. Taveuni was the end of the line for many things and in those days before the advent of the car ferry, motor vehicles that made it to the island were usually on their last wheels and had come there to die. I took a precarious enjoyment out of coaxing my Landrover up the rough track that had recently been cut to Des Voeux Peak for the installation of a telecommunications dish.

As the track climbs through the rainforests, from about the 600 metre mark up to the Des Voeux Peak summit standing close to 1200 metres, scarlet bunches of *tagimoucia* orchids flash at you from the mossy tree trunks, and for the last seventy metres of the climb the track cuts through volcanic cinder which crumbles away as you drive over it. The summit is part of the edge of an extinct volcano, and about three kilometres off to the north, Lake Tagimoucia can be seen glistening in the volcano's jungle-covered caldera.

If you clamber into the forest it doesn't take long to encounter the enigmatic and dapper little silktail. Enigmatic because taxonomists have been unable to agree on a place for this bird in the avian family-tree, and dapper because it is quite so, with its satin iridescent black coat and silky white tail. The silktails are found only on Taveuni and the adjoining hills of Vanua Levu. Like a lot of insectivores they seem fearless and inquisitive, and it is a special pleasure to sit on a tree-root up in the primeval forest on the very top of Taveuni with a friendly little silktail for company.

We had American ornithologists Bill and Ruth Beckon staying with us for a while in Waiyevo. I would drop them near Des Voeux Peak, where they would erect a pup-tent and carry out their ornithological work up in the cloud-filled forest. During one of these field trips they netted what they called a Taveuni monkey bat and claimed it was a new species. I first learnt of this on getting home from work one day when I went to our fridge for a beer. There in the blue glare of the fridge light, orange eyes staring at my throat, clawed-wings spread, thin red tongue protruding from white fangs, was an angry-looking bat. I lifted its black rubbery wing out of the butter and slipped a bottle of beer from under its furry torso. It was about thirty centimetres across and the angry look on its face probably related to the fact that its belly had been dissected so that our ornithologist friends could discern what its last meal had been.

Some years later I was sent a copy of the bulletin of the British Museum entitled 'A New Species of Pteralopex Thomas, 1888 (Chiroptera: Pteropodidae) from the Fiji Islands'. The bat in our butter had been bulletined by the British Museum, for the Beckons had indeed discovered a brand new species.

Then there were the ghosts, spirits and devils, who seemed to outnumber the mere mortals on Taveuni. Down at the south end of the island, people saw *veli*, the little people, indigenous fairies, all the time. As far as I was aware, *veli* did no-one harm, and such was the conviction of those that had sighted them, it would have been churlish to do other than express polite wonder at the latest *veli* incident.

At Waiyevo the resident *tevoro*, a devilish spirit, had the unfortunate habit of getting unmarried women pregnant. In view of their purely temporal powers, there was little the Waiyevo police could do to prevent his attacks on these apparently innocent women.

One night Marijcke and I were dining with a planter at the south end of the island. He had a charming Fijian wife, and members of their extended family were present at the dinner. Half way through dinner he said that one night last week a big ball of light had come out of the garden and hovered here in the dining room while the family all looked on in fear and wonder. There were nods of assent from the family around the table.

'And then it drifted out the door, back into the night.'

'It must have been ball lightning,' I ventured.

'Oh no, there was nothing sudden about it. It just hovered there,' he said, pointing to a spot in the middle of the room, 'as if it was surveying us, and then it left.' Long pause. 'It was Daucina.' And the family all nodded earnestly.

The dividing line between us and the spirit world was under stress in Taveuni. Daucina was a pre-Christian Fijian god who was personified as a glowing ball of light.

A certain *mata ni yasana*, an elected provincial official, who took himself very seriously, used to decry to me the ignorance of some of the members of his constituency. One day we were footing it to a village meeting in Lavena in the days before a road was cut along the coast to that village. Beside the ancient track we came across a vaguely phallic boulder just over a metre high, on top of which small leaves were secured under a round rock. One of our group picked a leaf from a nearby bush and added it to the leaves under the rock as a supplication to the *tevoro* that inhabited the boulder.

'That's the trouble with us Fijians,' the *mata ni yasana* berated his fellow travellers. 'How can we progress when we are held back by heathen superstitions?'

Around the corner, the track stretched ahead through a grove of very old, very high coconut trees. I was walking behind the *mata ni yasana*, when the man behind me shouted and jerked me back. A coconut travelling at terminal velocity crashed to the ground in front of me grazing the shoulderblade of the *mata ni yasana* as it plummeted. When he realised how close he had come to having his skull split open like a melon, the *mata ni yasana* became quite ashen; and when we reached Lavena he asked to make the *sevusevu* presentation, in which he paid homage not only to the Lavena people but every spirit that walked the neighbourhood.

In the far northeast corner of Taveuni district is the island of Naqelelevu. When I was district officer Taveuni, the population of Naqelelevu was about twenty hardy souls who lived out on the edge of human existence like Bedouins at a desert oasis. Their island was 140 hectares of inhospitable raised coral; inhospitable because the limestone rocks which cover it are in places as sharp as needles. It is pockmarked with rocky holes, and rough coral spires thrust up all over the place. The only land that is any good for planting is a narrow strip along the foreshore near the little village, and a restricted range of food crops were being grown there on my visits. These conditions had their compensations: succulent coconut crabs live in the limestone caverns, and through subterranean waterways sea water travels to two inland lakes in which the islanders kept big fish and turtles in live storage for times when the weather precluded fishing in the lagoon.

And what a lagoon. It is 22 kilometres long and 11 kilometres wide, and its barrier reef is up to 2 kilometres in breadth. The barrier reef can only be navigated through at its western end; and when you do so the island is still below the horizon, for it lies flat, off to the very eastern extremity of the atoll 'in the ocean's bosom unespied'.

In any one year very few boats take the passage through into that distant lagoon, and I always enjoyed the opportunity to do so. If there was a national census or a general election on, I would commandeer a government boat and head off to the Ringgolds with the semi-legitimate excuse of comprehensively covering my district. So it was that I took a general election polling team to Naqelelevu in 1976. There were only a dozen registered voters on the island but we were proud to be taking universal suffrage to even the most isolated communities of Fiji. However, when we arrived at Naqelelevu, we found that half the population were off-island attending a religious meeting of some sort. So while the crew of our boat went fishing further up the lagoon, we overnighted at the village and drank the supply of kava that we had presented as our *sevusevu*, which was now being served back to us as we talked long into the night on that lonely island outpost.

In the morning we set up the polling station in the dappled shade of a tree just above the high tide mark, with the glare of the lagoon side-lighting the scene and the rumbling of the barrier reef the constant background sound. The electoral rolls were placed on a small wooden table brought from one of the houses. Two chairs were found for the officials, who sat behind the table. One official was to take the voter's name, find it in the electoral roll and cross it out. The other official would call out the voter's name to allow for public challenge of impostors, and then give the voter his ballot paper. A third official stood by with a little bottle and paint brush, with which he was to daub with indelible ink the cuticle of the voter's forefinger; this was to ensure that the voter didn't flaunt the system by voting twice.

I use voter in the singular because only one of the villagers turned out to be eligible to vote that day. With absolutely no sense of the ridiculous the polling station was declared open. The voter went through the identification process and then turned to the little audience of seated villagers, ballot paper in one hand and daubed index finger protruding awkwardly from the other. Grinning selfconsciously, he stood there long enough for the audience to take their mental snapshots of his moment of importance, and then another official guided him to the white wooden polling booth that we had shipped with us.

The booth had been set up some distance from the table, giving the event an added sense of space and time. The official politely advised the protagonist to take his time with his vote. Inside the booth he did just that, while the rest of us on Naqelelevu that day looked on solemnly. Finally the booth started wobbling slightly as he went through the motions of placing his mark on the ballot paper. He emerged. Everyone pointed to the ballot box, and he dropped the paper into its slot. He then stood for a while in front of the box like someone who has just won a TV gameshow, with a sheepish grin and not knowing quite where to put his hands.

Voting done, and it was time for the officials to go through the carefully observed ritual of sealing the box and its padlock with twine and great amounts of red sealing wax. They glued a label onto the box and marked it as that of the Naqelelevu Polling Station, with its lonely ballot paper inside, thereby inadvertently eliminating the principle of the secret ballot. We packed up our gear, and bade farewell, sailing off to the south and leaving the islanders to their thoughts on the wonderful machinery of democracy.

THE GOVERNOR GENERAL'S PATH

BY THE END of June 1987, Fiji's pressure cooker was ready to blow again. The leaders of Bavadra's government had absented themselves overseas for most of the month, looking for external solutions and casting aspersions on the governor general's motives and legality. Meanwhile the army and the Taukei movement had learnt from their representatives' attendances of the Advisory Council meetings that the governor general was deadly serious about restoring parliamentary democracy in a manner which would be compatible with his responsibilities as the Queen of Fiji's representative, and many of them were not convinced this would auger well for their aspirations. While the main task of June had been to safeguard the nation's economy, it was now time for the governor general to provide a direction out of the political fire.

On June 11 Ratu Penaia had broadcast to the nation his plan of action to lead the country expeditiously back to parliamentary democracy. It was a plan which called for a high degree of trust from a nation on its knees. If aspects of it appear audacious today, it should be remembered that it was created in the weeks following the coup, when the threat of communal violence was ever present and the uncertainty of national direction was crippling both the economy and the national morale. The two boundaries within which the plan was mapped were that it had to travel within the laws of Fiji, and it had to have a realistic chance of acceptance by the divided communities.

In the June 11 address, Ratu Penaia made it clear that the commitment he had given to the Great Council of Chiefs in the aftermath of the coup for a review of the Constitution of Fiji had its motivation in the looking for ways to strengthen the political rights of the indigenous Fijians. However, he emphasised that no changes to the Constitution would be made in an unlawful manner, and he was adamant that the Fiji Indian community should play its full part in the solution. In doing so he called on 'all the faith and understanding that the people of Fiji, and their leaders, can muster.' This mustering would be the first step along the governor general's path.

The second step was to be the formation of a constitutional review committee, which would be a politically balanced body with a respectable input of legal expertise. It would give the public the opportunity to make submissions to it and after due deliberation would deliver its report to the governor general. The third step would be the formation by the governor general of a council of national reconciliation, representing the full spectrum of Fiji's political scene. This council would be charged with achieving consensus on constitutional changes and national reconstruction, based on the report of the constitutional review committee.

In order to legally implement the expected consensus at this council, an Act of Parliament would be required in accordance with the existing Constitution. As Parliament had been dissolved, the governor general would call new elections for the House of Representatives in order for them to pass this Act. Under a formula to be agreed and incorporated in the Covenant of National Reconciliation, a national slate of candidates would be put forward for the House of Representatives which would result in an uncontested election, in so far as the governor general could 'call on the goodwill and understanding of the people of Fiji' to support this path.

The newly elected House, in accordance with the Covenant formula, would lawfully pass the amendments to the Constitution, and directly thereafter seek dissolution of Parliament. The governor general would then call for fresh and fully contested elections under the amended Constitution as quickly as legally possible. 'Put your trust in the path that I am laying before the nation and I give you my word that your trust will not be misplaced,' concluded Ratu Penaia in his address to the nation.

If all this sounds a little extraordinary, remember that we were living in extraordinary days in Fiji back then, and the path set down was a legal approach without recourse to force.

The reaction to Ratu Penaia's June 11 address was encouraging. Both national newspapers enthusiastically endorsed the governor general's path and the Council of Advisers gave it their approval. But the missing voice of accord remained that of the deposed government, and thereby Fiji's Indian community whose leaders were members of that government.

Getting the deposed government, or in their absence, credible representation of the Indian community, onto the governor general's path became high priority at Government House. By the time the leaders of the deposed government returned to Fiji at the end of June even their most vocal ally, New Zealand's prime minister Lange, had advised them to go back to Fiji and support the governor general's efforts. The governor general's emissary to New Zealand, Mosese Qionibaravi, had reported back to us after his June 18 meeting with Lange that the latter had advised that it was untenable and unrealistic for Dr Bavadra to claim that he was still prime minister in the current political situation.

Dr Bavadra came to Government House on June 26 for his first meeting with the governor general after his return from his world trip and opened the door to dialogue with the NFP/Labour coalition that had formed the deposed government. A fuller meeting was arranged for June 29, and in preparation for this I put together a position paper for the governor general assessing the stance of the deposed government. The main thing to get over to Dr Bavadra and his political colleagues was the reality of the governor general's besieged position and how hard they were making it for him to restore national sanity. If through lack of support the governor general's role became untenable for Ratu Penaia, it was most probable the Taukei movement and the army would take over and declare a republic with a one-sided constitution. If the NFP/Labour coalition provoked civil disobedience leading to a breakdown in social order, the slide into communal violence could be rapid. It was by now clear that foreign military forces would not intervene. Continuing disruption of Fiji's economy would lead to economic hardship for Fiji's people and hardening of communal antipathy.

The deposed government's Supreme Court challenge to the governor general's actions implied that he should resign. Is this really what they wanted? There were two likely options if they were not prepared to cooperate with the governor general: a second military coup followed by a unilateral declaration of a republic, or, if he could hold off such a coup, for the governor general to proceed down his path to parliamentary democracy without them. The latter option would involve the appointment of an Indian advisory council to serve as the governor general's connection to the Indian community.

The June 29 talks were held at the governor general's *bure* outside Lautoka. Dr Bavadra was joined at this meeting by his political colleagues

Jai Ram Reddy, Mahendra Chaudhry, Tupeni Baba, Etuate Tavai and Harish Sharma. I took notes throughout the meeting, and it is plain from these that, while Dr Bavadra's camp was now committed to dialogue, there was still some way to go before they would give their full cooperation to the governor general.

At the meeting they finally gave an answer to the governor general's long-standing invitation for them to take up four seats on the Council of Advisers. That answer was no. They called for a change to the terms of reference for the Constitutional Review Committee so that they were not premised on the need for constitutional alteration. If such changes to the terms were made they would consider providing their representatives to sit on the committee. They were non-committal regarding the Supreme Court action they were bringing against the governor general's dissolution of Parliament. They asked the governor general to arrange and chair a meeting between them and Ratu Mara and his political colleagues. They asked for full investigation to be held on Rabuka's claim that they had a political connection with Libya, as they wanted to see their name cleared in this regard. Ratu Mara had previously said he wanted an investigation into the allegations of corruption in his government so that his name could be cleared, and Bavadra said that if this investigation was held they would be pleased to provide evidence to the investigation.

Even with his huge reservoirs of good temper, Ratu Penaia's patience with political posturing was wearing thin. He reminded them of the gravity of the situation, and said, 'The longer we prolong, I am afraid we are in for a very hard time.' Chaudhry's stance was, 'We cannot arrive at a solution overnight. The damage has been done, and the healing process must be on a basis that it is fair and honourable to all people.' Jai Ram Reddy's concluding remarks to the governor general were, 'If you see merit in what we are putting forward then there is very little between us at this stage. We must be seen to be doing the right thing.'

In spite of its inconclusiveness, the fact that this meeting had been held and the long-requested dialogue had commenced was heartening for Ratu Penaia. It had been a source of great frustration for him since the coup that his efforts to look after the interests of the Indian community had been thwarted by the absence of their leaders, and indeed the absence of one preeminent leader of that community with whom he could have an open, trusting relationship. He was a man who placed huge store on the sanctity and value of personal relationships.

After the meeting we discussed its dynamics and agreed that Jai Ram Reddy was the man who most clearly articulated Indian interests and on whom the mantle of leadership most comfortably fitted. Jai Ram was generally softly spoken and careful, but was forceful in his dialectic. He had a rather meek manner and often had a slightly bemused, almost hurt expression on his face. These outward appearances belied a dogged inner resolve, and his political courage had been evident from the time he defeated the former leader of the opposition, Siddiq Koya, in parliamentary elections for the Lautoka constituency. A lawyer by profession, his keen intellect appeared to operate strictly within a reverence for the law, but we felt he would allow himself to think beyond these confines if it was for the greater good. I rang his house and asked him if he would care to return to the *bure* to join Ratu Penaia for an evening drink, and he returned alone that evening for a couple of whiskies with the governor general. There was a genuine sense of desire to help each other at the end of that evening, and I remember Jai Ram saying to Ratu Penaia, 'You and I always got along very well when we were in Parliament together.'

During that evening Ratu Penaia floated the idea of an Indian Advisory Council to advise the governor general in the same way that Fijian opinion was carried through the Great Council of Chiefs. Jai Ram said he'd give it some thought. A couple of days later I phoned him to ask if he might be able to suggest some names to serve on such a council. On July 6 he wrote to the governor general in a letter that, though helpful in its tone, gave the expected advice that to create a separate Indian Advisory Council would not be seen as a good move as it would be perceived as an attempt to undermine and divide the NFP/Labour coalition. Jai Ram Reddy had probably rightly rejected the concept, but Ratu Penaia was pleased that dialogue was underway and that the message of his determination to bring the Indian viewpoint fully into the picture had been firmly received.

The commencement of the work of the Constitutional Review Committee held potentially big rewards. To get the committee underway would demonstrate momentum down the governor general's path. It would give the public a chance to air their views in legally constituted hearings with representatives of all major political elements present. It would demonstrate to Fiji, and the world at large, the legal and consultative nature of the governor general's leadership. If we could attain the participation of the deposed government's representatives on the committee, this would indicate they were now fellow travellers on the path, and, as a result, remaining international reservations and domestic blockades such as the potentially ruinous refusal to begin the sugar harvest could be expected to drop away.

The governor general decided that membership of the Constitutional Review Committee would be made up of sixteen appointees, with four to be nominated by the deposed prime minister, four by the deposed Leader of the Opposition, four by the Great Council of Chiefs and four to be appointed by the governor general. The governor general's appointees were the constitutional lawyer Dr Sahu Khan, Suva lawyer Kantilal Parshotam, Government House legal adviser Isikeli Mataitoga, and Rotuman representative Atfoa Varea. In addition he appointed the chairman – the ex-attorney-general, Sir John Falvey QC. Rabuka would sit on the committee as one of the Great Council of Chiefs' nominees. The committee was to commence its work on July 6 and report back to the governor general by July 31. It would be assisted by the soon-to-be-named expert in constitutional law, who would be provided by the Commonwealth Secretariat.

The governor general's emissaries to overseas governments and the Commonwealth Secretariat were all reporting international support for the governor general's leadership direction, but still we were frustrated by the lack of agreement with the NFP/Labour coalition on the terms of reference for the review committee. As late as June 29, in a letter from Viseisei village signed by him as 'prime minister', Bavadra was still opposing the need for a constitutional review, but said that if it had to be done it should be undertaken by 'a body of independent individuals, such as a royal commission of eminent jurists from outside Fiji.'

July 1 was a bad day. The country was rife with rumours of imminent Taukei movement violence and a second coup. We had to take these threats seriously, for the Taukei movement had grown increasingly wary of the governor general's path; it was not revolutionary enough for them and they could see Ratu Penaia was determined to bring the Indian political leaders in on it. Dr Bavadra rang me that evening to say that he had been warned and was worried about a second coup. He asked me to assure the governor general that he was working to get his parliamentary colleagues onto the governor general's path and he had brought forward a meeting in this regard from July 5 to July 3. It seemed the penny had finally dropped.

Bavadra asked for, and received the following morning, a letter from the governor general setting out the outstanding points regarding the review committee. The letter concluded with: 'I cannot emphasise too heavily, for the sake of our nation's future, the need for you to decide promptly on your participation in the path that I have put before the nation for a return to parliamentary democracy. In particular your provision of four names for the Constitutional Review Committee is required, if possible today, if this path is to be started out on and further dangerous delays avoided.'

During the first week of July I had several telephone conversations with Dr Bavadra and Jai Ram Reddy trying to satisfy them on a change in the terms of reference for the review committee. We set up a round table meeting attended by the governor general, Bavadra, Reddy, Rabuka, Bole and Sir John Falvey on July 8 in an attempt to break the deadlock on the terms of reference. Meanwhile, on July 3, Filipe Bole, Ratu Inoke Kubuabola and Taniela Veitata had held a meeting with the governor general. I didn't attend the meeting but afterwards Ratu Penaia told me the Taukei movement's message was, '*sa vakarau na dogo*' meaning that they were ready to cut clubs from the mangrove trees to use in widespread violence against their opponents. There was danger in delay and Sir John had begun the review committee's work on schedule on July 6, with our assurance that the four Bavadra appointees would shortly join.

In the interests of full participation of the deposed government's representatives, on July 13 the governor general issued a second letter to the review committee appointees changing the wording of their terms of reference. I quote the changes in full as an example of what it sometimes takes to achieve political face-saving. The relevant section now read: 'To review the Constitution of Fiji with the view to proposing to the governor general any amendments which will guarantee indigenous Fijian political interests with full regard to the interests of other peoples in Fiji.' They had previously read: 'To review the Constitution of Fiji with a view to proposing to the governor general amendments which will strengthen the political representation of indigenous Fijians, and in so doing to bear in mind the best interests of other peoples in Fiji.'

July 13 was a breakthrough day, and when I minuted Ratu Penaia at 10.35am to let him know that the four Bavadra appointees to the CRC, Jai Ram Reddy, Tupeni Baba, Krishna Datt and Ratu Mosese Tuisawau, had all turned up for duty and were participating in that day's meeting, he shot back a minute saying simply, 'Well done. PKG. 13.7.87.'

On the same day we issued a news release announcing that the governor general had ordered procedures for public and group meetings, proscribed under the Public Emergency Regulations, to be relaxed to allow the people of Fiji to get together for calm and rational discussions on the constitutional review. Until further notice, permission for public meetings for this purpose would not be required.

With the Constitutional Review Committee's work underway and the deposed government now following the governor general's path, the decision was made to postpone the July 17 deadline for issuing Writs of Election. Such writ issuance was legally required as a consequence of the governor general's dissolution of Parliament. The supervisor of elections delivered a letter to the governor general on July 16 giving the recommendation of the Electoral Commission that the writs should not be issued. The commission based its recommendation largely on the existence of a State of Emergency. Had the new mood of political cooperation not been clear for all to see, postponing the deadline would have been critical, as the governor general had to be seen to be upholding and acting within the laws of Fiji. But with all major political parties now represented on his review committee, it was now patently obvious that Ratu Penaia was working for the greater good of Fiji in not issuing the writs, and there was not a squeak of dissent when the deadline passed.

Professor Keith Patchett, an expert in constitutional law from Wales, joined the Government House team during the week in which the Writs of Election deadline fell. Patchett had been selected from a list of four experts the Commonwealth Secretariat had produced. He was funded by the Commonwealth and reported to the governor general. Finally we had someone on our team who was professionally qualified to advise the governor general on constitutional matters. Patchett advised that the postponement of the writs could be justified on the basis of the doctrine of necessity.

Keith Patchett made an immediate contribution to the governor general's path by pointing out that the governor general had the power to recall the dissolved Parliament for the purpose of making the required constitutional amendments, thereby obviating the need for further elections under the existing Constitution. Thereafter the recall idea became a preferred option to the uncontested election step which had originally been announced, and the governor general presented it widely as the most likely option for the Council of National Reconciliation to take.

The governor general assigned Professor Patchett to assist the review committee in its hearings. The review committee had a massive task, and throughout July they listened around the country to the views of political parties, religious groups and individuals. The Great Council of Chiefs met on July 20 to decide on the content of a submission to the review committee. Its deliberations became acrimonious and at one stage Ratu Mara threatened to leave the Council.

Rabuka was quoted in the *New Zealand Herald* on July 28 as saying that if Fijians didn't get control of Parliament, there would be 'widespread revolution.' He said he would have a hard job controlling the army because 'we might just go out and join them. Three thousand soldiers with arms, fighting for what we want. I would not stop them, I would lead them, and I won't be taking orders from anyone.'

Eventually the Great Council of Chiefs concluded its meeting in consensus and a submission was made to the review committee on July 30. The members and advisers of the Constitutional Review Committee demonstrated sincerity and commitment to their part in the exercise, considering nearly 1000 submissions during the seven weeks that they gave free service to the nation. But when Sir John delivered the committee's report to the governor general on August 17, it was not a unanimous one. The views of Dr Bavadra's appointees on the review committee were appended as a so-called minority report, in which they called for no changes to the 1970 Constitution. The so-called majority report advocated a series of constitutional changes, including many of the wishes of the Great Council of Chiefs.

Meanwhile we were working long into the night on the formative papers for the Council of National Reconciliation. Looking at my papers on the council today is like entering the twilight zone; these were plans for a bold ship that would never be launched. For all their futility, the plans still speak to me of the certainty with which we were walking down the governor general's path at that time.

As all this preparatory work was going on, the governor general's efforts to bring the opposing political parties into meaningful talks was making real progress. The success of these talks would result in a different approach to national reconstruction being taken, which would make the Council of National Reconciliation obsolete before its time.

Failure is an orphan they say, but let me take this one on. In the days of uncertainty after the coup, I accompanied the governor general to the Western Division from June 1 to June 3, where he held numerous meetings with the Indian community who had made it clear that he was looked to for national salvation. He met there with Dr Bavadra and Jai Ram Reddy, and at that time just two weeks after the coup, they were still holding to the unrealistic belief that the governor general should restore their government to office. We knew from what we had learned in and around the recent meeting of the Great Council of Chiefs, that such a course would have led to one of two scenarios: immediate communal violence and irreparable damage to the nation, or another army takeover. Good intentions were not enough. The governor general had to have a public plan of action. He was the man on the spot and, even if he'd wanted to, there was no-one to pass the buck to.

We were staying at the governor general's *bure* on the outskirts of Lautoka. I sat down at the dining table and wrote a short paper which was the origin of the so-called governor general's path. It would provide him with breathing space and give him the initiative of direction. I then presented the idea to the governor general on the basis that it was legal and provided a positive way forward. Obviously he consulted with others on the plan's legality and practicality, and considered other options, but at the end of the day there were few who were able to give him a neutral viewpoint. With this admission I put my wrists into history's stock for an inevitable pasting, perhaps deservedly so, for my advice to Ratu Penaia on this subject. The plan was so full of leaps of faith over deep pitfalls. And you see, Ratu Penaia was a man who would take up such challenges, even, or maybe especially, if they rested on the evocation of the basic goodwill of people and if he thought it was in the best interests of those whom he was charged to protect.

But if the launching of this ship of councils, committees and covenants never eventuated, the building of it did serve a purpose. It was a clear demonstration to the politicians of the strength of the governor general's resolve to bring about national reconstruction in a manner in which the elected politicians would have to play a full and constructive part, and it focused their attention on how such a forum of unification would operate. In addition it gave Government House the time and momentum needed to carefully convene the opposing political leaders into meaningful dialogue.

In the months of crisis and uncertainty in the aftermath of the coup, the existence of the governor general's path gave the nation a route to follow, and if the path was difficult and flawed, it was infinitely preferable to the chaos and carnage evident in other countries where governments have been overthrown by force, society torn in two and no direction of decency given.

THE NEVER SIMPLE TRUTH

OSCAR WILDE WROTE, 'The truth is rarely pure and never simple.' My learning curve in this area rose steeply at Government House, particularly in relation to the voracity and the veracity of the media.

The Australian and New Zealand television media had a history of miscolouring Fiji's political situation well before the coup, with the once venerable Australian Broadcasting Commission and Television New Zealand both leading players. Intentional or not, their slant against traditional customs and leaders in Fiji in favour of popular Eurocentric preferences came through time and time again, often insulting not just the former but the truth as well.

In the days after the coup d'état, it was reported that New Zealand television viewers were shown tanks driving through tropical streets juxtaposed with footage of the Bank of New Zealand's Suva building in ruins, thereby giving the impression it had been destroyed by civil or military unrest. But there were no tanks in Fiji. African film footage must have been used. And the truth about the bank was that it was under a construction contract, the messy building site pictured was in fact the bank building under demolition prior to the construction of a new one.

Amongst my other duties at Government House, the governor general's public relations fell to me. I worked at this role through speech-writing, public announcements, and encouraging the governor general to meet visiting journalists and TV crews. Ratu Penaia did a bit of media relations work, but not much. Even when he had been a rather reluctant politician, he was not given to pandering to the media, and as governor general he didn't have a politician's vote-getting agenda. He was averse to press conferences, they weren't his style. I could understand any Pacific Islander, used to the mutual verbal respect displayed at their own meetings, finding the manners at press conferences objectionable.

We couldn't rely on the adviser for information, Reverend Raikivi, to get the governor general's message across because of the Reverend's Taukei movement blinkers. Thus it became my job, within the tense strictures within which we were working, to rather inadequately inform the public on what was being achieved in the halls of government. Each release would begin with 'A Government House spokesman said today...' The Fiji public got nearly as sick of that phrase as they did the 'return to normalcy' cliché which was being used in every speech at that time. No doubt an apology to them is overdue.

The deposed government had a pretty effective public relations campaign going in Australia and understandably they were pushing an anti-Rabuka and, at times, anti-governor general line. The Australian Broadcasting Commission used a lot of their material and on one occasion in early June they quoted a minister from the Bavadra government as saying that a large number of Indians had been murdered or raped in the wake of the coup. This was too much for me; the domestic implications from this sort of disinformation were enormous given Radio Australia's wide audience in Fiji. So I rang Radio Australia's director, Peter Barnett, told him who I was and said that Radio Australia should check its facts before it broadcast such inflammatory stuff. AAP's respected correspondent in Fiji, Jim Shrimpton, had heard the same stories, checked them, found they were untrue and spiked them. I had run checks with key police officials that day, and it was clear that these reported incidents just had not happened. History has borne me out in that regard. I told Barnett that Radio Australia was 'the victim' of a campaign of rumours which dangerously distorted the situation in Fiji.

But the media almost always has the last word; and so it was when Radio Australia announced in their next news bulletin that the permanent secretary to Fiji's governor general, Peter Thomson, had 'ludicrously' accused Radio Australia of 'orchestrating' a campaign of rumours against the Fiji administration. No mention of their being 'the victim' of an orchestration. Just a simple twist from Radio Australia of being the object to it being the subject, and I looked a right idiot and the ABC's seriously culpable error went uncorrected.

Doyen of the Fiji media, Sir Leonard Usher, subsequently wrote in a letter to Sir William Heseltine, the Queen's private secretary, that 'the governor general's permanent secretary, Peter Thomson, rather overdid a protest by suggesting that the ABC was carrying on an orchestrated campaign against the Fiji administration'. Heseltine sent a copy of the letter to Ratu Penaia, who showed it to me and said, 'Len got that one wrong.' We had just too much on at the time to be battling the media's errors, be they deliberate or unintentional; so one had to let the rarely pure truth slide by.

On September 16 a front page story in the *Fiji Sun*, under the heading 'Give us the truth – Taukei', said that the Taukei movement leaders had demanded to be told the truth of what was transpiring in the coalition-Alliance talks and that their sources had told them that the coalition was still fighting to restore the Bavadra government and retain the 1970 Constitution. One of their most vocal leaders, Ratu Meli Vesikula, said that the movement was 'upset' because I was hiding the truth on what was actually happening in the talks. 'He is releasing important news from Government House which do not tell the exact events. Fijians are no longer amused over Mr Thomson's secrecy over the whole issue. We do not like to be told lies from Government House. Mr Thomson had better start telling us the truth.'

The Taukei movement wasn't letting up on me and the next day at a Council of Advisers meeting, addressing the governor general but looking across at me, Taukei movement demagogue Reverend Raikivi said, 'The press have got things off Your Excellency's desk, probably without Your Excellency's knowledge.'

So what was the truth? As far as Raikivi's insinuation was concerned, it was not only insulting, it was pure and simple hogwash. As far as Vesikula's charge was concerned, the truth was that at the end of the coalition-Alliance meetings I was given a communiqué, agreed by the two sides, to be released to the media verbatim, without embellishment of the sort desired by Vesikula. I carried out my orders. Ratu Meli had yet to learn one of the basics of human politics: don't shoot the messenger.

At a time of extreme national crisis it is not unusual for governments to impose censorship, and the feeling amongst a lot of Fijian leaders in 1987 was that censorship should be imposed. In the main their motivation was not suppression of truth, it was dousing of what they saw as potentially inflammatory press provocation. On the governor general's Council of Advisers, Bill Cruickshank was the one who spoke up strongly against censorship, but there were many who would have welcomed it. In balance the latter were misguided, but there was some merit in their misgivings. How do you reconcile the commercial demands of the empires of Murdoch and Packer for drama and controversy with a desperate national need for calm and consensus? Platoons of public relations consultants might have helped, but in their absence there was a great temptation to tell the foreign journalists to just jack off to where they'd come from.

If New Zealanders and Australians wanted a better appreciation of what their neighbours to the north were thinking, they would have to do better than be spoon-fed by the quick-answer television journalists that were dropping into Fiji in the 1980s. Before the year of the coup d'état, the Australian Broadcasting Commission's high profile *Four Corners* programme went to Fiji, interviewed everyone with a gripe and presented their pillory as a balanced view of Fiji's state of mind. The programme was so one-eyed in its opposition to Ratu Mara's government that the opposition parties in Fiji made videos of the *Four Corners* programme and used them as election propaganda.

The foreign media continually came up with the myth that Indians could not own land in Fiji. This was and is completely untrue, but they persevered with slipping the myth into their stories. Ten percent of Fiji's land is freehold land which our European forbears acquired from the Fijians prior to the colonial government. This freehold land is obviously prime land – our forbears were not inclined to buy swamps and mountain ranges – and freehold land can be bought and sold in Fiji by everyone from Indians to Eskimos. Seven percent of the land in Fiji is state-owned land and this can be leased by anyone regardless of race. Eighty-three percent of the land in Fiji is owned by customary Fijian social units whose land has been painstakingly surveyed, recorded and placed under the administration of the Native Land Trust Board so that it can be leased out to people of any race or nationality. It is, to my knowledge, as good a system of dealing with customary ownership of land as any that have been devised elsewhere, so why the media's perpetuation of this myth of unfairness?

For much of the mid-1980s the Australian media carried a persistent slant that corruption was rife in the Fiji government. I worked for sixteen years in the Fiji government and never came across an instance of corruption that was not punished. I'm not saying there was no corruption; wherever there is government there is likely to be some form of corruption; but Fiji did not have a corrupt government.

What made the snide comments of the Australian media in this regard so riling was that the level of corruption in Australian state governments, when I was living in Sydney in the mid-1980s, was so much more spectacular than anything that might have existed in Fiji. In the Sydney Consular Corps of which I was a part, it was common knowledge that ministers of various Australian state governments were on the take and that senior levels of the state police forces were in cahoots with organised crime.

I got the sneaking feeling that these hard-nosed Australian investigative journalists found it easy meat to run political corruption stories in off-shore developing countries. Their stories were believable because of the Western stereotypes on the subject, and if they ran a Fiji corruption line there would be no physical or legal threats to their persons or their careers, which may not have been so had they run similar stories on the wide-spread corruption going on in the courts, governments and police forces of Australia at the time.

The Australasian media portrayed the emergence of the Labour party in Fiji as the brave modern face of Fiji politics, a truly multiracial party based on socio-economic principles understandable and acceptable to their version of the world. The governments of Australia and New Zealand were both in the hands of Labour parties, and these parties had long provided intermittent periods of good government in both those countries. But the media was coming at it from their own preconceptions, not from the reality of life in Fiji. The reality was that the great majority of Fiji's populace put the security of their interests and their political faith in the hands of the racially-based parties: the Alliance party for the Fijians and the National Federation party for the Indians.

While both of these parties made a big play on the fact that they were multiracial, the reality was that they were each overwhelmingly dominated by one of the two races. Indians who attained high office in the Alliance party did not represent mainstream Indian thought, and the same was true of Fijians who rose to prominence in the National Federation party and the Labour party.

When the Fiji coup took place, it was understandable that Australians and New Zealanders and their media representatives would identify with the interests of democracy and the disenfranchised non-indigene. The tenets of parliamentary democracy were at the very heart of all that their forefathers had struggled for, and their European political cultures rested somewhat uneasily alongside indigenous ones within their own nations.

At the same time they recognised the irony that it was the stand of their historical friends, the indigenous Fijian, that they were opposing. There were few New Zealand families that did not have a friend or relative who had fought alongside Fijians against the Japanese invasion of the South Pacific. There were few that hadn't played against or had Fijian mates as part of their rugby teams. There were few that didn't think of Fijians as the salt of the earth. In contrast their relationship with the Fiji Indian, in whose defence they were mustering, had since the end of Empire been a mutually uncertain one, circumscribed by doubts and watchfulness, while at the same time admiring of principles and industry.

At a personal level in offices, clubs and within friendships and marriages there was no such uncertainty between the Europeans and Indians of Fiji, and the veneer of national ideology denied its existence. But its lingering presence was evident at a communal cultural level and it was quietly divisive. On the Indian side the antipathy had firm roots in the colonial soil. In colonial days the European was the employer and the Indian was the employed, and the former were remembered for their arrogance, their racism and their profiting from the sweat of Indian labour. The Indians had asserted themselves through strength of will and strength of family, through education and wise husbandry, and when the fruits of democracy came their way, they sent the colonial government packing and got rid of the Australian CSR company that had controlled their sugar industry.

Yes, we were arrogant. Yes, we were racists, and I think some of us may have profited. But on the whole far more fortunes were lost than made in Fiji. Looking over the generations of my own family and friends in Fiji, I can see no-one who made much money in the islands. But this does not excuse our arrogance, for which a thousand humble humilities have been due and should be demanded whenever vestiges present themselves. The indenture system under which the bulk of Indians came to Fiji was little better than slavery. We should have understood that better at the time, for many of us were escapees from the arrogance of social class and Anglo-colonialism ourselves. I think of the depressing rankle of the Scottish film *Trainspotters* where a low-life Scot says, 'Some people hate the English. I don't, they're just wankers. We on the other hand are colonised by wankers; can't even find a decent culture to be colonised by.' Bitter self-destructive words, but such is the working of the mind of the oppressed.

Imperialists, from Roman to Mogul to latter-day Russians, are by their nature arrogant. If they weren't they wouldn't have created empires. And does not the arrogance rest within us all? As the Spanish proverb goes: 'It is pleasant to command, be it only a herd of cattle.' So vigilance is required; for to imagine that new imperialists will not emerge, turning disproportionate economic power to military might, and in the flourishing of their ambition and arrogance take to conquering the rest of us would surely be to ignore the synthesising lessons of history.

Racism is not the preserve of British imperialists or Australian sugar company overseers, and Mira Nair's *Mississippi Masala* delves richly on that score. I was having lunch once in Sydney with Karam Ramrakha, the former general secretary of the National Federation party, and we were discussing some of the racial legacies of colonialism. Karam came out with a typically provocative remark: that India may well have invented racism, after all it is a country where wedding advertisements in newspapers still provide descriptions of brides with wheaten-coloured skin. And while it is not for me to presume, I believe that however hurtful the racism of the colonial experience was in the historical conscience of the Fiji Indian, there comes a time to let it be. But if further atonement is required, then let it be dealt with now so that the back-drop of resentment can be folded up and put away forever.

By the time my generation came around, the British Empire had irrevocably fallen, and like teenagers all over the world we were going along with anything The Beatles said was groovy. George Harrison was getting sitar lessons from Ravi Shankar and then off they went to the Himalayas with the Maharishi seeking spiritual enlightenment. We were somewhat superficially searching for Indian culture in Fiji at that time and noticed that, like the culture of Australasians of European extraction, it was but a pale imitation of the richness of the motherland. I identified then one of the many shared experiences that bound us together as non-indigenes in the South Pacific, and recognised the need to cultivate our own hybrid Pacific culture.

When I was working in the Ministry of Foreign Affairs in Suva in the late 1970s, there was a senior official in the ministry who was a bit of a mentor for those of us further down the ladder. He was the main organiser of our kava drinking sessions at the ministry and was a centre of attention around the *tanoa*, being a witty raconteur with a cheering disposition. Out of choice we would go to him for good advice on difficult issues confronting us. He was a Hindu from a rural community which was in a predominantly Fijian area and his social views were thus broader than your average town dweller. Like me he had gone to university in New Zealand. We enjoyed each other's company and often shared confidences.

One day he and I were having a few bowls from the *tanoa* and he was deeply troubled by a political issue that had tested his sensibilities as a Fiji Indian. He said, 'You know Peter, sometimes I think the only answer's for me to emigrate, and I reckon the only place I could go and be happy is in India.'

I knew him well enough to know this was a pipe-dream, and told him so, 'You're dreaming. I'm the one that might be happy living in India; for me it would be an adventure. But I bet you'd find it crushing. If you emigrate anywhere, it'll be to New Zealand.'

We had another bowl of kava and I thought again on how our lot as non-indigenes in the South Pacific was a shared predicament. We recognised that this was the home of the indigenous Fijian, in the very fullest sense of the word 'home'. Fiji was the physical crucible in which, over the millenniums, gene codes had been muscled into a race of people, *na taukei ni Viti*. Within these islands a rich language *na i vosa vakaviti*, the indigenous tongue, had evolved. No person of goodwill could conceivably want to detract in any way from these indigenous truths.

But what of us non-indigenes, the flotsam of Empire, who had been led to believe by our nation, by our families, by our own choices that Fiji was home? Whatever the ethnic cleansers said, there was no home country for us to return to. For us it was a case of love our home in the islands so much that you could reluctantly accept the veils of exclusion, or take the tough option and hit the road Jack.

Where your people have virtually grown out of the land you inhabit, the world must seem a very different place. Indigenous Fijians standing on their ancestral lands must have a sense of oneness with the land which we immigrants can only guess at. Looking around the slopes of the valleys in which their families have lived since before recorded time, surely feelings are evoked for the indigene which will never again be in the human experience of we the uprooted. For all I know, these feelings of indigenous place may be claustrophobic, and no doubt some yearn to be free of the bindings of ancestry, but it would appear that for the majority of indigenes the contrary is the case.

Meanwhile we, the descendants of immigrants, see our island home with a different kind of love. We recognise our transience of life and place, and like the Nobel Prize-winning non-indigenous St Lucian, Derek Walcott: 'one acknowledges with gratitude what's there. The inheritance of the continuity: that's the bounty. So you're not here, so what? Tomorrow the same sea will be bright and shiny; somebody will be saying it's great.'

The strident National Federation party politician, Vijay Parmanandam, once stood up in Parliament and said angry words to the effect that given a realistic opportunity the great majority of Fiji Indians would emigrate. At the time this appeared to me to be national heresy, but no-one in Parliament or the press challenged the truth of his assertion. It is chastening for me on reflection to realise that Parmanandam could have said that the great majority of Fiji non-indigenes would emigrate, and he would have been equally correct, for if I look at the families of Fiji Chinese, Europeans and *kailoma* the same holds true. It is a fact of island life the world over that unless they have compelling reasons to stay, be those of love or money, most of your children will want to get off the rock as soon as they can.

And emigrate we have; but not back to the mother countries from which our forbears voyaged to Fiji. We have chosen to continue our cohabitation as non-indigenes amongst the remodelled relics of the Empire around the Pacific Rim. Which has a curious irony to it when you think of the politics of disgruntlement, grounded historically with good but obsolete reason between the communities of the Fiji Indian and the Fiji European.

And I say again that where one's shared history has not been a happy one, be it one of trading in the misery of other human beings, or of being of the legacy of the exploited, there yet comes a time after atonements and advancements over the generations to say, 'I've got over it', to draw again from Oscar Wilde and say, 'We are all lying in the gutter, but some of us are looking at the stars', and live to be among the latter.

I certainly claim no monopoly on truth in all its shattering around the time of the coup and my mind is open to views of what was and might have been. I don't know, for example, why Ratu Epeli Nailatikau, the commander of the Royal Fiji Military Forces, would have gone off to Australia days before the coup to look at the launching of some other country's naval boat at a time of civil unrest of unprecedented proportions in Fiji, other than to say it was a measure of Dr Bavadra's political immaturity as prime minister and minister of home affairs that he let him go. I will say with absolute certainty in my own mind, as one who knew him since the time of my birth and worked with him daily as his immediate lieutenant in 1987, that Ratu Sir Penaia Ganilau gave Colonel Rabuka no hint of assent in the planning and execution of his coups.

That Rabuka acted essentially alone in the execution of the first coup is acceptable to me, as is the reasonably well-documented view that many influential Fijians were aware of the coup prior to its execution. That Rabuka correctly assessed and reflected the mood of the majority of Fijians when he carried out the coup is attested to by their subsequent reactions. So where does the culpability lie and who is so pure and innocent that they will be the one to point the finger of condemnation?

And what was the truth about the coup leader? He presented himself at the time as a simple soldier with a duty to carry out, who looked forward to the opportunity of quickly handing power over to the senior Fijian leaders. But the man who stood on the balcony of the Suva Civic Centre the week after the coup and raised his fists in triumph to the adoring crowd below did not appear to me to be a man who would easily relinquish power.

After meetings of the Council of Advisers, a few of the councillors would usually dally in my office, which was directly adjacent to the council's meeting room. The dallying was done around a *tanoa* and while some rounds of kava were going down, the councillors had a chance for a break from the anxious realities of the day. Rabuka would quite often stay on for a few bowls and I was impressed by the way he would listen to and contribute to the banter without any show of egotism. He was relaxed and comfortable. But I would observe in the others a suppressed excitement in sharing his fellowship. Like it or not, he had acquired an aura of charisma which people were drawn to. I once read that, after the Nuremberg trials, Albert Speer had said that human beings should beware of the very dangerous qualities of charisma. I saw its seductiveness working like the tidal pull of the moon around Rabuka.

His prowess as a communicator in person and on camera became quickly apparent, and he regularly made himself available to the media. He was self-deprecating and humorous, with a simple but unmistakable hold on authority and direction, and you were left in no doubt he had both the will and the power. For the majority of Fijians and many an international television viewer, Rabuka was the soldier-hero of male myth, taking up the sword in righteous resolve for his people and appearing to wield it only so far as it was necessary for the strong to protect the weak.

Rabuka said that in carrying out the coup d'état to safeguard the Fijian race, he was following a mission given him by God. Detractors were quick to hold up his comments as delusions of divine ordinance, for history has grown justifiably wary of claims made by kings and armies of having God on their side. But consider the position of a religious man who accepts the joys and tragedies of life as God's will. And look at the teachings of great scholars who over the centuries have argued the case for and against inexorable fate and free will, and perhaps one is less quick to deride those who believe they are carrying out God's work.

In Australia and New Zealand the old culture was rugby, racing and beer. In Fiji the trilogy was rugby, army and church, and Rabuka perfectly manifested that trilogy as a former member of the Fiji national rugby side, the soldier's soldier of the army's high command, and lay preacher of the Fijian Methodist church. Fijians had been looking ahead in vain to see from whence the next generation of their leadership would come, when in a flash the coup-maker rose like a mystagogue warrior from their ranks. He had the bearing, the *mana*, and his demeanour and words moved eloquently within the humbling demands of *i tovo vakaturaga*.

But what of his treason to the wider nation and his breaking of oath and word to those to whom he owed allegiance as an officer and liegeman? Time was needed to judge whether a pleasing countenance, an iron grip and his defiant defence of the indigenous Fijian interests could justify the mental torment, disenfranchisement and economic suffering resulting from his coup. And only time would tell if, in putting on the leader's mantle, he could also heal the wounds, succour the vanquished, turn sword into ploughshare and loathing to love.

FIJI PATOIS

ACROSS THE ROAD from Government Buildings there is a single-storeyed wood and iron building on the harbour's edge. Today the building's waterfront is being lost to a Suva City Council reclamation process which is creeping along Suva's foreshore and the shadows of multi-storeyed modern buildings now fall across its tin roof. Its present use is as a government office and it has taken on the drabness of appearance that such function usually bestows. Until 1960 it was the Boys Grammar School, and I attended it in the fifties decked out in our uniform of short-sleeved white shirt, khaki shorts and black sandals.

In our school days the building was flanked by grass playing fields on two sides. It faced large drooping *baka* trees which lined its frontage onto Victoria Parade and it had the seawall and the lapping waters of the ocean at its rear. On the other side of the main playing field was the boarding hostel for the boys from the islands and the countryside. Today the old hostel is still one of Fiji's finest buildings, labouring under its treatment as another dilapidated government department. The hostel nearly met an untimely end in 1958 when my friend Dougy Thompson from Vanaira and my brother John accidentally set fire to the cubby under the building that we had until then, but never again, used for classes in cigarette smoking.

When I think of Boys Grammar now I think first of food. Snake, the peanut vendor, was there every break shouting 'make it line, make it line' as we pushed and shoved to get at the wares in the baskets that he carried. Over the years he sold thousands upon thousands of little brown bags of roasted peanuts and chilli-laced 'hot peas'. The latter came in two varieties: the extra hot 'soft bean' which was an Indian version of mushy peas, and the garlicky 'hard bean' which he sold in small cones made from spirals of *Fiji Times* newspaper.

Every lunchbreak out on Victoria Parade, pulled up at the kerbside under the baka trees, there was a tiny dark-green Bedford van with the inscription 'Empire Cafe' on its side. At its open back doors a man sold us parcels of vegetable curry and roti, and golden pineapple pies which oozed a thick sweet syrup. We would take this food and go down to the seawall, on which we would sit, legs dangling over the side, while we ate our lunch.

From that lunchtime vantage point memorable scenes were taken in. I recall the waterspouts that danced a seductive turn around Beqa island for a day. Tornado towers of water snaking through the straits between the island and the mainland, the waterspouts rose up from the surface of the ocean into the clouds high above, from which, according to some Beqa islanders, fish rained.

Another day a big dead hammerhead shark was bumping against the seawall at our feet. Then there was an invasion of sea-prawns, and we all took to the water to harvest them. Standing on the seawall in 1959, we watched Fiji Airways' new aeroplane do an inaugural fly-over for the benefit of Suva's population. Up until then we had been used to seeing their three-engined Drover lumbering overhead. The new plane was a de Havilland Heron and with its glinting silver underbelly and what seemed to us at the time to be great speed, it was as if something from outer space had just sped over the coconut treetops.

On the foreshore of the main playing field was the Sea Scouts shed, and behind that I was witness to the most savage fights I have ever seen. A squabble during school hours could lead to the challenge 'after school behind the Sea Scouts shed!' Word would be whispered around the school and those that could, and would, turned up to witness the hostilities in the out-of-view arena between the shed and the seawall. And when those senior boys off the coconut plantations up Cakaudrove way or from the goldmines of Vatukoula fell to fighting, it was fierce. Angry fists, elbows, kicks, hair, teeth, spit, blood, and sometimes bitter tears. Witnessing those fights introduced a certain intimidated diffidence which stayed with me for the rest of my days.

On the playing field itself we played British bulldog. If you were selected you had to stand out alone in the middle of the field while anywhere between ten and sixty boys would line up on one side of the field. You would call out the name of one of the boys, who would then have to try to run past you to the opposite side of the field. If you managed to tackle the chosen one, you had then to lift him off the ground and declare for all to hear 'British bulldog!' at which point he became part of your team and helped you catch the next runner. If he evaded you, as soon as he reached the opposite side of the field the remaining boys charged like a jeering herd of wildebeests across the field to join him. You then tried to pick off one of these hoons as they careered across. The temptation was to go for weak and sickly victims as your chosen one, so that you could boost the strength of your cause by sheer numbers, but this tactic invited scorn. So you stood out there in the middle with all your critical peers waiting for your election of combatant, and you would choose between the dubious glory of being run over the top of by one of your physical superiors with the slim chance of nabbing him if he sprained an ankle, or going for one of your near equals, aware that your place on the school pecking order was then visibly at stake.

I am a *kaivavalagi*, the Fijian generic name for people of European origin, people from over the horizon. This label never gave me satisfaction in my search for identity. It is a bit of a mouthful, unlike the Polynesian equivalent *palagi*, and was much less specific than *kaidia* or *kaijaina*, the Fijian names for Indians and Chinese. In a scrum on the rugby field or in discussion with a drunk in a bar you might find yourself being called *kumala vulavula*, the derogatory Fijian name for white people referring to the pasty off-white colour of the boiled roots of a variety of sweet potato.

Most of the local *kaivavalagi* growing up in Fiji identified with the *kailoma*, people of mixed racial origins. *Kailoma* were the golden ones at school and at play, and it always seemed to me they were the ideal to which Fiji society was moving. One could see in the attitudes, language and behaviour of many young Fiji Indians, a similar leaning towards *kailoma* culture as our shared national culture. The first time I heard and understood the word 'miscegenation' I remember recoiling from it, confused by its negative slant on human progress.

But when coup-coup time came along, for a while the differences between indigenes and non-indigenes were accentuated and there was an emigration exodus of many *kailoma*, *kaivavalagi* and *kaidia* anxious to get on with their lives as individuals and families, rather than live within the confines of racial labels. Race is a fact of life anywhere in the world, but it takes on more importance than it should in places like Fiji at times like that.

It can be said with some veracity that the blame for the racial divide in Fiji lies principally with the *kaivavalagi* who created the situation whereby the indigenous people felt threatened by the numbers of non-indigenes in Fiji. There were elements of colonialism, such as the education system, which institutionalised racial differences, and more could have been done by the colonial government in the lead-up to Independence to emphasise the common humanity and shared future that all the races of Fiji were facing. However, it must be said that much of this institutionalisation was at the behest of the indigenous people and it would be rash indeed to say that racial prejudice was or is a failing confined to white people.

During the Bavadra government, the minister of information was also deputy prime minister. His name was Harish Sharma. He was a Nadi lawyer, a short man with a precise way of speaking and a slightly bemused expression on his face. I worked with him all too briefly and remember him with fondness and respect.

I saw him on a television programme in 1988 and with his typical honesty he was explaining the lack of intermarriage and cultural bonding between the Indians and Fijians. 'In fairness to other races, for some reason Indians find it very hard to assimilate with others,' he said. 'It is because of our background. Our forefathers came from India and there they had to put up with the caste system and they themselves could not intermingle and intermarry. North Indian would not marry South Indian and vice versa. Coming from that background it is difficult for the Indian community to assimilate with others.'

Given time these barriers get lowered and, at a personal level, love and friendship harbour stronger forces than cultural or political dictates. Maybe if we had all been required to speak Fijian as our national language the barriers would have come down faster, for language provides the entry and knowledge to culture and thought. But language is also power, so parents wanted their children to learn English and with that tongue to go beyond the restrictions of one culture to the imagined opportunities and freedom in the other.

Yet many of us whose mother tongue was English wanted to be more Fijian. That was why we positioned ourselves as *kailoma* and spoke the Fiji patois, the street language and a major point of difference between us and the expatriate *kaivavalagi* such as the young Australian and

New Zealand 'bank boys', who came to work in the banks for two year terms and were distinguishable walking around Suva by their white shorts and long white socks.

Fiji patois was mainly simple English with a heavy island accent. It was also leavened with Fijian words which were more pithy than their English equivalents, such as *mataqali* for your extended family, or with Hindi words like *paisa* for money. Many Fijian words had more bite than an English word and were therefore preferred – *lamu* for scared, *save* for weakling, or *boci* for uncircumcised penis were everyday Fiji patois. Sentences tended to begin with 'Bro' (rolling the 'r') if addressing a male, or 'Man' (pronounced 'men') in general address. In third person, people were described as 'fullahs'.

Someone over-refreshed with kava or alcohol is described in Fijian as *kasou*. In Fiji patois the English word 'full' is added, so that such a fullah is 'full-kasou'. 'Full-suit' describes someone who has got all dressed up for a special occasion, and 'full-struck' is when cupid's arrow has driven home; thus 'man, first time the fullah saw her, same time the fullah full-struck'.

A certain quaintness made the Fiji patois quite poetic at times. My Uncle Peter remembers a Savusavu friend of his saying to him after they had been reading the story of Jason and the Argonauts at Boys Grammar School, 'Hey bro, Jason was a brave like I haven't saw before.' Adjectives interpose for nouns and tenses get jumbled into what is an enjoyable flow.

Fiji patois was often inventive and referred, for example, to 'a want-to-be' long before Americans adopted the word 'wannabee' for a poseur. But use of difficult English words, or ones outside the Fiji ken, were eschewed and only used with some embarrassment by the speaker. Thus 'the fullah could run like a what' rather than 'he could run like a deer', for to use 'deer' would have been outside the Fiji milieu, whereas the use of 'a what' is a non-pretentious cover-all.

Another example of the mistrust of 'fancy' words involved the renowned Inspector Mumraj of the Police Training School in Suva, who was lecturing cadets on first aid. Pointing to body parts on a diagram hanging over the classroom's blackboard, his pointer fell on the throat area.

'What is this?'

'Oesophagus, sir,' said a bright cadet at the front of the class.

'Mmmmm,' said Mumraj suspiciously. 'Yes, down the back, what is it?'

'Windpipe, sir.'

'Yes, windpipe,' and looking down at the bright cadet he said scornfully, 'Oesophagus my arse.'

On the other hand, some English expressions that had long gone out of current use overseas remained prevalent in Fiji patois, such as 'he's a real skallywag.' To get the pronunciation of the latter right: roll the 'r' in real and say the word as 'rrill', and pronounce skallywag 'sikellywag'

Emphasis was provided with the word 'again', as when returning from seeing *Spartacus* at the Lilac Theatre, 'Man, the main boy was too good again' (i.e. he was excellent). The dominant interrogative was 'how come', as in 'How come the fullah don't want to drink kava? Fullah *save* or what?' If something was not good it was 'waste time', thus 'Hey bro, my bike too fancy again. Yours really waste time.' If something was inadequately made it was 'shot-shot', as in '*Sa!* The fullah's tin boat is shot-shot bro.'

A lot of the patois was borrowed from Fijian, which was only natural in that the plants, fishes, birds, and places which surrounded us all had Fijian names. Also certain types of behaviour, custom and thought could only be described in Fijian. Thus you always took a *sevusevu* when visiting someone's house, not necessarily the kava root presentation of its Fiji meaning, but a bottle of wine or whisky taken as a gift would be referred to as such.

In spite of the strict morality of the Methodist Church prevalent in the Fijian community, there is also a strong sense of sexual fun and banter, and women in groups are openly flirtatious. If you are walking along the road in Fiji and an open-sided bus goes by and some of its passengers are women in high spirits, they may call out to you, 'Nice *bola*!' The 'nice' is English and the *bola* is a Fijian invention with an enjoyable proximity to 'balls'. It is the equivalent of shouting out 'Hey handsome, how about it?' The invitation is usually offered in jest and represents another small victory in the war of the sexes.

Before the days of 'nice *bola*', which didn't surface until the late sixties, Fiji patois used 'kashine' as an expression of attraction to another. '*Ka*' is the Fijian for 'thing' and 'shine' is English. If a girl shouted 'kashine!' to you across the road it was usually to get a rise out of the girls who accompanied her. The face-saving response was 'kaspark!' which was a retort of mutual attraction and it would set up hoots of delight from the girl's friends as her bluff had been called.

'Kashine' was a late fifties and sixties phenomena, and before that the phrase was '*kua ni kana*' meaning 'stopped eating', which really meant 'I'm so in love with you I'll never eat again unless you requite my love'. '*Kua ni kana*' was accompanied, or could be silently symbolised, by a motion of the forefinger horizontally across the throat. It too was usually offered in jest; the same young man is walking down Victoria Parade outside the Boys Grammar School and a dark green Nasese bus drives by with its open windows, carrying Fijian girls in lavender uniforms home from school. And one of them spots him, her big brown eyes widening, and slices her finger across her throat, and he quickly responds with the same gesture; and she laughs and throws her head back as the bus continues on its way down the road towards Nasova.

Buckingham Palace

On May 16, 1987, just two days after the coup d'état and the governor general's defiance of it, Ratu Penaia had received a message from Buckingham Palace: 'The Queen wishes you to know how much she admires your stand as her personal representative in Fiji and the guardian of the Constitution. Her Majesty is following developments with the closest attention, and hopes that you will keep us in touch. We are here to help in any way we can.'

In the months ahead, this message was a constant source of inspiration for Ratu Penaia as he struggled through the racial and political morass, searching for a solution which would be both domestically workable and at the same time acceptable to the Queen in her position as head of state of Fiji and head of the Commonwealth.

During this period Ratu Penaia had frequent telephone conversations with Sir William Heseltine, the Queen's private secretary. It was my responsibility to write reports on the Fiji situation to Sir William, which were despatched to him under the governor general's signature. The first such report was sent off on May 27; it expressed thanks for Her Majesty's support, gave the background to the governor general's actions, and outlined his plans.

Looking back on this first report, it is salutary to observe the thread of allegiance to the Crown running through the events after the coup. The report describes the initial actions of the coup and makes mention of Rabuka's intention to retain the office of governor general and the links with the Crown. It goes on to explain the governor general's taking of executive control of the government of Fiji, on the advice of the chief justice and the judges of the Supreme Court, and the ensuing battle of wills that he then had with Rabuka's military government and the Great Council of Chiefs.

Four days of intense negotiations followed as the Great Council of Chiefs discussed the pros and cons of the maintenance of the military government. It was clear that a great number of indigenous Fijians saw the military government as the best means of ensuring that indigenous Fijians would never again lose political control of Fiji. During this period of negotiations the spectre of racial violence and an irreparable division of the communities of our nation became very real. The destruction of the economy of Fiji was also imminently at hand. It became clear to me that the only alternative to turn away from this spectre was to reach an agreement with the military government and the Great Council of Chiefs, which would ensure that the executive authority in the management of the affairs of our nation remained firmly with the governor general.

The report goes on to record how Ratu Penaia achieved such agreement and subsequently had the resulting Council of Advisers swear oaths of allegiance to Her Majesty; and it notes that the Great Council of Chiefs had concluded its meeting with a resolution reaffirming their loyalty to the Queen.

It then describes the governor general's ongoing dialogue with Dr Bavadra and his colleagues of the ousted government, and his determination to work to bring them around to joining the path that he had set out on towards national reconciliation. On May 21, when Ratu Penaia was down at the Great Council of Chiefs arguing for the survival of the Constitution, I took a call on his behalf from Dr Bavadra, who had been released from army detention on the night of May 19. I wrote Dr Bavadra's message down for the governor general's attention on his return. In the message Bavadra says, 'Let me say once more how much I appreciate and admire your actions in the last week and all that you have done to heal our country and protect Fiji's sacred democratic institutions and the rule of law. I have told the nation of my complete trust in you and my sincere belief that you, as the chief executive of our nation in this time, will do what is right to restore peace to Fiji. I have urged the people of Fiji to share that trust.'

Bavadra's call was received two days after the governor general had published a proclamation in the *Fiji Royal Gazette* dissolving Parliament and declaring vacant the offices of prime minister and the ministers of the Crown. With this and other messages from the unseated government, Ratu Penaia had good reason to expect he would have their support in resolving Fiji's crisis to the satisfaction of the Queen of Fiji.

To many onlookers, the strength of Fiji's ties to the British monarchy were somewhat bizarre when viewed against the international backdrop of post-Suez dissolution of Britain's imperial past. From bank notes to public holidays, and from royal precursors in the names of clubs and services, to road names and parks, the British royal family seemed omnipresent in Fiji. Calendars on office walls showed scenes of Balmoral or Windsor, and most Fijian homes had framed pictures of the monarch on prominent display.

When looked at with a critical eye, for Fiji's non-indigenes loyalty to the Crown was in large measure one of self-interest. Fiji's demographics were a creation of the British empire and allegiance to the Crown was a back-stop for legitimacy of presence. And as long as the indigenous people put their faith in the monarchy, the non-indigenes could confidently expect the rule of law, and the basic decencies embodied in the Crown's legacy, to prevail.

It is perhaps easier to understand the indigenous Fijian attachment to the Queen if you consider the hierarchical nature of their culture. At birth a Fijian is registered in the *Vola ni Kawa Bula* which assigns him to the *mataqali*, the land-owning unit, into which he or she has just been born. This *mataqali* is forever registered as a member of a particular *yavusa*, a collection of *mataqali*, which in turn is part of a larger traditional grouping, the *vanua*. Most of these social units are led by a *turaga*, a chief; thus, depending on the level of social unit involved, the existence of the *turaga ni mataqali*, *turaga ni yavusa* or *turaga ni vanua*. Above the *turaga ni vanua* are paramount chiefs and above these, the three pre-Cession geopolitical confederacies are led respectively by the three preeminent chiefly titles of Fiji: na Vunivalu na Tui Kaba, na Roko Tui Dreketi, and na Tui Cakau. The structure is like a pyramid, but at its top were three titles, not one. The pyramid shape was therefore not complete until Cession, when the British monarch was placed at its apex. Had Fiji not been ceded to Britain, had foreigners not settled in Fiji, had the neighbouring king of Tonga not then conquered Fiji, the completion of this pyramid would have been done in another way. Presumably at some time thence one Fijian chief would have risen above the rest and become the indigenous king of all Fiji, just as had occurred in the Pacific Island kingdoms of Hawaii, Tonga and Tahiti.

In the South Pacific the importance of past deeds lives strongly in the present and those that went before are not so easily forgotten as they are in the urban cultures of the West. A Samoan proverb says, 'Stones rot, but words last forever.' A few years ago the governments of Samoa and guano-rich Nauru were having a spat over money. Nauru was coming in for some heavy flak in the Samoan Parliament when a minister rose to deliver an apocryphal coup de grace to Nauru's prestige by saying in that pitiful Micronesian country they didn't even have genealogies. The Polynesian attitude behind such a comment is that without genealogies how can people know what their past stood for, or what their place is in the present, or indeed why they should bother to prepare the way for those that will come after them?

In a part of the world where genealogies are revered, where your place on the land and in society is delivered at your birth, the picture of a monarchy like Britain's, with lines of responsibility, trust and experience going back into the mists of history, is one which surrounds itself with respect in a way that no self-promoting elected minister of state could easily expect to attain.

When the chiefs of Fiji ceded the islands in 1874, it was to Queen Victoria not the British government. With Cession, the rights to property went to the monarch, but Queen Victoria decreed that land ownership should be vested in the names of the customary owners as existing at the time of Cession. In 1970, when the instruments of Independence were formally handed over to Fiji's first prime minister, Ratu Sir Kamisese Mara, it was by Queen Victoria's direct descendant, Prince Charles, and not a British minister of the day. In the years since the departure of the British colonial administration, links with the British government had all but withered away, but the bond with the British royal family remained strong and the Queen responded to Fiji's loyalty in kind, through visits, messages and support.

Conscious of her responsibilities to the people of Fiji when things were falling apart in September 1987, she released a statement acknowledging the allegiance of Fijians to the Crown and saying she would be 'deeply saddened if those bonds of mutual loyalty and affection, which have so long held the Fijian people and the British monarchy together, were to be severed.'

Perhaps it was its very absence that made the monarchy so perfect for

Fiji. In a nation of disparate cultures cohabiting in a climate of watchful tolerance, grouped together as a result of historical venture on a collection of islands in an isolated corner of the Pacific Ocean, the common allegiance to a head of state linked to that historical venture but above and beyond the complexities of its aftermath, was convenient and comforting for all. A locally-elected president would have to struggle to achieve the same neutrality or sense of detached majesty. Constitutional monarchy, albeit with an absentee monarch, had served Fiji well, and the only reason the Republicans got the hearing they did in Fiji in 1987 was the seemingly impossible position for the Queen in the scheme of the constitutional demands of the indigenous Fijians that year.

When Dr Bavadra visited London in early June seeking an audience with the Queen to plead for her assistance in restoring his government, he received a message from Buckingham Palace but not an audience. The message said it went without saying that Her Majesty greatly regretted the events of May 14, and went on to note that in the meantime the governor general, upon whom the Fiji Constitution conferred the responsibility for executive authority as the Queen's representative, with the support of the chief justice and the other Fiji judges, had asserted his authority. 'Recognising that it was impossible to return the situation as it was before the illegal seizure of power, he had done his admirable best to find a way back to normality.'

The main point of the Queen's message is one which would have led Fiji to a far less painful year in 1987 had it been heeded better by the ousted government and its allies, the ruling political parties of Australia and New Zealand. 'Her Majesty's view is that such a return to constitutional government can best be achieved by supporting the governor general in his efforts to find a solution. If the Constitution is to be amended in some way, it can only be done in Fiji, and it is the governor general's efforts on which the best hope of a settlement, agreeable to all parties in Fiji, depends. Her Majesty therefore feels that in lending her support to the governor general in the actions which he has taken so far, not only is she following the only course open to her but also taking the course which is best calculated to serve the long term interests of Fiji and all its people.'

Following on from Bavadra's London visit, Buckingham Palace made two suggestions to the governor general. The first concerned the Council of Advisers. It noted that Dr Bavadra was obviously distressed at the thought of working with those who forcibly deposed him and those who supported them. 'It would help if the imbalance in your Advisory Council could be redressed to some extent.' This was good advice and offers were made accordingly to Dr Bavadra and his colleagues after their return from overseas.

The second suggestion was that it might be helpful to the governor general for some expert legal assistance to be made available to help him 'sort out the tangle which the coup and the dissolution of Parliament have created for you'. The Palace said they would be very happy to enquire of the Commonwealth Secretariat to see if they were able to provide such technical assistance if the governor general thought that would be useful. The offer was warmly accepted and resulted in the aforementioned July arrival in Fiji of Professor Keith Patchett, an eminent constitutional expert, who was attached to the governor general's Secretariat and was to prove a valuable resource for the governor general in his approach to the Deuba Accord.

From my observations throughout the crisis, Buckingham Palace gave the governor general wise advice when it was needed and accepted his advice in the same manner. Some eminent criticism has been made on the nature of these communications after the second coup, but I am unable to comment on this since I was out of the picture by then.

Our Fiji passports used to read, 'The Governor General and Commander-in-Chief in and over Fiji requests and requires in the name of Her Majesty the Queen all those whom it may concern to allow the bearer to pass freely without let or hindrance and to afford the bearer such assistance and protection as may be necessary.' Hollow words? The question has been asked whether the Queen of Fiji did enough to protect the welfare of her subjects in Fiji in the year of 1987, but I believe the more relevant question for historians to address is whether the Queen did too much? Did she over-step the mark which requires the monarch to act on the advice of her ministers?

She backed the governor general when her main faith in doing so had to have been her implicit trust in Ratu Penaia's personal integrity and loyalty. She stood behind her representative when he was forced by circumstances to make unpopular decisions and was regarded by the Australians and New Zealanders as having questionable motives. When the ousted government announced its intention to take the governor general to court for having illegally dissolved Parliament, and we moved outside the provisions of the Constitution when the governor general was unable, as required, to issue election writs within two months of Parliament's dissolution, the Queen's support did not waver.

Extreme circumstances usually require extreme measures to put them right, and that is what happened at Government House after the coup. The dissolution of Parliament was an extreme action, but it was the duty of the governor general under the law to maintain the executive role vested in Her Majesty under the Constitution, and Buckingham Palace stood firm in its support. A weaker man might have called for the assistance of the armed forces of Australia and New Zealand to try and restore the deposed government, and then watched the ensuing bloodbath on television, while he prepared to live the rest of his life in a country where the wounds would have been cut Balkan-deep.

There was inherent understanding between Buckingham Palace and Government House that, while the governor general had taken all executive authority in the nation upon himself, his solution to the crisis would be one of national consensus and one which the Queen as head of the Commonwealth could accept. These were immutable principles to which the governor general attached himself in the trying months that followed in the aftermath of the coup.

The Queen's influence on post-coup Fiji went further. It was noticeable that the Great Council of Chiefs and the wide majority of the Fijian people continued to hold firm to their links with the Crown and that in the main it was the firebrands and extremists amongst them who didn't. The desire to retain those links partnered a will to maintain the standards of human decency and traditions of respect for others that had prevailed in Fiji for so many years. And it was a mark of the man, and the questions surrounding him, that in spite of his overthrow of the Constitution itself, Sitiveni Rabuka searched long and hard for a way to remain a faithful subject of the Queen of Fiji.

In practice a politician's responsibilities lie with his or her electorate, and politicians have to be seen by that electorate to be effective in promoting the electorate's interests. The monarch on the other hand, through her governor general, is responsible only to the law that exists to defend the rights of her subjects. It has been instructive in my life to experience first-hand the contrasting effectiveness of a monarch's representative and elected politicians at a time of national constitutional crisis. Our country was falling apart after the coup d'état in May 1987 and the governor generalship, with the timely advice of the judiciary, and the moral and legal backing of Buckingham Palace, saved the day.

THE DEUBA ACCORD

'YOU, THE PEOPLE of Fiji, deserve much from your leaders for your calm perseverance over the last three months. Now is the time for those leaders, whatever their political persuasion, to show the nation the qualities of statesmanship that we know they possess.'

These were the words of the governor general when on August 31, 1987, he made a radio address to let the nation know how things were going with progress along the governor general's path. He thanked the people of Fiji for displaying the patience, trust and understanding and said that it was these national qualities which had brought us peacefully through the crisis and were helping create a gradually improving political climate. Then he announced that prior to convening the Council of National Reconciliation, he had arranged for talks to be held on September 4 between representatives of the government and the opposition of the dissolved Parliament as a means of preparing the ground for the council's work.

The month of August had been spent preparing for these talks. Dr Bavadra had initially called for one-on-one talks between himself and Ratu Mara, with the governor general as convenor. Ratu Mara had said no, if Bavadra wanted talks within the context of representation based on the dissolved Parliament, then they should be joined in talks by representatives of their respective parties, the NFP/Labour coalition and the Alliance party. Some Taukei movement activists within the Alliance party, such as Apisai Tora, were opposed to the talks, but Ratu Mara called for a constructive approach. The Alliance party's pre-election secretary-general, Jone Veisamasama, issued a statement to the press saying that before the talks could take place the NFP/Labour coalition should apologise to the Alliance and Great Council of Chiefs for some of the things they had said about them. Just when the talks seemed on the verge of getting underway, some new condition like this would pop up. The nation's patience was wearing thin.

There were calls for Rabuka to be included in the talks; but he and the governor general had conferred on this, and it was agreed that it would be better for Rabuka to stay out. Rabuka had recently been officially confirmed by the governor general as the commander of the Royal Fiji Military Forces and promoted to full colonel. As commander and adviser for home affairs, he had a direct relationship with the governor general which would keep him fully in the picture. Rabuka's confirmation as commander had raised some eyebrows at the time, but in confirming this Ratu Penaia had only recognised the obvious, which was that the army accepted Rabuka as its leader. For stability and security's sake it was better to regularise the situation by making the confirmation. Ratu Penaia recognised the qualities in Rabuka which inspired the army's loyalty to him, and it was better that he bring Rabuka into the camp of legality than have him out there on the perimeter looking in.

On September 4 the meeting between the representatives of the Alliance party and the NFP/Labour coalition finally got underway in the Government House drawing room. The governor general was in the chair and Ratu Isoa Gavidi, Professor Patchett and I were present as the secretariat. The NFP/Labour coalition delegation was made up of Dr Bavadra, Jai Ram Reddy, Dr Rakka, Etuate Tavai, Joeli Kalou and Mahendra Chaudhry. The Alliance team was Ratu Mara, Tomasi Vakatora, Apisai Tora, Filipe Bole, David Pickering and Ahmed Ali.

Ratu Sir Kamisese Mara is a man whose mental prowess matches his two-metre-tall physical frame. Even had he not been groomed as a young man for national leadership, even had he not been born to be paramount chief of the eastern islands of Fiji, he would still engender the feeling that it was inevitable this prodigious man would lead Fiji. And lead it he had for the last twenty-one years. If you were not in awe of him, you were at least very wary of him; if you didn't fearfully defer to him, you at least gave him the respect he had earned. His vindictive bouts of rage were legendary. It was, therefore, with the sense of an impending storm that I began scribbling the notes of the meeting, which got underway with an argument between Bavadra, Reddy and Chaudhry on one side and Ratu Mara on the other.

Following his opening remarks, the governor general had invited Bavadra to speak. Bavadra thanked the governor general for his kind words of welcome, but omitted to thank him for all he had done for Fiji since the coup. Bavadra said that he wanted to 'make it clear that we are here representing the aggrieved party in the sense that we were democratically elected and ousted by a military coup. I would like to see that that feeling is appreciated by members of this meeting'. He said that the starting point of discussions should be the retention of the 1970 Constitution and the restoration of his government.

When it came his turn to respond, Ratu Mara thanked the governor general for convening the meeting and on behalf of his party and the people of Fiji thanked him for his provision of leadership since the coup. He said that they hadn't come to dictate to him, but to do all they could to help him. Then he launched into, 'Dr Bavadra talks about being the aggrieved party. Everyone here has been aggrieved. I have been branded as the architect of the coup.' And then, looking daggers at Bavadra, 'We all know where that allegation has come from.' Turning to the governor general, he then referred to the Supreme Court challenge by the deposed government against the governor general's dissolution of Parliament, 'We are also aggrieved that we are meeting here when there is a court case hanging over your head. This case is resented by Fijians. It will be pointless to go on discussing if the court case intervenes and our talks are useless.' He said the discussions should start with the question of the court case and then the recommendations of the Constitutional Review Committee.

Bavadra replied by addressing Ratu Penaia. 'The question of the court case has attracted widespread attention. I am accused of insulting Your Excellency. My frank and honest opinion of the case is that you dissolved Parliament in a way that was not constitutional. I saw the case as a way to correct what I saw as wrong from a constitutional point of view. I must say it was not meant to insult you in a personal capacity. I felt it was my duty to do this as the leader of a duly elected government.'

Jai Ram Reddy added, 'I am surprised that this has come up this early. It is common knowledge that any aggrieved party is entitled to go to the courts. It is a lawful action. We have not sued the person, it is the office. You are not even named in the action. It is "Bavadra vs Attorney-General". I would submit, and this is an undertaking, that the court case is really a secondary matter for which there will be no reason to proceed with…we don't want this case to be heard. It is too early to ask us to withdraw the case now. We don't have the army, we only have the courts…'

Ratu Mara's storm was visibly building. 'I don't want to launch into a temper. Who has the army to call upon? We don't have the army at our call.'

Reddy countered, 'Ratu Mara has read more into this than I intended. This inference was not intended.'

But Chaudhry cut in with, 'The opposition is overwhelmingly in control of the government.'

The tornado of wrath building around Ratu Mara was about to unleash itself when Tom Vakatora interceded with some calming words about accepting reality, supporting the governor general's efforts and the need for a political solution rather than one from a court room. Discussions continued without making much headway and, after a break for morning tea, David Pickering suggested an adjournment to allow both sides to consider the aired views. It was agreed we would meet again at Government House on September 8.

While the meeting had been going on, the Taukei movement had undertaken some street theatre by making a *lovo* oven, guarded by traditionally-attired Fijian warriors, in front of Suva's Government Buildings. They let it be known that the people responsible for the court case against their high chief, Ratu Penaia, would be cooked in this ground oven. When Bavadra's aide, Richard Naidu, approached the *lovo* he was beaten up by the warriors. In retaliation some Bavadra supporters clashed with Taukei movement activists. Soldiers chased the Bavadra supporters and fired warning shots into the air.

Following on from this, threats of arson and physical beatings were made against Bavadra himself. He became alarmed and phoned me on September 6 to say that if we couldn't guarantee his safety, his party would not be at the next round of talks.

Assurances were given, but when the allotted time came on September 8, only the Alliance party representatives turned up at the Government House drawing room. Rather than waste the occasion, the governor general used the meeting to discuss with the Alliance their constitutional questions, using Professor Patchett as the provider of expert advice. The Alliance wanted to know whether a caretaker government had the power to legally change the Constitution, with or without the other party's participation, and Patchett was saying that it would be very difficult if the NFP/Labour coalition was not part of that caretaker government. Ahmed Ali was trying to make the point that the support of the Indian community was not necessarily just with the NFP/Labour coalition, but Patchett countered that they demonstrably had the legitimate Indian support. It was pointed out that a unilateral caretaker government was blocked by the existing Constitution, and Ratu Mara replied that the only solution would be to remove the Constitution. The discussion continued, and Patchett at one point was answering a quandary arising from a point of law and, quoting Dickens, said that in this particular case 'the law is a ass.' Looking coldly at Patchett, Ratu Mara said, 'The lawyer's an ass.'

The governor general said that the next meeting would be held on September 11, and let it be known that if Bavadra and his colleagues did not turn up, he would have to start looking at unilaterally forming a caretaker government.

In his letter of September 9 to the Queen's private secretary, Ratu Penaia wrote,

While the achievement of political consensus will obviously be very difficult, I am nonetheless convinced that it can be achieved given goodwill and patience. If I do not succeed in getting the two parties together, the other option I am having to consider is that of forming a caretaker government of my own choosing with membership which will command the respect of the community at large. I would obviously prefer that the two political parties recommend the formation of a power-sharing caretaker government, but if they cannot agree then I may have to go ahead regardless. The judges of the Supreme Court had earlier advised me that such a course was open to me.

The question of the review and retention or amendment of the Constitution of Fiji remains open. I am advised that it may be preferable for a greater passage of time to be allowed for before any firm decisions are made on this matter. This question will of course be a major element in the achievement of political consensus in the current round of talks that I am arranging between the coalition and the Alliance.

The September 11 meeting was held on schedule and was fully attended. Early on in the meeting Dr Bavadra reiterated that his side wanted the Constitution to be unchanged and his government to be restored to office. That set them all off again trading one-liners. After a while Ratu Penaia quietened things down and recounted to them the decisions and actions he had taken since the coup. He then pointed out that Rabuka had given two reasons for the coup: the first to forestall civil bloodshed, and the second to get changes in the Constitution to strengthen the political rights of indigenous Fijians. Ratu Penaia said that if peace was to be restored in Fiji, then the desire of the Fijians for strengthening of their political position would have to be satisfactorily resolved. 'If I hadn't recognised that, I don't think I would be sitting here today.' He said he was unable to accept the possibility of restoring the Bavadra government, as it would only put Fiji back into the coup scenario again.

Jai Ram Reddy called for the finding of some common ground. He said no benefit came from individuals taking a position at the beginning which they kept until the end, as had happened with the Constitutional Review Committee. The Council of National Reconciliation would fall into the same trap. 'If there is to be consensus the chances of finding it are much greater in a smaller group. A solution has to be found within the purview of the current committee.'

Ahmed Ali responded, 'Does Mr Reddy feel that there is some scope for change in the Constitution?'

Jai Ram responded, 'It is an unfair question at this stage.'

'Thank you,' said Ali, 'You have answered my question.'

The Bavadra team made the point that they had no mandate from their people to agree there should be changes to the Constitution. Discussions then fell into talk of a second coup, the threat of communal bloodshed, the time bomb the country was sitting on and the role of the army. Ratu Penaia pulled the meeting out of a tail-spin by saying that any leader should be prepared to take the initiative and then be accountable to the people. He said, 'We must look for consensus. I'm not here to force anything on anyone. If we come here with predetermined feelings, we will get nowhere. I am in the unhappy position of shouldering a burden that has been thrust upon me. I want to share this responsibility.'

Jai Ram asked whether, from the governor general's perspective, the question of changes to the Constitution was necessarily linked to the question of providing a caretaker government.

Ratu Penaia replied, 'It is relevant to it.'

Dr Bavadra, addressing the governor general, said, 'Forgive us if we go back to refer to our people. We are here for the people. Please spend a bit more time on discussion. This is only our second meeting.'

Then Jai Ram offered to prepare a paper for presentation at the next meeting on the question of constitutional change. This was accepted by the meeting and it was agreed that we would reconvene on September 15 at Government House.

After the meeting Mahendra Chaudhry, Filipe Bole and Etuate Tavai stayed on at Government House to drink kava with the governor general and some of his secretariat. Chaudhry was second only to Reddy as the architect and articulator of Fiji Indian opinion. His support base was the trade unions and sugar farmers, and he was a skilful and fearless negotiator. I didn't know him well, but had a healthy respect for his abilities. He must have had a little for mine, for upon his assumption of the position of minister of finance of the Bavadra government, he asked that I draft his speech assuring foreign investors the new government would continue to welcome and protect the rights of foreign investment. I was at the time of his request still the permanent secretary for information.

Filipe Bole was a relatively recent arrival on the political scene but had long been a respected civil servant, filling such posts as permanent secretary for education and Fiji's ambassador to the United Nations. He was regarded as being amongst the spearheads of the Fijian intelligentsia and was one of the early driving forces of the Taukei movement. Seeing Bole and Chaudhry chewing the fat around the governor general's *tanoa* gave me a strong sense of the possibility of political consensus.

Ratu Penaia had pushed hard for the next meeting to be held on Wakaya Island. Before the September 11 meeting we had discussed the desirability of getting the political leaders onto an offshore retreat so that they could talk without distractions. Wakaya is a privately-owned island and I had cleared with its owners that it would be available for our retreat. However, Dr Bavadra wanted the next meeting to be held in the Western Division. This was opposed by the Alliance team, so it was agreed that we would hold one more meeting at Government House and then go to Wakaya. That weekend, radical elements of the Taukei movement began their threatened arson campaign in Suva and shops in central Suva were set alight. I had a call from Dr Bavadra, who made it clear he had real fear over threats to his life and the likelihood of further violent demonstrations in Suva. As a concession to Dr Bavadra's sensibilities, we changed the venue for the September 15 meeting from Government House to the Hyatt hotel near Korolevu in the Western Division.

In his opening remarks at the Korolevu meeting, Ratu Penaia expressed his sympathy for the aggrieved feelings of the deposed government and Jai Ram Reddy picked up on this, responding that they were most grateful for his expression. Jai Ram had prepared and presented his paper on constitutional change to the meeting and it opened a way forward by mentioning the possibility of the appointment of a government representing a wide cross-section of the nation. The remainder of the meeting was spent discussing the parameters for such a caretaker government. It was agreed that it should be bi-partisan and drawn from the elected members of the last Parliament. In answer to a question from Bavadra, the governor general said that if the bi-partisan caretaker government was formed, the Council of National Reconciliation would not be convened as it would then be redundant.

The Alliance team said that it would be essential that the constitutional changes be simultaneously addressed 'in order to satisfy the coup instigators'. Reddy said, 'We need to look at the Constitution with a view to reviewing it. The caretaker government could set in place the machinery to review the Constitution in a bi-partisan way. Our first priority should be to define what a caretaker government is.'

The governor general then set out his prescription for a caretaker government. He would select its composition in consultation with the leaders of the two sides of the former Parliament. It would be made up of elected members of the two sides, with the two sides represented equally in numerical terms, and he would be allowed the right to select a limited number of others from outside the ranks of the two sides. The members of the caretaker government would be given the powers to perform the function of ministers. The caretaker government would be given limited legislative powers for voting bills of supply and other emergencies. It would have a life of up to twelve months. At the same time, as a matter of necessity, a full review of the Constitution would be carried out. The caretaker government would govern until the question of constitutional change had been resolved by consensus, put into legal effect, and elections held for a new Parliament. The very nature of the proposed government, that of a 'caretaker', required for its legal justification the review of the Constitution.

It was agreed that the meeting adjourn so that further consideration could be given to the form of the caretaker government and so that participants could be clear on what is was they wanted to achieve. The governor general tried the Wakaya retreat venue idea again, but Bavadra's team was reluctant, so it was decided to meet next at Pacific Harbour on September 22.

The following day the governor general met separately with Colonel Rabuka to brief him on the progress of the talks and what could only be described as a major break-through in the previous impasse. Before the meeting I gave the governor general my assessment of the army's position, which was that it would go along with the expected caretaker government outcome, but that its confidence needed to be bolstered throughout the process. My reasoning was the army would recognise that it had successfully removed the Bavadra government from office, and the results of the coup would become legally and internationally acceptable as a result of the formation of the caretaker government. Most importantly the constitutional review that would be set up by the caretaker government, while bi-partisan in structure, would be charged with examining ways to safeguard and improve the lot of the indigenous Fijians. The army had a critical role to play in preparing for the achievement of the desired caretaker government agreement during the following week; it was up to them to see that civilian calm was maintained while the talks progressed. Also the Taukei movement would have to be made to understand that the interests of indigenous Fijians were being kept at heart by the governor general, in accordance with his undertaking to the Great Council of Chiefs.

Running in tandem with the optimism leading up to the Deuba meeting, was a sense of dread that the forthcoming consensus could be outstripped and undone by external events. Over the weekend Dr Bavadra was continuing his Operation Sunrise meetings, which were meant to demonstrate the strength of grassroots Fijian support for his leadership. Apart from die-hard Labour supporters, no-one was deluded by this stance. Meanwhile the Taukei movement extremists saw that they had to play their hand now or lose out big time. On September 18 they began arson attacks and looting of Suva Indian shops. The army dutifully stepped in, setting up road blocks and closing public bars and nightclubs. Suva sports fixtures for the weekend were cancelled and shop windows were boarded up as Suva citizens braced themselves for trouble. The security forces made arrests of looters, and a Fijian bank robber was shot in the leg by a soldier before being arrested. The Taukei movement said the unrest was inevitable given the frustration of the goals of the coup and said that it had been 'unnecessary' for the army to shoot a Fijian.

The rumour mill had been working overtime and, in spite of the Korolevu meeting, there was a public perception that political consensus had failed and that the governor general was going to hand over power to Colonel Rabuka. Who knows where this rumour started, but by September 21 it was strong enough that a respected Indian reporter from Radio Fiji rang me to say that as the hand-over to Rabuka had already been done, would Government House be issuing a statement today? We relayed messages to Jai Ram Reddy and Dr Bavadra emphasising the gravity of the situation, and stressed that we had to be able to tell the people of Fiji at the end of tomorrow's deliberations that consensus had been achieved.

I had booked Villa 37 at the Pacific Harbour as the venue for the next meeting. Pacific Harbour is a beach and golf resort that had been created from swampland in the early 1970s, located in the *tikina* of Deuba about an hour's drive along the coast from Suva. We had selected it as the talk's location because there would be fewer distractions there than at Government House, and Bavadra didn't want a bar of Suva. As we drove into the resort on the morning of September 22 I spotted my old classmate Wayne Hill, Bavadra's security guard, organising his men on the roadside and gave him a grim wave.

The next two days were spent in intense negotiations within Villa 37. The governor general directed proceedings through a pre-planned agenda, cajoling, sympathising, extracting compromises, giving undertakings and demanding the best of the negotiators. By the evening of the first day we were able to put out a news release that agreement had been reached to form a bi-partisan caretaker government.

The following day the negotiations continued, with Dr Bavadra making a play for the leadership of the caretaker government. This was totally unacceptable to the Alliance side and you could see that Dr Bavadra's side were not giving the bid much seriousness. Thereafter the dynamic that had been developing since the bi-partisan talks began three weeks earlier was plain to see. The NFP/Labour power lay with the leaders of the Indian electorate, Jai Ram Reddy and Mahendra Chaudhry, and for the remainder of the day's decision-making it was they that called the shots on their side. A subcommittee was formed to look at the final contentious issues and Bavadra was omitted from it. While the deals were being done in a side-room, Bavadra was sitting in one of the villa's bedrooms, and whenever I went in there to mollify his frustration he would say, 'Would somebody tell me what is going on?'

We took lunch at the Pacific Harbour golf club and, as we sat out on its veranda above the eighteenth hole, the atmosphere amongst the politicians was convivial. Apisai Tora sat at a table by himself, so I joined him and we had lunch together while he expressed his doubts that this caretaker government could hold together or be acceptable to the Fijian people in their current state of raised expectations. He then did his best to convince me that all of this stuff was irrelevant anyway because a meteor was soon going to strike the earth and would wipe out most of its inhabitants. He had the date of the meteor's arrival and the details of its size. He was utterly convinced, and looking back on it now I should have placed a bet on the meteor's non-arrival. But then if I could go back in time, there were a few other things I would have done differently that momentous week.

That afternoon the deal now known as the Deuba Accord, was finalised. A caretaker government would be formed and be known as the Council of State for Fiji. The Council of State would be chaired by the governor general, Ratu Sir Penaia Ganilau, who would also be its chief executive. The Council of State would be drawn from the membership of the dissolved Parliament with equal numerical representation on the council of the former government and the former opposition. Councillors of state would for all purposes be the equivalent of ministers under the

1970 Constitution. The Council of State would govern for a prescribed period during which time a bi-partisan constitutional review was to be carried out, under the chairmanship of an independent chairperson from overseas. The review would arrive at a new Constitution which would have to satisfy the diverse interests of Fiji's people, taking into full account the aspirations of the indigenous Fijians for betterment of their constitutional, economic and social interests.

The relief was immense, and an impromptu drinks party was organised for the negotiators around the villa's swimming pool. Ratu Penaia was out to enjoy himself, and his mood was infectious. Only Tora disassociated himself from celebrating. As the drinks went down, the smiles grew wider. I heard Jai Ram saying to Filipe Bole, 'You won't find me difficult to work with.' Former adversaries were putting arms around each others' shoulders and having their photos taken. A big celebratory cake was delivered to us by the Pacific Harbour hotel and the press were allowed in to take photographs of Ratu Penaia, Ratu Mara and Dr Bavadra beaming over the cake.

An army officer came up to me, shook my hand and congratulated me, saying he was hugely relieved a solution had been found. Keith Patchett was elated and he, John Tevita, Ratu Isoa Gavidi and I posed for a secretariat photo. While we were standing out on the villa lawn Ratu Isoa, who had stood unwaveringly loyal to the governor general throughout the crisis, said quietly to me, 'If this agreement doesn't work, you should be very careful. There will be people out to get us.' Coming from him this was a sobering thought, but as I mingled back into the party, amongst the laughter and holding of hands, euphoria took over again. In what I was seeing all around me in the happy faces and voices of these national leaders, I couldn't help but believe that we were on the cusp of an new era of sharing our national experience, an era which would see the opening of our hearts to one another, and glad acceptance of our common destiny.

BALI HAI PROFILES

LOOKING OUT FROM Nadi airport's tarmac you see the start of a chain of islands known as the Yasawas which for some two hundred kilometres form a rocky barrier along Fiji's northeastern boundary. Around the north end of the Yasawas in 1789, post-mutiny, Lieutenant Bligh's seamanship passed the test as he fled in the *Bounty*'s launch chased by two Fijian war canoes. A short sail from the route of this chase, less than 200 years later, Brooke Shields emerged dripping from the Pacific Ocean onto the beach of the Yasawan island where *Blue Lagoon* was filmed.

I have spent many of my holidays in the Yasawas, and more particularly the Mamanuca Group, which lies at the southern end of the island chain. These holidays started from my primary school days, when my father would take some of his sons with him on his sojourns in the islands to delineate the boundaries of the ownership of traditional land and fisheries rights. In the course of this work he sailed around in a little ketch called *Fairwind* in the excellent company of such men as Ratu Naulivou, George Mate and Joseva George. Deliberations in the villages were a protracted process accompanied by many ceremonial presentations and days of discussion around the kava bowl. We boys would befriend villagers of our own age and spend our time swimming, fishing and mucking about.

On one such visit, in Matacawalevu village on the shores of the famous Blue Lagoon, I remember squatting down next to half a dozen huge sea turtles; these had been placed on their backs outside the village house that was allocated as our sleeping quarters. Men would bring buckets of seawater occasionally to splash over the turtles, which would then vainly slap their sides with their leathery flippers. In high Fijian ceremonies of welcome there is a point in the proceedings at which food is presented, and turtles are one of the types of food that it is acceptable to present. The Matacawalevu turtles had played their part in the ceremonies and were awaiting the earth-ovens. The snapshot I retrieve from my mind's memory bank is that of waxy tears rolling down from the turtles' sad blank eyes.

When my father became the Commissioner for Western Fiji in 1962, the Mamanucas and Yasawas came within his division, so as teenagers we were able to spend a lot more time in the islands. By this time spearfishing had become a passion of mine, and whenever possible I would go diving with friends off the islands and reefs of the Yasawas and Mamanucas. Fiji waters are pretty shark-infested and, unlike some of my diving friends, I never lost my unease around sharks. Nowadays we are supposed to appreciate their beauty, but close-up I've always found them repulsive, evil, snake-eyed people-eaters. In spite of my love of skin-diving, I was nervous in deep water and always kept a wary look over my shoulder. I had good reason to be nervous when diving near the Yasawan village of Kese.

Peacetime's highest British award for bravery, the George Medal, was awarded to a Kese villager, Josateki Tunisau, in 1964. Josateki had been spearfishing off Kese with other fishermen when a shark attacked one of his colleagues. While others made their way as fast as possible to the safety of the shore, Josateki swam to the mauled man and, with the shark circling him in a spreading pool of the dying man's blood, cradled the man in a one-and-a-half-kilometre swim to the beach. I believe only divers who have been in the water near an aggressor shark can fully appreciate the benevolent strength of Josateki's will as he struggled along in that deadly crimson pool.

I turned twenty-one years of age in the Yasawas. On that occasion I made the passage between the islands of Naviti and Yaqeta in a small fishing boat with my friend Robbie Watson. We drank a bottle of rum between us, singing ourselves hoarse, to celebrate my coming of age, which was not a great idea as the weather was ugly and we had over 100 kilometres to cover that night. The only reason we were out there was to make an urgent delivery of some engine parts to his brother. The latter had a deep-sea fishing boat, which had broken down with a full load of tourists on board and was stranded in an anchorage in the northern Yasawas. There was a point on that squall-filled night, after narrowly missing a reef, where we agreed that we would welcome the dawn of November 18, 1969.

At the south of the Yasawa chain is Waya Island whose rocky peaks contest with the profiles of Moorea and Borabora in the portrayal of the romantic South Seas island. But it is the island of Monu in the Mamanucas which took the prize when its towering volcanic spires were chosen for the montage of island scenes at the beginning of *South Pacific*, the 1958 pineapple-hued musical melodrama of the year.

Today there are tourist resorts on many of the islands in the Mamanucas, but when I worked at Castaway Resort on Qalito Island in 1968 it was the only hotel in all of the Mamanucas and Yasawas. It had been established a few years earlier by Dick Smith and was at that time the fashionable tropical island for the chic set from Sydney. My elder brother Andrew was the resort's assistant manager and Dick gave me a job as one of the resort's boatmen. My duties involved such chores as sailing the catamaran on day-trips over to the idyllic desert island of Mana and teaching bikini-clad women how to waterski in the lagoon. I guess I'd have to say my career has been on a downhill slide ever since.

While I was working on Qalito I had many friends amongst the Fijian staff, and about a year later when I was passing through Fiji en route from the British Virgin Islands, where my parents were then living, to university in New Zealand, I went out to Castaway to see my friends. Down in the staff village we drank kava, and then I was given *sau ni tavako*. The latter translates as 'cigarette money' and it was customary to give members of your community money and clothing to provision them for a voyage to far-off places. Thinking back on it, I am moved by the natural generosity of spirit of those people as we sat there in the *bure*, so humbling and so typical of the concern for the welfare of others inherent in Fijian culture. Apart from some pocket money, I was given a red and white *bula* shirt and a pair of khaki shorts.

The next day I was leaving the island and I donned my new clothing which proved to be several sizes larger than my then skinny frame. The date was February 1970 and I was adorned with mutton-chop sideburns and blue John Lennon sunglasses. Looking back on it, even in the context of the times, it can't have been a good look as I wandered barefoot around the resort waiting for the boat which would take me back to the mainland.

I went down to the beach, sat in the shade of a coconut tree, removed my sunglasses and shirt, reclined back on an elbow and took in the languid scene across the light blue lagoon, the reef submerged at high tide, and the royal blue of the straits between us and the low outline of Mana Island. Mana was four long thin horizontal lines of colour; the lower one the white of waves on its reef, the next the powder blue of its lagoon, then the ivory of a long sandy beach, topped by a green line alternating between olive and jade. Off in the hazy distance the wild Bali Hai profile of Monu danced in the vaporous tropical air.

I heard the ski-boat before I saw it, recognising the tone of its engine and the way it strained when a strong skier would cut well out to the side of the wake in a slalom, moving faster than the boat and throwing up a sheet of water; this caused the rope to go momentarily slack, then taut, putting a strain on the engine. I heard the clunking sound of the hull flying through the chop and the slap-slapping of the ski on the water's surface. About 400 metres out, off the northeast point of the island, the boat came into view, followed by a figure on one ski aggressively slicing from one side of the boat to the other.

They took a course parallel to the resort's beach and then the boat did a sharp turn to prepare to enter the passage into the lagoon. The skier took the outside curve, thus travelling at twice the speed of the boat, and then as the boat straightened its course, cut back across its wake; so that as the boat sped through the passage the skier was again rocketing out on a tangent, this time over the submerged coral reef. At this point I saw from her streaming dark hair, long limbs and string bikini that the skier was a young woman.

She dug in her rear heel, leaned inwards almost flat to the water and her ski threw up a three-metre-high wall of glistening water, which seemed to hang there as a backdrop as she traversed the boat's wake one last time. Letting go the rope, she glided across the shallows to a stop at the lagoon's edge, stepping from the ski onto the sand directly in front of my mesmerised, open-mouthed, smitten person. She looked down at me, took me in with her wide green eyes, smiled curiously and walked up the beach.

Every move and look of her just slew me. I sat there trying to keep my cool, my hands spread in the sand for stability as I craned my neck to follow her progress up the beach. As they say in Fiji, I was 'full struck'. Behind the round blue sunglasses there was some kind of kerchunking chemical reaction going on in my brain. Later on that fateful day, none too subtly befriending her mother, I discovered she was only fourteen; so we had to wait another three years before we could marry and live the life of love together for which, for some blissful reason, we were destined.

But enough of that. As Huxley once said, 'There is something curiously boring about somebody else's happiness.'

Arrest at Musket Cove

POUNDING SOUTH FROM Castaway Resort in a powerful speedboat, arcing through passages within the barrier reef, in fifteen minutes you come to a sheltered harbour between the islands of Malolo and Malololailai. On the beach of the latter is Musket Cove Resort, home of the Musket Cove Yacht Club and haven over the years for countless yachts cruising the South Pacific. The resort takes its name from the siege with muskets of a Fijian village on the shores of the harbour in 1840. The attackers were the US navy, under the command of Lieutenant Charles Wilkes, and they were on a mission of punishment for the murder of some of Wilkes's fellow officers.

Once you leave this harbour in a westerly direction, you are out of Fiji waters; next stop Vanuatu, 800 kilometres across the blue Pacific. Each year, from Musket Cove to Port Vila in Vanuatu, a yacht race is held which attracts a big following of cruising yachts, from sleek ketches to doubtful luggers. The commodore of the Musket Cove Yacht Club, Dick Smith, my employer some twenty years before, had asked me to come out to the island to start the 1987 race, and it so happened that the race that year was to start on the weekend following the Deuba Accord.

Since the Wednesday night party after the Deuba Accord, my main task had been the drafting of the governor general's speech announcing the new government structure. The speech was ready by Friday morning, September 25, and Ratu Sir Penaia had Radio Fiji record it on Friday afternoon for broadcasting at 6pm. In retrospect it should have been broadcast the night before, as the hearing of it may have altered the subsequent course of Fiji history. The speech set out in detail what had been agreed at the Deuba Accord and explained what lay ahead on the governor general's path for the nation.

I don't have a copy of the speech but my draft heading notes sum it up:

GG kept faith with people of Fiji throughout crisis. GG's duty and allegiance to the Queen unshakeable, and her support of his efforts had been vital. Thank leaders of Fiji political parties for qualities of statesmanship shown in Deuba Accord. Explain new Council of State of Fiji, its politically balanced composition and main aims, including constitutional review. Affirm position of the Great Council of Chiefs and the strengthening of indigenous rights. GG has received support of Rabuka and the army. Public to get behind security forces and let government get on with the job. Thanks to out-going Council of Advisers. Time to put aside bitterness and suspicion. Period ahead will demand Fiji's best qualities. Thanks to people of Fiji for their patience and trust.

During the preparation of the speech I had taken calls from various people, including Dr Bavadra, who had stressed points that needed to be made in the speech. Apisai Tora had rung me from Sabeto to say that he was amongst a big gathering of very disgruntled Fijians and that I should ensure that there was a strong emphasis in the speech about the strengthening of indigenous rights. When the speech had been approved by the governor general, with his permission, I then took the weekend off and drove down to Pacific Harbour to catch a light aircraft that would take me to an island resort for a break with my family.

The plane flew me to Nadi to pick up Marijcke, our children, James and Nicky, and our friend from Cambridge University days, Stephen Hooper. I was unaware as I winged it over Viti Levu that on the stroke of 4pm, Rabuka was executing his second coup d'état. When the others boarded the plane at Nadi airport they broke the news to me. We continued the flight out across Bligh Water to the Mamanuca Group and on arrival at the Malololailai airstrip we jumped into Dick Smith's truck and drove to his beachside office, where I got on the phone to Government House.

I had difficulty getting through to the governor general; our normal Government House lines weren't replying and when I did get an answer, there was a voice on the other end I didn't recognise. I identified myself and asked to be put through to the governor general. There followed five minutes of muffled conversations in the background as various people were consulted. Finally Ratu Sir Penaia came on the phone, and it was clear from all the whirring and clicking in the background that our conversation was being listened to by others in Suva.

Ratu Penaia was putting on a brave face, but I could tell from his tone that he was pretty despondent. All his work of the last five months, taking a country from the brink of madness and ruin, talking political enemies into a joint caretaker government and undoing a military coup d'état was now destroyed. How else could he feel? Only days before the Deuba Accord, Rabuka had given Ratu Penaia his assurances that the army would back the governor general and the results of his labours. But what good were words now?

I said I would make arrangements to get back to Government House immediately. He demurred and said that I should have a good night's rest and he would ring me in the morning to tell me what he wanted me to do. I mustered as much enthusiasm as I could and encouraged him to stand by all he had achieved since the first coup.

I wandered over to the Musket Cove bar to join Marijcke and Stephen down by the harbour's sandy edge. We drank Cuba libres and watched the sunset turn the harbour's limpid waters pink and mauve. Fish were plopping in the tide while yachties rowed ashore in the stillness of dusk, oars clunking on the sides of their skiffs, voices bouncing across the water as they called out to one another in anticipation of the evening's festivities. Above them big black fruit-bats were gliding in on rubbery wings, across from Malolo to raid the resort's fruit trees.

We talked about what would have motivated this second coup. Presumably Rabuka would have been faced with the same pressures as those preceding the first, but was the threat of communal violence as real this time around? The Fijian leadership had been restored through the Deuba Accord. There was, however, no doubt in my mind that the tide of passion for greater indigenous rights had yet to peak, and that the second coup would allow its flood to spread further across the land. And then there were the aspirations of a new generation of Fijian leaders who had tasted power after the first coup and no doubt saw the Deuba Accord as a scotching of their ambitions; it was in the fever of millenarianism that they stood the best chance of advancing their careers. This younger generation had now sat around the same executive tables as the Fijian leaders whom they had previously held in awe, and saw that they could foot it with them. A changing of the guard was underway.

Yachties and tourists were now converging on the bar, and a string band took its place by the dance floor. Flares were lit and a glistening pig was put over the coals for roasting. The band started playing, blue and orange cocktails were flashing and the pre-race party got underway. The mentality of the evening was sailors in paradise and Coup-Coup Land was another world of no concern to them. I felt out of place and exhausted, so Marijcke and I retired early.

We were staying in a tourist *bure* in the centre of the resort and Stephen was to bed down later that night on the couch in the *bure*'s lounge. James and Nicky were staying at Dick's house up on the hillside overlooking the resort. I was glad that my family was out of Suva that night. Who could say what would be going on back there when darkness had fallen? I felt sure that heads would roll in the capital, but at least out here on the island, in the cocoon of the tourist industry we would be safe.

As we lay there in the gloom of our *bure*, listening to the laughter and music filtering through the palm trees from the party, my thoughts turned to a review of the likely scenarios of this second coup. I could come up with none which were other than dismal. We had speculated at Government House that if another coup took place it would be more cut-throat than the first. The military and Rabuka's kitchen cabinet would know who they wanted to take out of the picture this time around, and I had received enough warnings from Fijian friends to suspect that I would be one of them.

I fell down and down into the deep sleep of the toil-worn.

Then Marijcke was shaking me, whispering urgently to wake me. I crawled out of a cavernous well of unconsciousness. It was still night time. The resort was silent and I guessed it was somewhere between 2 and 3am.

'There are soldiers on the island. They've come to arrest you.'

No, this is a dream; I'm going back into my well. Marijcke shook me again, 'Wake up they're coming to get you.'

This time I sat bolt upright and pulled my *sulu* around me. Stephen and the resort manager, Margie Thaggard, were standing at the *bure* door alternately looking at me and glancing nervously into the darkness outside. Margie said the soldiers had come to her quarters and ordered her to show them where I was sleeping. She said it was no use bluffing as they knew I was at the resort.

I walked to the door and peered through it. In front of us was a lawn the size of a small football field ringed by coconut trees. Underneath these palms, silhouetted in the moonlight, were uniformed men with guns in their hands. They were all looking across the field in my direction. My stomach felt suddenly heavy.

Why did they have the field surrounded? Did they think I was going to make a run for it? Why would I do that? What was it they were going to do to me? I felt sick with apprehension.

I pulled on a shirt, tightened my *sulu* and told the others to wait in the *bure* while I went out to the soldiers. 'No way,' said Marijcke, ' I'm coming with you.'

Stephen was of the same opinion, so the four of us set off across the lawn towards one of the armed men. It was a long walk, and all the way across I kept thinking of those words of warning I had received.

The soldier I approached turned out to be the sergeant in charge of the platoon, and as I walked up to him the other soldiers converged on us.

'Are you Mr Thomson?' he asked.

'Yes. What do you want with me?'

'You have to come with us now. We have to take you to Lautoka.'

'How?'

'In the *Boubale*.'

So this was the standpoint. They had sent the *Boubale*, one third of the Fiji navy's fleet, out into reef-strewn waters in the middle of the night of a coup d'état to apprehend me. I asked myself why they hadn't phoned me and told me to come in on one of the resort's speedboats? There could be no good afoot for me in going with these men. This was not an offer of transport, it was an abduction. I glanced around. Some of the soldiers were gripping their guns nervously. There was no way I was going willingly with them on the *Boubale*. Who knew whether I would ever get to Lautoka?

I summoned a tone of authority, looked the sergeant in the eye and said, 'First I have to phone your superior officer in Lautoka.'

The sergeant hesitated, he had his orders and he could now carry them out whether or not I agreed, but he wasn't used to this sort of situation. Behind his blank expression he was thinking carefully. The 'senior officer' bit gave him an out. He assented, and we walked through the sleeping resort to Margie's office.

The four of us then crammed into the little office with the sergeant and four soldiers. The latter had difficulty pointing their guns anywhere without digging barrels into someone's ribs or pointing them absently at one of us. The sergeant took the phone and began the laborious process of getting through to the army camp in Lautoka. Eventually a Captain Kalou came on the line, and I was given the phone. I asked him what his orders were. He said they were to apprehend me and escort me to a meeting of permanent secretaries in Suva. This 'meeting' was plainly a ruse, but I went along with it and said that I would catch the first morning plane from Musket Cove and attend the Suva meeting under my own steam. He said this would not be possible and that I was to go with the soldiers on the *Boubale*.

I remembered that the army's commanding officer in the Western Division was Lieutenant Colonel Tuivanuavou, whom I had known since I was a kid, and I demanded that he make the decision. Then I overheard Kalou on the radio telephone talking to Tuivanuavou who was driving around in a car somewhere. After some discussion between them I heard his crackling instruction to Kalou, 'Tell Thomson if he gives me his word of honour that he'll be on the 6.30am flight out of Musket Cove in the morning, I'll accept it.'

I did so. Kalou gave the sergeant his new orders and, as silently as they had appeared, the soldiers disappeared into the night. Musket Cove resort would awake in the morning unaware of the night's military visitation.

Back in our *bure* we agreed that Marijcke would stay on the island with the children. With all the uncertainties ahead in Suva it was better for them to be out there; and as a back-up, if worse came to worst, New Zealand friends of ours had an ocean-going yacht in the harbour and they could sail out of Fiji waters in no time at all.

Stephen insisted that he would accompany me to Suva. He spoke fluent Fijian, having done extensive fieldwork in Fiji for his Cambridge anthropology doctorate. He would be able to pick up extra information and keep Marijcke informed if I were put out of action.

I was drained. Unable to sleep, I lay on the bed, dreading the first light of dawn and the sound of an approaching aeroplane.

The time for our departure arrived and Stephen and I set off. The light aeroplane stopped at Nadi Airport then continued on to Pacific Harbour.

On the way to Pacific Harbour, Stephen and I were the only passengers on board, and the Australian pilot took us for tourists. As we flew along the southern coast of Viti Levu he gave us a scenic commentary over the intercom, pointing out the various hotels and geographical features as they passed below us. He gratuitously advised us that we needn't worry about yesterday's coup, as they never hassle tourists after coups in Fiji.

We landed on the gravel strip at Pacific Harbour and he taxied back to the thatched shed that served as a terminal. As he cut his engines, out of the bushes leapt half a dozen men dressed like guerrillas. Some had woollen balaclavas over their heads. All of them were theatrically aiming their guns at the aeroplane.

'What the...!' said the Aussie pilot as the soldiers yanked open the door and stuck gun barrels into the plane.

'You, Thomson?' one of them grunted at me.

Stephen and I were led away at gunpoint. Looking back at the plane I saw the pilot was still gripping his flight controls, staring open-mouthed at his departing passengers. In no time he had his engines fired up and was scurrying down the strip for the safety of the skies. He was out of there, mate!

We were bundled into the back of a truck and driven off in the direction of Suva.

RETURN TO NAVUA

THE TRUCK CROSSED the new Navua bridge and turned off the main road onto the raised road which ran along the east bank of the Navua River. Evidently we were heading not for Suva but the sleepy river township of Navua. I spotted the large maroon saloon that Dr Bavadra had been driven around in during his 'deposed prime minister' period. It was abandoned on the side of the road, and I wondered with some trepidation what they had done with him.

As we weaved along the riverbank road looking down onto the broad river, I remembered driving along this road in another truck fifteen years earlier. In 1972 I had just been appointed district officer Navua when Hurricane Bebe, one of the worst to affect southeastern Fiji this century, struck the district. As Bebe bore down on us, I had spent most of the day coordinating the collection of people from their flooded homes on the Navua plains. The river, normally some 200 metres from bank to bank, had spread to a mass of water 13 kilometres across from Nakaulevu to Lobau village. Here and there a few soggy islands, including the township, had stayed above the flood level.

We were collecting people in flat-bottomed river punts powered by outboard engines and operated by their Fijian 'river taxi' owners. The willingness of these men to undertake dangerous, unrewarded rescue missions throughout the day exemplified to me the brave and charitable spirit with which so many Fijians are endowed.

As evening approached and the hurricane's full force was coming on us we called off the rescue operation. Shortly afterwards a distressed Indian lady begged that we bring the remainder of her family from their inundated house out on Tokotoko Back Road. We asked for one of the fatigued boatmen to volunteer his services and chose one from the handful who did so. I decided to go with him in order to get a first-hand assessment of the state of the flood.

The Navua river was careering past the township with ochre waves nearly three metres high and bristling with madly rolling uprooted trees and huge clumps of bamboo speeding by. Our destination was eastward away from the river across the flooded Tokotoko rice farms. We found the house just as the last smear of storm-dimmed daylight left us, took on our passengers and headed back in the direction of the township.

Halfway back our propeller hit the top of a submerged fence post and the engine's shear-pin snapped. The boatman began the tedious task of trying to shape a piece of wire into an approximation of a shear-pin and as he worked away I contemplated our chances. As later meteorological statistics were to show, the rain was driving horizontally at 193 kilometres per hour. We had lost our sense of direction as our punt yawed and rotated powerless in the darkness, and we were being sucked along by a watery vortex concocted by the collision of the main flow of the river against the incoming wall of the sea's storm-tide. I calculated that this vortex was inexorably taking us towards the main river's wrath. The person in the bow was given the job of holding on to the odd branch or post that we drifted into but his grip would be lost in ensuing gusts. I felt glum and mentally fatigued.

It was a long, bleak twenty minutes before our engine started again and we moved cautiously forward through the dark storm. Our main fear was ending up in the river, which our punt would not have survived. But we had to go with the current that was pulling us towards the river because the township also lay somewhere in that direction. So we proceeded, eyes stung by the wind and rain, searching for any sign that we might have missed Navua and were about to enter the river's torrent.

A light was spotted and we steered towards it. The vision of that beacon and the sense of relief it gave are firmly fixed in my memory. The light was from the second floor of the hospital, and as we putted past the flooded first floor I looked up at the light and saw, through the rain-streaked glass, a Coleman's pressure lamp and in its glow the face of a Fijian nurse peering anxiously out into the hurricane.

We made our way back to the police station which was the headquarters of our emergency services operation. In the small hours of the morning the wind was beginning to abate when Constable Maharaj burst into the station and stammered, 'Bridge has gone, sir! Bridge has gone!'

The Navua bridge was a venerable structure called the 'sixpenny bridge', because it was peppercorn-gifted to the government by the

Vancouver Sugar Company when the company closed down its Navua sugar cane plantations in 1921. It had a fifteen-metre high, steel superstructure and was the pride of the district. We climbed into the cab of a PWD dump truck, which growled slowly along the raised riverbank road, its headlights illuminating the muddy bow-wave advancing before us. When we came to the point in the submerged road where it turned sharply left to approach the bridge we ground to a halt. Huddled in the front seat of the truck, we gaped like the mesmerised front row at a magic show when some immovable object has just been made to disappear. Our monumental bridge was nowhere to be seen, vanished, just the torrent of the river raging by in our headlights.

Fifteen years later in the back of an army truck we arrived in Navua, swinging past the riverbank market place and the stubby river jetty where the boats from Beqa island were berthed. We turned at the police station, then drove between the mosque and Thomson Park to the makeshift army camp. Thomson Park was the district's main sports field and was named after me by the townspeople when I was away from Fiji for a year doing my postgraduate studies at Cambridge. The park had been my pet project, converting it from two rice paddies to a football ground, and I had spent my weekends working with volunteers to make the conversion. Even so I still self-consciously cringe as I think of this landmark bearing my name when so many other names from the district would have been more appropriate.

Arriving at the army camp, we drove through a barbed wire perimeter and pulled up in a cloud of dust. It was about 8am. The camp was makeshift, with lots of barbed wire, canvas tents and wooden crates. Reclining on the latter were Rambo poseurs. They were dressed in semi-uniforms, a bit of army-issue fatigues shared amongst them, bandannas around heads and necks, ammo belts, that sort of thing. Too many Viet Nam war movies. Those from our truck who had been wearing balaclavas now had them rolled up off their sweating faces to make berets of them. They were clearly enjoying the opportunity to throw guns around, take prisoners and strike heroic poses. One had the definite impression that this was military at the fringe, and I felt distinctly uneasy being the prisoner of these cowboys.

On the other side of the army camp was Vashist Muni Memorial School, where Marijcke and my brother Richard were teachers in 1974. Looking across to the school, I had the sad thought that some of my captors might be their former pupils. In the days before Thomson Park, the district rugby competition used the school ground to play on, and I remembered the wild tackling and passing when Richard and I played for the Veivatuloa team, in our Cambridge blue jerseys, against the other village teams.

On the other side of the camp were the green rice paddies stretching for two kilometres or so across the Navua flats to the line of coconut trees on the horizon which marked the beachfront and the location of the Naitonitoni Government Station. Before the road was cut through from Suva to Navua in the 1930s, the district was serviced by a ferry which came down the coast from Suva each day. The ferry's terminus was Naitonitoni where it transferred passengers onto a long wooden jetty extending from the grey sandy beach.

At the end of the jetty is the district officer's residence, the court house, a collection of government cottages and some net-festooned fishermen's dwellings. During the day Naitonitoni's exposure to the southeast tradewinds sets up a constant rustling commotion in the coconut palms and white caps fly on the blue channel stretching from there to the purple peaks of the fire-walking island of Beqa, some thirteen kilometres distant.

When I lived there in the early 1970s, Naitonitoni had an insular quality to it. A seaside village surrounded by watery rice paddies. Every hour or so a bus would come bumping down the gravel road from Navua, turn laboriously where the road came to a dead end at the jetty, and drop off those passengers who needed to pick up a licence of the various varieties that we dispensed from the court house: dog-ownership, liquor retail, hawking, marriage, death, and so on. Apart from days when the magistrates court was in session or the District Development Committee was meeting, Naitonitoni was a pleasant backwater where time passed nice and slow.

It had not always been so pleasant. Its name Naitonitoni means the dipping place, *toni* being the Fijian verb to dip or steep in water. Last century and beyond, cannibalistic people of the district were in the habit of using a deep freshwater pond next to the district officer's house as cool storage for *bokola*, the oven-bound human corpses for an impending feast.

When as a bachelor in 1972 I was about to take up residence in the rambling old district officer's house at Naitonitoni, the prime minister's wife, Adi Lady Lala, told me not to stay there alone as it was a haunted house. Apart from the disturbing past of the pond, the house itself was the scene of supernatural occurrences, and a colonial official had once taken his own life in the dining room. Adi Lala had lived in the house for several years in the early 1950s when she married Ratu Mara who was at that time the district officer.

An old family friend, Meli Ramacake, was bunking in his office in Navua township so I asked him to come and live with me at Naitonitoni, which he gladly did, and continued to do so after Marijcke and I were married in 1973.

I was never that disturbed by the ghostly goings-on in the house, taking the attitude that if I was ever confronted with an undeniably life-after-death apparition I would then calmly but quickly dedicate myself to a religious life. But some of our house guests were profoundly disturbed, and breakfast sessions were often a time for the recounting of terrifying nocturnal happenings. I remember an American Peace Corps engineer who had spent the night repeatedly waking up screaming in an imaginary room of blood. He left on the first bus after breakfast. There was another guest who claimed he was being smothered close to the point of asphyxiation in his bed. Maybe it was something in our water tank?

At eight o'clock each night we turned off the thumping diesel generator which serviced a couple of the houses at Naitonitoni with electric light. Once the generator was silent, the night sounds would have crystal clarity: the slap of the waves on the slick sand beach outside our open window, the snaky rustling of the coconut leaves overhead in the evening air currents.

One such quiet evening, the night air was ripped with violent screaming and guttural gurgling sounds directly above us. It sounded like a large pig was being clumsily put to death with knife blows to its flailing throat. In our attic, or perhaps on the roof? Meli and two of my brothers were with me playing cards in the dining room and as the horrifying din continued, we gathered our scattered wits and took torches in clammy hands to look for the source of the sound. Shortly into our search the racket stopped, and we were unable to find any explanation for it on the roof or in the attic. I remember stunned faces in the torchlight as the hushed night continued and we returned to our candlelit card game.

When Marijcke came to live with us at Naitonitoni she told me that she thought Meli was being visited by a lady at night. This was news to me and I asked her why. Marijcke had gone to the bathroom with a lantern around midnight. You had to be wide awake going into the bathroom because *dadakulaci* sea-snakes would sometimes get in there and lie under the wood-slat mat or in the cool corners behind the claw-foot bath. Coming out of the bathroom one stepped onto a twelve-metre-long veranda at the end of which was Meli's bedroom. The door to his room was a gauze-covered mosquito screen.

Moonlight was falling through a window onto the bed where Meli lay and standing next to his bed and bending over towards him was a lady in a pale Edwardian gown. As Marijcke moved down the veranda she saw that the lady was old with long white hair, just looking down at Meli's prone body; and then as Marijcke moved closer the apparition was gone. We told Meli about this and he quite matter-of-factly said he was often visited in his sleep by this old European lady who did nothing more than look at him in a curious lost way and caused no disturbance to his nocturnal slumbers.

Down in Navua township we would divide our leisure time between the Farmers Club and SS Khan's store. They were next door to each other. The club was the venue for alcohol consumption and SS Khan's was for playing draughts and drinking kava. One of our workmates, Ratu Namosimalua, a scion of one of the great chiefly families of Fiji, had had a problem with the bottle and was going through a drying-out phase in Navua. He was the stalwart of SS Khan's veranda and, even though the Farmers Club was only a few steps away, it was always understood that no-one would bring their glass with them from the club when they came to check on the progress of the draughts contest. This was an unspoken rule which was quietly adopted out of respect for Ratu Namosimalua's peace of mind.

We would play the Spanish version of draughts with king's long move. There was only one board and the winner would keep his seat on the well-worn bench in front of the board until a challenger defeated him. SS Khan was a genial Muslim store-keeper, with white-grey hair and smiling eyes. Apart from the fun of it, the only benefit he got from our use of his front veranda as the Navua draughts venue was his sale of packets of ground kava and Pall Mall cigarettes.

His family would mix up the kava for us in a white enamelled tin basin. I can see the basin's chipped blue rim and clearly hear the hollow resonating twang from the basin as the liquid was swirled within the thin metal. The kava was dispensed in *pyala*, little enamelled tin bowls, and we would get through three or four basins in the space of an hour as we puffed away on our Pall Mall, watching the play on the board, with a slow wave to the occupants of the occasional punt gliding past on the river.

SS Khan's schoolboy son was our draughts champ. When one of us beat the boy, SS would grin, eyes twinkling and touch the side of his friend Ratu Namosimalua's thigh with the back of his hand. They would have a little chuckle and then Ratu would take a long pull on his curved tobacco pipe, blow the smoke out of the corner of his mouth and say, '*talo*', the command for another round of kava to be served.

The Farmers Club in those days was not much more than a wood shack with a small bar and a scraggy pool table. Old Ram Deo was the club secretary and barman. He had a face like a frog, bulging eyes and big lippy smile. The bar offered Fiji Bitter, Gordon's gin or Dewar's White Label whisky. That was it. The company was usually good and very low-key, for the more progressive types went to the double-storeyed, concrete-walled, linoleum-floored Navua Club further up the river. At the Navua Club they had an electricity generator and the interior was lit by bright fluorescent tubes. Down at the Farmers Club, Ram Deo poured the drinks and pumped up the hissing benzene lamps if we wanted to play pool after nightfall.

Through the window next to the club's bar could be seen a tin-walled house across the road, surrounded by mango and coconut trees. I was driving past this house one day when I saw a gesticulating group of people peering into it. I stopped my utility truck and went across to investigate. Hanging by the neck from the house rafters was a young Indian man. The group of people, some of whom were his relatives, were wailing around helplessly, so with the assistance of a Fijian man who happened by I untied the body and lowered it to the ground. I was further shocked on recognising the distorted face of the dead man in my arms as that of the happy one who only the week before had come to Naitonitoni to uplift a marriage certificate for his forthcoming traditional Hindu wedding ceremony. Evidently and tragically things had not gone as planned.

There was an old wooden theatre in the township that showed Hindi movies. The theatre had a generator which provided enough electricity for the projector and a few light bulbs to dimly illuminate the bare wooden benches inside. Above the front door was a sign displaying the theatre's name 'Laxmi Talkies', and under that the proprietor's name 'Prop. Ghellabhai & Sons'. Providing sound with the moving pictures was still considered an innovation worth promoting in Navua in the early 1970s. Another sign I liked was outside one of Navua's many little Hindu temples; painted in English and Hindi was the message, 'Drunkards Are Strictly Prohibited'.

Further along the river bank was the rice mill, full of hessian sacks, piles of unpolished rice, straw-dust and field mice. Outside the mill's big front doors was another popular place for drinking kava, especially if there had been a problem in the Indian community and the sage words of Master Mangaru were desired. 'Master' is the honorific given in Fiji to school teachers, which profession Mangaru had followed until taking up the position of secretary of the Rice Milling Cooperative. Navua had a large population of dark-skinned, Tamil-speaking South Indians, called *Kaimadarasi* in Fiji, and Master Mangaru was of that stock. He would sit on his chair outside the mill, cross-eyed and cross-legged, hands clasped neatly over his knees, and give us the soft-spoken, diligently thought-out advice that was needed to sort things out so that they were fair to all concerned.

Past where the road turned at a right angle away from the river towards Naitonitoni was a muddy track which continued along the river bank. Beside this track was strung the hamlet of Naitata. In the middle of the hamlet was a mandir, a Hindu temple, where each year, as part of the Hindu calendar, fire-walking ceremonies were held. Our gardener Jai was the leading exponent of fire-walking in Navua. He told me that what had led him into it was his son's inability to walk as a young boy. Jai went through the preparatory rituals and then carried his son through the firepit. His son commenced walking soon afterwards and Jai had continued each year thereafter to lead the walkers through the fire.

The firewalking day would begin on a gravel shoal in the Navua river near the old bridge. Fijians going over the bridge in buses would irreverently yell down '*Koida, koida!*', their interpretation of the '*Govinda*' chant taken up by the firewalkers to evoke that god's blessing. After ablutions and prayers in the river's purifying water, the chanting built up and drummers with flat drums battered out a hypnotic rhythm. The head priest stabbed metal skewers through the tongues, cheeks and necks of the firewalkers and daubed red paste and yellow turmeric onto their glazed faces. The thin cotton tee shirts and loin clothes of the men and the saris of the occasional women participants, bright yellow from dousings of turmeric water, clung to their bodies as they began trance-dancing to the drums. Red sashes at their waists warned of danger and garlands of yellow marigolds and wilted red hibiscus flowers whipped across their chests.

Brass *kalsa* pots were filled with water and sacred leaves, then the burnished *kalsa* with their thick green thatches were lifted onto the heads of Jai and a few others who led the procession up from the river, dancing through the township chanting, with cymbals clashing and drums clattering. The crowd gathered and moved along the muddy Naitata track to the *mandir*, where the skewered dancers encircled the firepit in front of the divine effigies of the temple. Blue flames licked up from white charcoal in the long pit, the drummers were beating to a crescendo and dancers were being flogged with a heavy jute whip by a priest; and then into the firepit went Jai followed by the red and yellow procession. Again and again through the ecstatic flames they would go, and then the exhausted firewalkers spread out like fallen flowers on the grass in front of the effigy that the head priest bought out of the temple and cradled over his shoulder. The effigy is of Maha Devi, the Great Mother, source of energy, compassion and terrible revenge.

One last memory of that night when Hurricane Bebe raged over us came from a few hours before dawn when the wind had died down and the flood level was starting to creep back from its highpoint just in front of the police station. I splashed across the road in my gumboots and stood next to the market, shining a flashlight out over the brown surge of the river.

Something white caught my eye jutting out of the flood-waves racing down towards me. The object was flung by a wave into a swirling eddy and came circling over to where I stood. It was the wooden sign which used to hang about half a mile out on the road to Suva; the one that had been erected by the Navua Jaycees, who as far as I could gather had come briefly into existence, erected this sign and dispersed forever.

The sign was one of those ones which has a town welcome message on one side and a town farewell on the other. Bobbing there at my feet was 'Navua Hopes You Will Return'. And so, as I waited full of rue and foreboding in the Navua army camp in 1987, surrounded by barbed wire and cowboy soldiers, I thought, 'Well guys, I'm back'.

Mountains Tower Up

A TELEPHONE CALL was received in one of the canvas tents and the order was given for us to get back in the truck. Stephen and I clambered into the rear with a motley assortment of guards and guns and parked our backsides on the metal benches. The truck rumbled off along the dusty Tokotoko Back Road in the direction of Suva. The shapes of individual rice paddies we passed through and the way they jigsawed together over the Tokotoko flatlands were so familiar to my eye and I felt so very much a part of them. A cloud of road dust plumed behind us and drifted its bitter-tasting grit out over the pure young rice plants emerging from the shallow waters of the paddies. To my sense of unease was now added a forlorn feeling that I was bidding farewell to all this.

Our vehicle bumped over the bridge at Lobau, and I caught a glimpse of the smooth brown river surface curving away through the mangrove forest. If you follow the river for two kilometres or so down to where it meets the sea, you are on the foreshore of my old mentor Esava Duasuva's domain. From the foreshore you clamber up a steep slope to Qaributa, his homestead, which looks out to the mountains at Mau and the main sea reef off Veivatuloa.

Esava loved music and had trained his sons to play acoustic guitar and sing harmonies uncommonly well. In the sixties their recorded music was often played on the Fijian radio broadcasts and the name of their performing group 'Caucau ni Qaributa' was well-known throughout the islands. When I lived in Navua, I used to play in Veivatuloa's rugby side with Esava's sons, and after a game we would sometimes end up back in my house at Naitonitoni, drinking kava, playing guitars and singing in the soft light-pool of a kerosene lamp.

Caucau is the night breeze that comes down off the sun-heated hills to the coolness of the sea. It is a beloved wind because it comes in our hour of need when the prevailing tradewinds have ceased. In the close hush of such a night, humidity rises like steam from a pudding. Sweat beads form on prone bodies. Mongrels bark their half-hearted messages through the stillness and the whine of a passing mosquito is like the siren of a minute ambulance veering by. Just when the atmosphere is getting too claustrophobic to breathe, down from the hills, wafting through the vine-tangled jungle, gliding silently along nocturnal river valleys, across the star-reflecting rice paddies comes the *caucau*, gently cooling and soothing us to rest.

Esava was an elected member of the Namosi Provincial Council. He didn't have much of a formal education and he spoke only a little English. He was short, thickset and bald. He was a clear thinker, practised hard work and sincerity, believed in service to his fellow man and had a warm sense of humour. When I was living in Navua he was about sixty years old and he took care to give me the good advice I needed to work with some degree of insight into Namosi affairs.

His constituency was down on the Veivatuloa coast but he would sometimes accompany us on our visits to the villages in the Namosi hill country. In those days in the early seventies there were no roads to the villages in the interior, and the strenuous walks up muddy tracks would take their toll on the overweight or unfit. Esava would be telling stories and cracking jokes as we wound our way up the hillsides, while some of our party would be struggling behind gasping for breath.

On one such trip we were sitting at the top of one of these climbs enjoying a rest and admiring an inland view of the jagged Korobasabasaga mountain range. I was looking through my binoculars for peregrine falcons, which could sometimes be seen riding the air currents near Mount Voma where they were known to nest. Esava was deep in thought for a long time, observing the lay of the land and the clouds riding up over Korobasabasaga's peaks. When he spoke it was to say that he'd been a serious student of music all his life, had considered the songs and deliveries of many a singer, and he had decided that one performer stood above all the rest. Knowing of his musical prowess we waited respectfully for the completion of this revelation. 'Jim Reeves,' said Esava, with a faraway look in his eyes, perhaps listening in his mind's ear to distant drums. For the rest of the day's walk, whenever I exchanged glances with my friend Ratu Leone he'd giggle at me, 'not bloody Jim Reeves!'

Ratu Leone Matanitobua was a direct descendant of Koroduadua the feared

195

cannibal lord of the mountainous lands of Namosi. On a clear day Namosi's peaks could be seen from Suva Harbour from whence they loomed as a dark challenge to coastal order. After Christianity took hold in Namosi, intrepid Victorian travellers would visit Koroduadua's Namosi stronghold and then describe in tones of eager grimness the empty cannibal ovens and the trees surrounding the old pagan temple. In these trees, jutting out like speckled dead branches, were embedded the bones of the victims of cannibal feasts past. Fairy-ferns grew from nooks in projecting fibulae, and moss was seen to dapple a jaw-bone popping out of a joint in a tree trunk.

Koroduadua was the Tui Namosi, king of the *matanitu* of Namosi. Matanitu were independent political states and at the time of the Cession of Fiji to the British Crown there were ten *matanitu* in Fiji. Namosi was the only one of these headquartered in the mountains of the interior. Koroduadua was dead by the time of Cession, but his son Matanitobua, the new Tui Namosi, was one of the thirteen signatories of the Deed of Cession and was subsequently presented with a sword as a gift from Queen Victoria. Ratu Leone had this sword in safe-keeping.

Ratu Leone is dead now, fallen prematurely, but he became Tui Namosi in his time and was a treasured leader of his people. He was about the same age as me and was a good-looking man with a mischievous sense of humour. Unusually for a Fijian he had red hair and, like most of the Namosi people, as a result of a conversion decision taken last century by a previous Tui Namosi, he was a staunch Roman Catholic. After the second coup d'état in 1987, at the Great Council of Chiefs Ratu Leone referred to the sword which had been given to his great great grandfather by Queen Victoria and denounced the arbitrary breaking of the links between his people and the Crown. We shared the perhaps anachronistic view that oaths and tradition mean too little to too many today.

I have a black and white photograph of Ratu Leone, which is as clear as the day I had it developed in 1972. He is standing on a rock in the middle of some wild rapids of the Navua River. Our punt carrying hurricane relief supplies between Namuamua and Waibogi had just capsized in the rapids, losing its outboard engine. Ratu Leone's well-muscled body is balanced on its rock plinth like a Roman statue in the middle of a foaming fountain, his precious gumboots in his hands. Across the years and the screen between the dead and living I salute you, Ratu.

The track from Navunikabi to Wainimakutu village up the far reaches of the Wainikoroiluva River called for the river to be forded more than twenty times, and with the frequent rain storms it took a while for travellers to dry out in the village of one's destination. It was cool enough up there in the hills for fires to be lit inside the houses and we would sit in front of these drying out and enjoying a smoke. The fires had to be carefully tended for the houses had thatched roofs and were set in hearths close to the woven reed walls of the dwellings.

From Nakavika to Namosi village, the latter being Koroduadua's old capital, the track took us over the natural rock bridge of Namodo under which the Wainikoroiluva thundered and past which *ika droka*, the good-eating flagtail fish, cannot venture. Once during the dry season Ratu Leone and I ran the length of the track in our gumboots all the way from the abandoned village of Nakorowaiwai, with its spooky old stone *yavu* in the root clutches of huge *baka* trees, to Namosi village, a distance that usually took several hours to walk. That was a favourite track, for it took one up over the watershed of the Navua and Rewa rivers and down through a towering ravine into the gorgeous river valley in which the Namosi capital, the Catholic Mission and its surrounding villages were set.

Up where the track passed over the watershed, there was supposed to have been a shaddock tree whose branches spread either side of the watershed so that some of its fruit rolled down into the streams that fed the Navua river and some rolled down to those that fed the Rewa. *Moli kana*, shaddocks, were quite common in Namosi and we would help ourselves to the fruit off the trees that we found near the tracks. The fruit is like a grapefruit grown to the size of a pumpkin and, inside the fruit, the large segments are just like a huge orange but without much sweetness. Returning along the banks of the fast-flowing Wainikoroiluva we would throw the shaddocks into the waters for a bit of fun. They bobbed along the river like green rubber balls and we would pick them up downstream later in the trek when we felt like a snack.

We made a point of regularly visiting all the villages in Namosi Province, some of which like Nasoqo, Wainilotulevu and Naraiyawa seldom had visitors from the coast. One night in Wainilotulevu I was told of a *tabua* which had a long and venerable history from the time it was found last century on a reef near Kadavu island. Ratu Leone asked the villagers to show it to me and in the morning a long object wrapped in layers of old tapa cloth was laid in front of us. Layer upon layer of bark cloth bandages were unwound to reveal before me not a whale's tooth but a metre long elephant tusk, smoked and oiled to a deep mahogany brown, with a rope attached to each end so that it could be presented as a ceremonial *tabua*; surely the only one of its kind in Fiji.

Nothing came into those Namosi villages that couldn't be carried on horseback or on the backs of the hardy human inhabitants. As a result corrugated iron was a rare sight and the internal combustion engine didn't exist. The villages were well kept, with the building and maintenance of the thatched dwellings still being a communal responsibility. Spending time in these riverside villages at night was a wonderful experience. You sat, slept and ate on the soft springy floor of a *vale vakaviti*, the floor being of packed earth covered with plaited bamboo and dried grass, on top of which several layers of pandanus mats were laid. Outside a mist would usually have filled the mountain valley, muting all sounds but that of the river rushing by over boulder-filled rapids. A fire would have been lit in a wall hearth and pungent wood-smoke would be filtering up into the thatch above.

Tramping through these same valleys and hills with a Fijian guide in 1913, Rupert Brooke stepped out from a Namosi village on a clear night and then wrote, 'Fiji in the moonlight is like nothing else in this world or the next. It is all dim colours and all scents. And here where it is high up, the most fantastically shaped mountains tower up all around…'

When we visited these isolated villages Ratu Leone and I tended to go with a team comprised of officials from the various arms of government of relevance to the villagers: a doctor, an agricultural extension officer, a policeman, a woman's interests officer and so on. The arrival of such a group of visitors was always an excuse for some entertainment for all concerned, and after the ceremonies of welcome and the village meeting had been dispensed with, the visitors were then required to fill the roles of both audience for the village dance groups and dance partners for the village ladies as a string band beat out a punchy rhythm. We were also the recipients of vast amounts of kava served at all times, except during meals and the very limited sleeping periods allowed. At Nakavika village, if we tried to avoid the kava torture by sleeping in or dilly-dallying in an adjacent dwelling, the women of the village would douse us with pots of water.

This was all done with a huge sense of fun and, with Ratu Leone around, there was no way we were going to do anything but participate. After one particularly kava-soaked visit to Nakavika, I planned that when next we were to pass that way we should take a little-used track which wound along a jungle-covered ridge to the west of the village. It added up to an hour to our trek to the villages to the north of Nakavika, but the joke would be on the Nakavikans when they found we had avoided their torture-by-kava techniques.

Half-way through our diversionary tactic, trudging up that muddy ridge somewhere near its highest point, we came across a small clearing that had been cut in the jungle and the Nakavika hard-cores had carried buckets of water and all the kava paraphernalia up there; they were seated about the clearing with big expectant grins on their faces. We took our liquid punishment for an hour or so before resuming our journey and Nakavika had scored another notable victory to fuel the stories which were told up in the Namosi villages that year of 1973.

Ratu Leone professed innocence in the forewarning of the Nakavikans, but his sense of humour was deeply suspected in that and many of the other cultural jokes to which the government team would be subjected. For instance, a feature of Fijian custom in the old days was that most tribes and clans had totems which might take the form of an animal or a vegetable. In many parts of Fiji, memory of these totems has slipped away, but in Namosi the totems are still remembered and it is *tabu* to talk about the totems or behave towards them in a disrespectful way. Having said that, in the interests of village hilarity and secretly encouraged by Ratu Leone, our Namosi hosts would set us up to inadvertently show disrespect to their totems.

For example, in Nakavika the river prawns were the totem, and someone visiting the village for the first time would innocently eat the prawns served up by the villagers at dinner. Then all hell would break loose and mock anger at Nakavika's totem having been eaten would result in the innocent transgressor having to accept *ore*, traditional punishment. In Nakavika the *ore* would be eating all the remaining prawns with shells, heads and claws intact and then having to drink kava from an enormous coconut shell called Bilo Savusavu.

In the case of Namosi village itself, the totem was a wild yam called *tivoli* which was difficult to differentiate from the other yams served there. For the diners in the know, unless you were very sure about your yams, you would avoid yams altogether and go for the taro instead. Meals were eaten off a long table cloth laid on the floor with diners sitting cross-legged either side of it. For all the informality of the setting, mealtimes were quite ritualised. Because of traditional relationships, some people could not eat when others were eating. The cooks and servers congregated at the domestic end of the house observing the diners and replenishing dishes. Diners sat according to rank on either side of the cloth, with the places of honour at the furthermost extremity of the cloth from the domestic end. Grace was always said before the meal, and impeccable manners prevailed.

The uninitiated would hoe on into the yams until one of them inadvertently consumed a *tivoli*. The transgressor, usually one of those seated in places of honour, would then be shocked by a bellow from a woman at the serving end of the evening's repast, her formerly beatific face transformed to that of an avenging Amazon, and scooping up another steaming *tivoli* from the serving plate she would storm down the line of seated diners and ram it into the victim's groin.

There were other cultural complications that one became aware of. A regular member of our team was the assistant health inspector, who was from Noco in the Rewa delta. Now the Rewa people didn't have many material resources, since their ancestral home was amongst the mangrove swamps. In spite of this they had acquired considerable influence in Fiji and in doing so had relied solely upon their wit and charm; others would say their devious cunning. Their articulate speech has served them well in politics, in the pulpit, and of late in business, but it has lead the rest of Fiji to uncharitably label the more complicated or drawn out utterances of Rewans as 'RB' (Rewa Bullshit).

Our assistant health inspector, tall, gaunt and grey, aged beyond his many years of late night carousing, had amongst his sanitary duties the upgrading of village toilets. This was a task of no small relevance, as many a fly-infested open-pit toilet was encountered in those days. In honour of his profession the villagers gave him the irreverent title of Vuniwai Valevou, meaning toilet doctor, in spite of the fact that his main concerns were preventative medicine and mosquito control. During the village meetings they would insist that he address them in full on his long-drop speciality and would ask as many questions as they could to keep the subject going, in order to enjoy the teasing banter to which they invariably subjected him.

Vuniwai Valevou was up to it and he would use his rapier Rewan wit with flair and a certain arrogance in holding the villagers at bay. He got little assistance from his government colleagues in this regard; most of us would just sit there enjoying the jokes, but Ratu Leone could be relied upon to make sure that Vuniwai Valevou was given more than ample time on centre stage. For all the mutterings of 'RB', his audience delighted in his twisting and turning of words and ideas.

Ratu Leone would often arrange for us to drink kava at the schoolmaster's residence at Namuamua, because the schoolmaster was from Lau and was therefore *tauvu* to the Rewan toilet doctor. *Tauvu* relationships are customary ties of common ancestry which loosely link people from specific regions of Fiji. The main manifestation of a *tauvu* relationship is for one party to mercilessly, usually in a humorous way, take the mickey out of the other party in the *tauvu* relationship.

The grog sessions at the Lauan schoolmaster's house were marathon events. It has to be remembered that with no electric lights, television, cinemas or pubs, the night's entertainment up there in the hills had to be home grown. *Yaqona* was the main cash crop of the area, so kava was in plentiful supply, and the peculiarity of the region was that instead of sun-drying the kava and pounding it, the plant was pulled straight from the ground, peeled and rubbed on a rock until it was a mushy ball. The latter was then passed into the house in which we were drinking, where it would be immersed in water and squished around. The result was a more potent brew than normal kava and was called *yaqona drokadroka* or 'green grog'.

Vuniwai Valevou was at his most combative in his *tauvu*'s home and he would always ensure that he took the seating-place directly next to the side-entry door. This was a position of medium rank in a Fijian house, and it was easy for him to justify it as an appropriate spot for him to occupy. All attempts to move him further up the house away from the door were resisted by him with deference to Ratu Leone's chiefly rank and the more senior officials present.

Then the kava drinking would get underway. Vuniwai Valevou was no slouch in the drinking department, indeed he was known from time to time to be afflicted with a hint of *kanikani*, but he would have to be on his guard, for as well as verbal attack he would be the victim of a liquid onslaught from the host.

The kava ritual is done in rounds, with each person present drinking once in each round, but with different amounts of liquid in the *bilo* for different people. Thus over an evening one drinker might have only drunk the equivalent of a couple of pints, while others might have swallowed several bucketfuls. Vuniwai Valevou was always served a *bilo* full to the brim and he would take it without complaint, but by sitting next to the doorway he was able to consume only a little of the draught and in the dim light pour the remainder, supposedly only the dregs, out into the night. His slight of hand was suspected but he denied it in tones of mock umbrage.

One night the kava was flowing freely and he was entertaining us with tales of Lauan stupidity, when the schoolmaster had some accomplices sneak up to the doorway in question and place a sheet of corrugated iron on two rocks outside the door. During the next round of kava when Vuniwai Valevou was drinking his bowl, the room fell silent as he took a light swig and ejected the bulk of the contents out the door. The liquid fell upon the iron with a loud splash, at the sound of which the room erupted to shouts of shame and the Rewan was dragged from the doorway to a place where he could no longer do anything but drink his unfair share of the greenest of grog on into the long night.

Amazing as it might seem on a Pacific island, I met old people up in those villages who had never seen the sea and whose only taste of seafood had been out of cans of Japanese mackerel. Yet for all this isolation, most were relatively well-informed on national and international issues, thanks to the reach of Radio Fiji.

Boxing is a popular sport in Fiji and Radio Fiji used to give it generous coverage. In the villages of Saliadrau and Navunikabi I remember impassioned debates as to who was the better fighter, Joe Frazier or Mohammed Ali, and all the detail that armed these verbal jousts came from radio programmes and the odd magazine or newspaper that made its way up the Wainikoroiluva.

And over the radio came news of development roads being cut into other parts of Fiji that showed potential for economic growth. The European Community in particular was providing funds for big roading projects. What had been unthinkable now became a tantalising possibility, a road could come over those jungle-covered mountains and across the river gorges into the valleys of Namosi. We talked long and hard on the implications of such a road and, to balance all the positives, I sometimes painted a picture of urban drift and social decay in villages devoid of young people.

There is no turning back the tide of progress when it is rolling in, and within a few years of my leaving Namosi the necessary funds were allocated by the powers-that-be in Suva and roads were cut into Namosi and the Wainikoroiluva. Great was the joy of the villages as they shared in the material benefits that that came with these gravel arteries. Bundles of dried kava, taro and cassava bounced out of the valleys towards Suva market in the backs of trucks, rather than on the backs of people, and corrugated iron and sawn timber came back in the trucks. But before too long it became apparent that there were more young people going away on the trucks than there were returning, and many of those that did come back returned with attitudes that didn't sit well with the old communal ways. Flying over those valleys a mere decade later I looked down on corrugated iron houses in villages that had shrunk, overgrown sites of hamlets that had disappeared and creeping bulldozers scarring the rain forest with landslides and clearings in their extraction of the hardwood trees on the slopes of those once pristine valleys.

I held my sad thoughts in check, for who can deny the human urge to better one's lot in life. I thought of my own ancestors making the descent from the austere beauty of the Scottish Highlands to crowded coastal towns, before the long sea voyages of their descendants to far-off lands. And like the Namosi people, for all those that fell by the wayside, some came on to better things.

The army truck crossed the coastal boundary of Namosi on the ridge past Wainadoi and Suva Harbour hove into view. We stopped at the navy base on the mangrove coast at Kalokolevu where our guards received further instructions, and then on we drove towards Suva. I took one last wistful look out the back of the truck at the peaks of Namosi rising behind the littoral hills, then turned my face to the capital and the fate that awaited me there.

IMPRISONMENT

WE DROVE UP to the gates at Queen Elizabeth Barracks. Our driver took instructions from the sergeant at the guardhouse, the white boom-gate swung up and our truck entered the camp. We came to stop in front of an office into which, surrounded by our posse, Stephen and I were led like a couple of outlaws. After some questioning, Stephen was told he was free to go. He told me he'd let Marijcke know where I was and set off.

Without any explanation I was then led back to the guardhouse and on entering it saw two rows of empty prison cells leading off it. So this was the permanent secretaries meeting I had been summoned to attend, a meeting of one in the brig normally reserved for drunken soldiers. I was momentarily confused, relieved that I wasn't being put up against a wall for target practice, but incredulous that I was going to prison without a word from anyone. A hand on my shoulder guided me into a cell and, as its iron-barred door slammed shut behind me, a wave of humiliated disbelief swept over me.

The cell was 2 metres by 1.5 metres. It was a plastered cement box. Its exterior wall had two tiny windows set high up for what transpired to be ineffective ventilation; it was not yet 9am but the building was already filled with hot dank air. The windows were without glass or gauze and were crossed with iron bars. If you stood on tiptoes you could see out of them to a reed-filled gully, and in the distance the back views of some Samabula houses. The interior wall had the door of iron bars set to one side of it. The door was bolted and secured with a heavy lock and chain. The only other opening was a drainage hole at the floor level of the exterior wall, presumably for those times that the cell's rough cement floor was hosed down. A previous occupant had scrawled his name on the wall, 'Kabekoro, 1982.'

There was a stench in the cell. I thought it might be from the human excrement that had been smeared up the side wall above the mattress. I noted the excrement had been smeared in the shape of a spreading tree and on closer inspection saw that it had been there too long to be the source of the malodour. There was no doubt about it, the smell came from the mattress. I politely asked for a replacement one, but was ignored. Later in the day, mental and physical exhaustion brought me into contact with this five-centimetre thick mattress. Going down on it was like lying on top of a limp, dead toad. Its sour smell was an accumulation of years of sweat, vomit and urine from inebriated soldiers, and to these olfactory elements was added the effects of mildew and age on its damp, coconut-fibre innards. For a pillow I used the only other furnishing in the cell, which was a mottled grey woollen blanket.

Close on the sense of humiliation when the iron door closed behind me had been a shock of outrage. 'Hang on,' I muttered to myself, 'this is wrong, I want out of here. I want out of here now.' But reality was the lock and chain on the door and its rusted steel bars. There was plainly no point in remonstrating with the know-nothing, see-nothing guards. And then came the intimidating realisation that I was totally under the thumb of these men in uniform clumping around out there in the relative freedom of their military occupations.

To a certain degree the fear and uncertainty of the previous twelve hours abated, as incarceration behind bars now seemed the likely extent of my fate. This was compounded when later in the day Robert Keith-Reid was bustled into a cell across the corridor, bringing news of the imprisonment of the mayor of Suva, a Supreme Court judge, and assorted trade unionists and provocateurs.

I'd known Robert since Suva Grammar School days, where he was a few years senior to me. We'd never spent much time together socially and we'd been on opposite sides of the table with me in government and he Fiji's leading investigative journalist. He was a fearless critic, with a tendency to see things in the negative. I was glad of his company and someone with whom to share such uncertainties as why we were at the army lock-up and not down in one of the civil gaols with the other prisoners. He wasn't amused when I speculated that he'd been put in with me just to keep me company, especially later on when we overheard comments that other political prisoners had been released.

We debated what the second coup meant for Fiji's future. We shared grim jokes. I speculated what 'Political Prisoner, 1987' would do for our

CVs and whether we would have to tick the affirmative box when visa applications asked 'Have you ever served a prison sentence?'

Two drunken soldiers were dragged in and thrown into adjoining cells. One of them was reasonably communicative. His name was Kavelutu, and he and his mate had been on an AWOL drinking binge. There was some comfort to be had from the fact that the army was disciplining its own. The other soldier was too busy filling his cell with vomit to communicate.

The afternoon heat was slowly cooking us in the hot box of the prison and my shirt-back was wet from sweat. When it became obvious I wasn't going anywhere for a while, I stripped down to my boxer shorts. I put my sandals and sunglasses to one side. I looped my belt through the bars of one of the windows and hung my trousers and shirt through the belt loop.

Then night fell and my cell turned into a convention centre for mosquitoes. While I was awake I could deal with this by slapping and waving my itching hands around. Sleep was only going to be possible with the woollen blanket as a total body cover, but after a few minutes under that, every skin-pore turned into a flowing faucet of perspiration. Emerging from the blanket the cloud of whining insects descended again. It didn't take long for their angry little bites to drive me back into the sauna of the prickly blanket and the wet, stinking mattress. There I would lie in a sweat-ball for as long as I could endure, scratching my welts and cursing, before coming up for air. So the night was spent in a round of semi-sleep, fitful swatting of the insect-filled air and declarations of eternal war on the mosquito race.

If the first day in prison had been about fear, uncertainty and disbelief, the second day was dominated by quiet rage. Dawn had broken and the mosquitoes retreated for twelve hours. I tried to catch up on lost sleep but was jolted awake by a loud metallic clatter by my head. I opened my eyes to find the barrel of an M16 fifteen centimetres from my face, pointing at my forehead. A soldier being issued with a gun from the guardhouse armoury, had carelessly leant his gun against the wall and it had fallen over. He picked it up, ignoring my look of incredulity.

My jaw was on fire from last night's mosquito torture. As I sat there stroking the stubble emerging through the welts on my face, a large, yellowish toad, covered in its own welts and warts, stared at me from the corner of the cell, then made a crawling exit through the drainage hole.

The prison was regularly filled with clouds of diesel smoke as vehicles stopped at the guardhouse to have their details taken by the guards. A big truck stationary for three minutes with its engine running and its exhaust pipe funnelling diesel fumes into the open doors of the guardhouse would fill our cells with choking fumes. At times it was like living in a road tunnel in a traffic jam. There was nothing to be done but grin, cough and bear it.

Equally gruelling was the noise level. Not only were we located day and night at the fulcrum of the traffic movements of the military government, but we were at the only point of human contact for citizens who had urgent requests of this de facto government. The bureaucracy down at Government Buildings was in a state of paralysed uncertainty and all decisions were being taken by the army. A small crowd milled around the outside of the gate, people who had lost family members, people who needed approval to leave the country urgently in the face of the blanket ban the army had placed on overseas travel by Fiji citizens, tradesmen who required exemptions from the curfew restrictions which had now been imposed, journalists seeking interviews or information, gawpers, spies and even peanut hawkers.

The telephones in the guardhouse rang constantly with queries, requests and instructions. They had those old-fashioned shrill call-bells which threatened madness to all listeners if no-one picked up the receiver. Bad for the soldiers sweating and swearing through their harried shifts in the guardhouse, but worse for us prisoners who lived through it twenty-four hours a day.

At one point I heard an officer shout at someone on the phone, 'This is our government, our army and our country, we'll do what we fucking like.' His arrogant incompetence struck like a blow and I muttered, 'Welcome to Coup-Coup Land.'

The regimen of prison life was becoming evident. No exit from the cell except to go to the toilet. Meals slid under the bars of the door to you. The body language of the guards showed their disdain for you, their lack of eye-contact their insecurity. One of the sergeants on duty that second day was a man who had worked with the supervisor of elections next to my old office at the Ministry of Information and he had often stopped by there to partake of the contents of our *tanoa*. Now I asked him if he might get permission for me to phone my wife, just to let her know that I was okay. Too small of spirit to even say hello in a way which acknowledged that we were human beings that had once shared a cup of fellowship together, he mumbled something incomprehensible and did nothing about it.

The toilet was situated in a lean-to near the front gate, and as this was the only permissible outing, the call of nature took on a welcome note. I'd pull on my trousers in the cell and call for attention. A guard would take me out to the toilet and check my pockets before and after my visit to the outhouse. This was all quite an entertainment for the crowd at the gate. '*O cei na kaivalagi oya?*' would be heard from people inquisitive to know who I was.

Each day I would see Stephen Hooper in the crowd and would subtly give him the thumbs up, heartened in the knowledge that he would be letting Marijcke know that I was alive and kicking.

Back in the cell, frustration and anger were building. All the ineffectual rhetoric was running through my mind: what right did they have, what had I done wrong, who had accused me, how was this mess going to be set right? I paced and paced and paced. In the small space in which I had to promenade, pacing meant two steps and turn, two steps and turn, two steps and turn. I did this hour after hour, getting into a rhythm to control my rage and assuage my boredom. I remembered the awful sight of big cats in small zoo cages pacing and pacing with wild, trapped looks, on the verge of a burst of panic or fury. I pictured myself as a leopard concentrating all my senses and my venom on the rhythm of the pace, the muscles used for each step and turn, honing them to perfect timing as the hours ground by.

In the afternoon I managed to get my dead toad mattress exchanged for a less objectionable one. I lay down to get some sleep, gazing at the excrement tree rising up the wall beside me. Phones rang, guards shouted, truck engines roared and down there with my head at floor level through all that noise and commotion, one sound stayed with me as I drifted into sleep. Like distant sleigh bells jingling through a Pushkin landscape, the sound of the tiny, tinny rollers on the buckles on the soldiers' sandals tinkled as they moved around the guardhouse.

When I awoke, a sergeant, who I took to be from Naitasiri, had come on duty. He was broad-set, bow-legged and bad-tempered. He didn't like the fact that Keith-Reid and I were in cells near enough that we could hold conversations. With a rattle of keys and some curt commands he moved Robert to a cell at the far end of the corridor so that we could only shout the odd bit of information to each other before being told to shut up. This man had no idea who we were or why we were in his prison, it was enough that we were there and we could feel his malice.

Kavelutu and Whisper had been set free, presumably to face subsequent charges. Robert and I had given Kavelutu's mate his name because, other than vomit, the only emissions from his mouth the whole time he was in the can were a couple of whispered remarks to Kavelutu.

Day number three was Monday, and I spent most of the day in a mood of depression. The only news I garnered was what I could overhear the guards discussing. '*Sa sogo taucoko na baqe*' – the banks had been closed, presumably to stop a run of withdrawals. The outer wall of Robert's cell faced the camp's main road, and through the ventilation bars he too overheard the odd snippet of news from passers-by. In this way he learnt that the other political prisoners had been released yesterday and today. 'Why not us?' he shouted at the guards.

In the history of human rights abuse our experience was a minuscule irrelevant atom. Unlike millions of political prisoners before us we were not subjected to beatings. We were fed. We had a roof over our heads. But the humiliating, depriving experience of incarceration was ever present. Four days of uncertainty don't seem like much, and in the greater scheme of things they weren't, but if you're interested in the physical sensation involved, map out a floor area in front of you 2 metres by 1.5 metres, and picture a smelly mattress 90 centimetres by 60 centimetres taking up most of the room. Then walk around in the remaining area for a few minutes. You have nothing to read, no radio to listen to, no view to distract you. It's not bad for a while, but after half an hour it starts getting to you, after an hour it can drive you up the wall, but the hours and days will still pulse balefully by.

Around about lunchtime the sound of a big convoy of trucks growling past the guardhouse woke me from the sleep that had been compensating me for another mosquito-plagued night. I was lying on my back with my head wedged against the iron bars of the cell door. The cell was sweltering in the midday sun and I was sweating. Pools of tepid water lay over my eyes and I wiped them off with my forearm. Blinking through the salt I became aware of two dark holes above me and I tried without success to focus them into one. They hovered there above my head.

Gradually the fleshy features of a malevolent face materialised around them and I realised I was staring up through the bars of the cell at a set of cavernous nostrils. Broader than the barrels of a double-barrelled shotgun, from my vantage point these two dark tunnels seemed to go inward and upward forever.

The face belonged to the Naitasiri sergeant and he was crouching over me in my cell. I had the feeling he had been studying me for some time. Maybe he thought I was sick. He continued to stare down at me now that I was awake. Time passed. '*Bula*' I tried. The sergeant gave a dismissive grunt, straightened up and hulked off down the corridor towards the sunlight.

Something in his manner said 'cargo cult'. The world had tipped upside down when a Fijian would not return the customary greeting of health to even the lowliest of mortals. The cargo had been delivered, but I wondered if the biscuits would be infested with weevils when the boxes were finally opened.

I lay there looking at the excrement tree climbing up the wall beside me. Its branches stretched out in a broad canopy. After a while I saw it as a flamboyant tree, rising out of the filth of Suva's bus station, its trunk scarred and covered in grime and tattered election posters. The spread of its canopy was in brilliant crimson flower, from which dropped blossoms, fluttering down into the muddy trash below.

Later it became a tree in a moon-lit village square in some far-off place, its branches filled with twinkling lights and under it a gathering of people in celebration with accordions and guitars, bottles of wine and dancing. Underfoot was crushed white shell and a narrow street wound from it down to a small harbour with fishing boats at its quay. I saw my children, grown to adulthood, seated happily amongst the people.

Happiness. It had been a while. Somewhere in there the umbilical chord to my homeland was cut. I ventured for the first time the belief that I could be happy living a life somewhere completely different. I took in, like a deep breath, that love and happiness, and family and friendship, could be just as rich in another land. A path appeared ahead which forked off from the one I had been treading. There was no sense of foreboding or particular promise about it. It just opened up there ahead, while all along I had thought that the one I was on was the only one allotted me.

Through all the depression of that day a small reprieve came in the form of an old team mate of mine from Gaunavou Rugby Club. He was an army NCO, had heard a rumour that I was in the lock-up and stuck his neck out to check up on my welfare. His rank was too junior to enable him to do anything about my status, but his concern was heart-warming and he promised to call my wife to tell her I was okay. I felt a bit choked after he left. 'Never, never, never, never, NEVER say die' was our Gaunavou refrain, and it took a rugby club mate to show some humanity around this place.

The fourth day of imprisonment started with more of the same, but by now my mood was one of resignation. Then, about midday, things started to happen. Captain Nukubati, whom I knew from his duties as the musical director of the army brass band, came into the guardhouse. He was surprised to see me and asked how long I'd been there. After four days of no bathing, shaving or change of clothes I guess we didn't look that sharp, and he offered to send down to our homes for a change of clothes and some toiletries for Robert and me. An hour passed and then a precious little bundle arrived in my cell: a shirt, shorts, towel, shaving gear, a banana and a Doris Lessing novel, *The Making of the Representative of Planet 8*. Things were looking up. I showered, shaved and put on the fresh clothing, ate my banana and started reading my novel.

When the soldier had arrived at my house to pick up this bundle, our housekeeper Makareta had gone into a panic and grabbed the first book she saw. It was a good choice. Lessing's subject was the icing over of a planet and the gradual death by freezing of its inhabitants. Walled up in the little hotbox of my prison, an icy breeze blew from the novel's pages.

Later in the day when I was starting to really get into the flow of the novel's narrative, I heard a familiar voice in the guardhouse arguing with the sergeant. It was Susan Douglas, the director of Fiji Red Cross. She had been in my class at Suva Grammar School. I could hear her now referring to an international convention that allowed Red Cross to inspect the welfare of political prisoners. Susan was allowed to see us briefly. She had a grim look on her face and I guessed she'd had a tough time of it over the last few days. She asked us to quickly list our prisoners' requests. I asked for a few things and said my main request was to be allowed to get out of the cell for the first time in four days to stretch my legs and have some exercise. Susan said she'd see what she could do and left.

Then it was back to the snow-covered progress of the Lessing novel. Yes, now I really was cooling my heels. At about 5.30pm an officer came into the prison and told me to get up as we were being released. For a moment my reaction was one of reluctance: I had a good book to read, I was on holiday from the turmoil, couldn't I at least be allowed to finish my book? Reality kicked in with a jolt and I called down the corridor of cells, 'C'mon Robert, we're out of here.'

And then the officer gave us the bizarre instruction to clean up a bit because we were going up to the Officers' Mess for drinks with Brigadier Rabuka.

On the way up the hill to the Mess I said to Robert, 'For God's sake, when we get up there no questions; we have a drink with them, polite as you like, and then we go home.' He grunted what I thought was agreement. Assembled in uniform in the Mess, drinks in hand, were the upper echelons of the army's officer corps. I knew half of them personally – people I had worked with in public service or hung out with socially. This was their first get-together since the second coup, and for all the bonhomie I detected an air of unease. One very senior officer, whom I had always thought of as a hard-liner, said quietly to me, 'The first coup was justifiable but this one is not.'

My response surprised me, 'Maybe so, but the well-being of this country now depends on the integrity and cohesiveness of the men in this Mess.' I was thinking of Africa and the gruelling effect on that continent of military coup after military coup carried out first by generals, then by majors, until even mad sergeants with names like Idi Amin felt fit to assume national command at the point of a gun.

Rabuka entered the Mess and took up a position to which officers approached deferentially for this or that. He was clearly no longer one of them. With the second coup he had shown that he was not prepared to relinquish the power he had so audaciously assumed with the first. The Mess was too small for him now, no room here for messianic politics, and whether it was awe and hero-worship or suspicion and fear, the aura around him kept others away that night.

I was continuing my gin and tonic circuit of the Mess as if I was at a cocktail party, keeping an eye on Robert, who was clutching his drink and glowering around the room. I found myself talking about the Fiji crisis as if it was happening in an another country; after four days in our host's slammer, it was so dislocating to now be attending his party. Everyone was either very polite or silent in response to my chat, and they were no doubt wondering, like me, what the hell Robert and I were doing there.

Rabuka was standing by himself, and eventually my old colleague from District Administration days, Colonel Buadromo, suggested I should go and talk to him. I crossed the room and was received in an imperious but friendly manner by the *generalissimo*. He said that he hoped I didn't mind being deactivated for a few days. I stopped myself short of thanking him for his consideration. We talked awkwardly about what he was now going to do about the machinery of government and state of the national economy. He was noncommittal about the future of the governor generalship, 'I'm not sure. We'll have to see.'

After a little while I saw Keith-Reid crossing the room with a belligerent look on his face and on arrival he blurted, 'Why did you do it, eh, why did you have this second coup?'

Rabuka didn't reply. Time to leave.

Robert shot with his next question, 'Why did you lock me up, what did I do?'

'Tear him for his verses,' said Rabuka absently.

'What?'

Then Rabuka explained with a sly grin, 'Don't you remember Cinna the poet in *Julius Caesar*? "Tear him for his verses," the Roman mob said. The poet wasn't one of the plotters but the Romans punished him anyway, for his bad verses.'

Though stunned into quizzical silence, steam was building in Robert's mute expression. I was riveted in bemusement at this Shakespearean turn, wondering how far the analogy went. Did he see himself as Mark Anthony to Mara's Caesar? Observing the state of play, Captain Isikeli Mataitoga approached us and said he would drop Robert and me at our homes. I said my brief goodbyes and then we were standing out by the flagpole at the front of the Mess looking down across the parade ground at the prison block that had caged us for the last four days.

Mataitoga came out of the Mess to say that he had arranged a driver to drop us, as he had other things to do. He took me aside and said that one of the conditions of my release was that I was to stay away from Government House and not attempt to communicate with the governor general. I would be monitored in this regard. I took some small satisfaction from the fact that at least Mataitoga was now showing his true colours.

So there I was leaving the Officers' Mess with a couple of gins under my belt, a seemingly proud rooster; but as I piled into the army transport and was driven down from the Mess past the prison and out of the gates of Queen Elizabeth Barracks for ever, I knew in my heart that I was already a feather duster.

DECLARATION OF THE REPUBLIC

ON SEPTEMBER 29, four days after the second coup d'état, a statement was issued from Buckingham Palace saying that Ratu Sir Penaia had spoken that morning by telephone to the Queen's private secretary and had assured the Queen that he remained at his post of governor general. 'For her part, Her Majesty continues to regard the governor general as her representative and the sole legitimate source of executive authority in Fiji.' The statement said the Queen had been pleased to give her support to the political settlement reached the previous week by the governor general and the two political parties, and much regretted that this process of peaceful change in restoring constitutional normality had been overturned by illegal action and the use of force. It proclaimed that 'anyone who seeks to remove the governor general from office would, in effect, be repudiating his allegiance and loyalty to the Queen.'

The night of my release I rang Government House and left a message for the governor general that I could be contacted at my residence. He rang back and I told him that I was under army instructions not to go to Government House or contact the governor general. He said he'd see about that and would call me back. But he didn't call back, and over the next few days the feeling of a *fait accompli* came over me.

Information was hard to get; the army had shut down the newspapers and imposed a curfew. Friends who visited us that week at our Domain home were stopped at an army road-block down the road for questioning on why they had been to see us. I presumed that my detention by the army, and their continuing surveillance of me, was to ensure that my work on behalf of the governor general was terminated. This was only a presumption, because I had not been told why I had been imprisoned and to this day I have never been given an explanation. It was increasingly obvious I wasn't going to be allowed to function again at Government House, and there was no way I was working for a military government, so I conferred with my family and we decided it was time for a new start.

On Friday October 2, I found myself at the back gates of Government House, where the new secretary for the Public Service Commission, Poseci Bune, had his office. I handed him my resignation from the Fiji Civil Service, and he accepted it with alacrity, slipping my letter into a drawer while we talked, seemingly lest I should change my mind. A sixteen-year period of my life's work had come to an ungracious end. I made my way out onto the back-road leading away from Government House, and walking away up the road, I got close to the spot where as a kid I had tipped out of my box-cart and permanently scarred my hip. I was looking in vain for a faint sign of the pot-hole I had been avoiding at the time of the accident, when striding up to me came Ratu Epeli Nailatikau, commander of the Royal Fiji Military Forces until his overthrow on May 14.

He had an incredulous grin on his face, 'Hey Peter, what the hell's going on here?' He pointed up to Berkley Crescent and the top of Cakobau Hill where platoons of soldiers were drilling. There was some kind of military exercise underway, with orders being shouted and the sound of heavy boots crashing in unison on the tarseal as platoons moved on the double here and there. Out of habit I went to give him one of my don't-know-but-I'll-soon-find-out lines when it hit me that, stripped of office, I had no special means of finding out what the exercise signified. Like the vast majority of Fiji citizens, all I could rely on now was rumour and speculation.

We heard garbled news over the next few days of meetings between Ratu Penaia, Ratu Mara, Dr Bavadra and Colonel Rabuka, with various suggestions of political compromise and power-sharing arrangements, but it seemed self-evident to me that the second coup's destruction of the Deuba Accord would mean that an acceptable compromise was now highly unlikely. On October 5 the impact of the Taukei movement's Methodist fundamentalist domination of the new regime surfaced, with a government broadcast warning that Sunday picnics would no longer be allowed. More visions of life in Coup-Coup Land.

On the morning of October 7 we awoke to find that while we were sleeping, just before midnight, Rabuka had declared Fiji a republic. 'Whereas the People of Fiji have expressed their desire to have a new Constitution for the advancement of their beliefs, rights and freedoms, and trusting in Almighty God and His blessing upon this Decree, I hereby proclaim that as from this day forth Fiji is declared a Republic.' Inevitable as it was, and even though we had all been expecting a republic to be declared on the October 10 anniversary of Fiji's Independence, it felt to me like the earth had shifted under our feet.

The next couple of weeks were spent preparing for emigration, cashing in any assets we could in preparation for whatever lay ahead of us overseas. The Fiji property market had crashed, so what little we had in that regard had crashed with it, and cash reserves, like my Fiji National Provident Fund account, were hit by a further devaluation of the Fiji dollar, making a total devaluation of thirty-three percent over the last four months. It is amazing to me how humans react. You spend your life painstakingly compromising and working to build up your meagre savings and investments, and then when over a third of it is snatched away by forces beyond your control and the rest is about to be consumed by relocating your life, most of us just give a dismissive shrug, move along and thank God for our health and the love of family.

We needed tax clearance, approval to take funds out of the country, visas, somewhere to stay overseas and someone to adopt our dogs in Fiji. We had friends to farewell, bills to pay, and a lifetime's packing to be done. Through my father I applied for and received a British passport from the British High Commission in Suva, and because Fiji's laws preclude holding two nationalities, I went down to Government Buildings one last time on October 14 to hand in my Fiji passport to the Ministry of Home Affairs.

The day before, I had been given permission to go to Government House to say farewell to Ratu Penaia. What could you say? He was despondent and I felt I had to be apologetic about throwing in the towel. He said he understood. He asked me what I was going to do and I said that I wasn't sure but that we'd go to New Zealand first to visit with family and then maybe I'd try and get a job in London with the Commonwealth Secretariat. He thanked me for my work and gave me a typically heart-warming letter of recommendation. Then he said, not for the last time, that I should write a book to keep the record straight about what had happened up at Government House in 1987. I said that I would, and we said our farewells.

On October 15 Ratu Penaia resigned as governor general. In a letter to the Queen he said, 'This I do with the utmost regret; but my endeavours to preserve constitutional government in Fiji have proved in vain, and I can see no alternative way forward.'

The Commonwealth Heads of Government meeting was underway in Vancouver, and as a result of the governor general's resignation, Fiji's membership of the Commonwealth lapsed on the basis of 'established Commonwealth conventions'. Rabuka's military government was in control, with its twenty-four member Council of Ministers dominated by Taukei movement leaders. In some of their decrees they were calling themselves 'the interim military government', but increasingly it was just 'the military government.'

The Queen issued a further statement, this time from Vancouver, accepting with regret Ratu Penaia's resignation, expressing her gratitude to him and praising him for 'his courageous efforts to avert changes to the form of government in Fiji by force'.

The Queen's statement said, 'the Queen accepts that it is for the people of Fiji to decide their own future and prays that peace may obtain among the people of all races in that country. Her Majesty is sad to think that the ending of Fijian allegiance to the Crown should have been brought about without the people of Fiji being given an opportunity to express their opinion in the proposal.' Therein the rub, for if that hasty declaration of the republic on October 6, 1987 had been put to a vote, it remains my firm belief that the great majority of the people of Fiji would have rejected it. To be fair to those in power at the time, there was no way a referendum could have been held; nevertheless, the birth of this republic had the air of the arrival of a premature illegitimate.

Sure I'm a monarchist, but not irrationally so. When in the near future Australia votes to turn itself into a republic, and turn I believe it will, I will have no regrets. The nature of Australia's past and the course it is set upon make a republic the logical choice for that country. But in Fiji we never got the chance as a nation to choose.

The reluctance of Fiji's populace to cut their links to the Crown continues to be manifested in Fiji to this day in the annual Queen's Birthday public holiday; and the orange Fiji five dollar note which I am looking at as I write this, with its *bunedamu* perched in its bottom left corner and its Fiji coat-of-arms in the top right corner saying '*Rerevaka na*

Kalou kei doka na Tui' (Fear God and honour the Monarch), is dominated by the face of Queen Elizabeth. It is signed by the governor of the Reserve Bank, Ratu Jone Kubuabola, and was issued in 1995, eight years after the declaration of a republic severed Fiji's links with the Crown.

Back in October 1987, as I packed up to leave my home town for what would probably be forever, I couldn't stop thinking on how we had mucked up so badly. Where just a short time ago we all thought we were living in paradise, suddenly here we were in a country where half of us felt like political refugees while the other half stormed around in angry confusion. I thought of Ratu Sukuna's analogy of Fiji as a three-legged stool, with the three communities all needing to be sturdy and firmly in place if the stool was going to stand. The stool now had a couple of broken legs and was propped up against a bar where the customers were cowered and the barmen looked decidedly dodgy.

It is human to want to assign blame, but no-one was blameless, and wherever I looked I could see symptoms of the problem. Every second person I met was making righteous assignment of blame, but these same people were blind to their own contributions to the breakdown. To most onlookers Rabuka was the main culprit, but he came to be where he was only because the majority of Fijians felt the way they did, and had he not been around things could have been much worse. Anyone who felt they were totally innocent would have done well to sit down around a bowl of kava and have a long listen to what someone from the other side of the tracks had to say about them.

In 1987 the Fijians were at a wild and critical crossroads. As an indigenous community they had both the power and the will to assert their position in Fiji. Through the army they had the power. That they had the will was clearly demonstrated by the train of events that year. If you think of people in similar circumstances around the world, it is only when a community has both the power and the will that audacious assertion can take place; one without the other won't do the trick. While my heart understood it, there was no way my brain could accept it, and it was time for my family and me to go walkabout.

LAY OF THE LAND

WE SPENT OUR last week in Fiji on the island of Wakaya with our friends the Millers, in their house above the arc of Homestead Bay. While trying to board our plane to fly to Wakaya we had a spot of bother when the plainclothes soldiers at Nausori airport said that I was on their list of banned travellers; but after some over-the-phone negotiating with army headquarters I was advised that I was now removed from the list and was allowed to fly.

Wakaya felt like a sanctuary. I spent my time spearfishing with Tui, Panapasa and Rob Miller out in the Koro Passage, or beachcombing with my family along Wakaya's pristine beaches. In the evenings we drank kava and sang the old songs with the Wakaya Club's string band. Dilip Jamnadas visited from Suva, and under his expert eye my recipe for curried duck was enhanced and the results enjoyed.

The day before our departure, Marijcke and I spent most of the morning swimming with our kids, James and Nicky, in the gin-clear lagoon in front of Wakaya Club. The tide was coming in and as we dived among the coral heads the sea was full of fish. Flashing rainbow runners were hunting around the edges of sparkling shoals of fry. These shoals were as big as small clouds and if you swam into them you were completely surrounded underwater by a silvery glittering mass. Kicking your body into the mass it would part like mercury and form again behind you, suspending you in a liquid blue womb with yielding walls of shimmering fish flesh. In spite of all the marine activity there was no sense of danger within this lagoon and it had long been a favourite place to loll about in. I had suggested to my family on various occasions that into these waters it might be appropriate they scatter my ashes when the day in question arrived.

Drying off on the white sand beach along from the club, we sat under a *dilo* tree and gazed across the straits to the rocky peaks of the island of Ovalau and below them the old capital, Levuka, strung along Ovalau's foreshore. We were joined on the beach by three elderly guests of the Wakaya Club. A German-American man, his sister and his wife. They had been watching the four of us swimming in the lagoon, and introduced themselves formally to us, one family to another. They showed great interest in Fiji and our place in it, and as we conversed over the next hour I answered their questions with care and explained what had passed in Fiji in that year. I told them about my surrender of citizenship and our impending emigration to whichever points of the compass we were to be drawn.

Pointing across to Levuka I described to them how last century my great, great grandfather, Captain William Scott Petrie, had dropped the anchor of his sailing boat, the *Westward Ho*, and taken his family ashore to their new home in Levuka. From this home and a subsequent one in Suva he spent the next ten years sailing the South Pacific in his trading vessel.

Captain Petrie never returned to the granite ramparts of the Scottish port from which he hailed, and his body was laid to rest on the shores of Suva harbour. His wife Emma was to outlive him by forty-nine years and was the family matriarch for the next three generations of our Fiji family. Their eldest daughter Maud was my grandmother Connie's mother; their second daughter Dora married Sir Hugh Ragg who some say was the founder of the Fiji tourist industry; and the third daughter Florence married Robert Boyd, the commissioner of Native Lands. Shortly after the arrival of the Petries in Levuka a son, John, was born to them. He had but a brief spell in this world before his tiny remains were buried in the Levuka cemetery overlooking the same blue straits that underlaid the direction of our vision.

The three German-Americans exchanged such knowing looks between themselves that I deduced our story-telling had evoked emotions relating to events and places beyond my own family's uncertain circumstances. After some coaxing from his wife, the old man told us of their own departure from their family's ancestral home in a Germanic part of what is now Poland. They had fled in advance of the Russian army, which was rolling towards them at the end of the Second World War. He told of their subsequent emigration to America, the success of their ventures in that adopted country, the retirement house in Miami and the vacation retreat on a canal in Venice. 'But for all the good fortune that has come our way, we have always this feeling of loss inside, for we have never been able to return to live in the land that is our true home, the land where we would feel whole. You should prepare yourself for the forsaken feeling that is the lot of the exile, as you may never be quit of it.'

Sleeping was difficult for me that last night. A sense of no return was over-coming me. I had always mistrusted the taking of fate into one's own hands and was troubled about this deliberate movement towards a door which once passed through would change a life, for better or worse, forever. I thought of that line from Camus where each studied shot from his gun is like a rap on the door of his undoing. I was gutted, feeling myself moving from a life which had been governed by what I could give, to one in which the dictate would be what I could get.

The next day we left Wakaya in a light aircraft and flew off in the direction of the international airport at Nadi. The first island we flew over was Moturiki, and I looked down at the village of Uluibau. A man named Jona Moli lived in that village. I would not have existed were it not for his quick wit and steel nerves in saving my father's life in a jungle battle with the Japanese Imperial Forces on the island of Bougainville.

To the south of our flight path lay a battleship-like island, *nai yanuyanu vakaturaga ko Bau*, scene of childhood visits with my father's friends of the *Mataqali Vuikaba*. I recalled the day I went ashore there as a twenty-four year old with the one hundred-strong delegation from the vanua of Namosi to the *reguregu* following Ratu Tui's passing away. It was the day before the little island would be packed with officialdom and foreign dignitaries attending the funeral of state. The Namosi delegation had waited its turn to pay traditional respects in the temporary accommodation allocated to us, while all the tribes of Fiji paraded silently past to the site of the *reguregu*. It was not until well into the night that our turn came to make Namosi's presentation and we sat humbly before the Bauan representatives in their cross-legged solemnity at the foot of the hill of tribute whales' teeth that rose like an ivory volcano behind them.

Our plane flew on over the main island, across the broad Rewa river flowing down from the fields of Vunidawa, over the silver-flashing waters of the Wainikoroiluva which I had forded so many times on my way up the *liga ni bai* of Namosi, and then the long curves of the Sigatoka river emanating from the source of our shared conception at Nadarivatu, somewhere off in the purple mists of the mountains to the north of our flight path.

After landing at Nadi we checked in at the Air Pacific counter and obtained our boarding passes. In spite of my now possessing a British passport with a New Zealand visitors visa in it, I felt some trepidation as I approached the customs desk to complete our departure formalities. Here was the last point of the regime's influence over me, and anything could happen. Sure enough there was a problem. A message on the computer screen told the operator to summon security. A young sun-glassed Fijian in jeans and sports shirt sauntered over, by his manner quite obviously a newly-empowered plain-clothes soldier. He told me that I was not allowed to depart from Fiji.

The intercom was summoning passengers for flight FJ440, departing shortly for Auckland, New Zealand. I was explaining to the security officer that the instruction on their computer had been superseded, that I had been given clearance to leave Fiji by the Ministry of Home Affairs. No sign of communication, just the mirror of his sunglasses. Marijcke and James were looking anxious and silent tears were starting to roll down Nicky's face. The call over the intercom said all passengers on flight FJ440 should now be boarding the aircraft.

I demanded to see the army officer in charge of the airport and a sergeant was summoned. It was incredible to me that the control of Fiji's most strategic international transit point should be under the orders of a not very bright sergeant. I stretched the truth and told him that Colonel Rabuka himself had sanctified my departure from Fiji today; on the sergeant's head it would be if he did not allow me to board my plane and depart Fiji. The sergeant was quite impressed by this line of argument, but it was my word against the explicit orders on the computer screen. I said that if we rang Queen Elizabeth Barracks in Suva I would be able to prove to him that I was free to leave. Therein lay the depth of his quandary, for on that day, Friday October 23, the telephone service in Nadi was out of action and it was not possible for him to contact his superiors by phone.

The final call for flight FJ440 was made. The sweating sergeant sent orders to the control tower that the flight was not allowed to depart until he had given it clearance. A Boeing 737 loaded with sweltering tourists was now sitting out on the tarmac. An army driver was despatched to try and locate an officer who could relieve the sergeant of his dilemma. My family were told they could board the plane but they refused to leave without me.

I carried on with my remonstrations in an increasingly melodramatic fashion and recall adding to the farce when I was caught in mid-speech between some automatic doors which kept opening and shutting on me, not sure whether I was coming or going, whether I was free or trapped, I kept up my diatribe while the doors beat a crazy rhythm on me. Observing this spectacle Nicky apparently stopped crying and started laughing, and has ever since had ownership of this vignette.

Some twenty minutes later, to the great relief of that tense little scene in the customs room, Captain Pickering turned up. I knew him from various points in the Deuba Accord negotiations to which the army had assigned him certain security duties. I gave him my word that I had obtained all of the necessary clearances from the government in Suva and on that basis he over-rode the instructions on the computer and gave the order that we were to be taken directly to the plane.

Our sense of relief and freedom on boarding the plane was strong enough that it subjugated the embarrassment of facing that planeload of angry over-heated passengers. The jet engines roared and down Nadi runway we rolled, lifting off from Viti Levu into clear blue skies, the canefields of Martintar to our left and the silhouettes of the Yasawa Islands trooping off to the right of us. We banked by Denarau and flew over Momi Passage's wide swathe through the barrier reef, setting course southwards to New Zealand.

Since that day I have been back to Fiji on many occasions, at times as regularly as once a month. At first I was dismayed at my lack of feeling for the islands; I had hardened myself to the cold world of the émigré and was at a point of emotional distance from the Fiji scenes, the people, the scents and tastes that had meant everything to me. And then, eight years after my departure, one of my cousins died when he drove his car into a power pole near Nabukavesi driving home late one night. I went to the funeral with my eldest aunt, Dorothy, and youngest brother, Douglas, both Suva residents.

We stood there on the flanks of Lovonilase cemetery overlooking Suva Harbour and put that beautiful young man into his grave. I looked around at the grieving graveside gathering and I felt a rush of empathy for these, my people. I turned away and looked over towards my grandparents' graves, tasting again my saline tears when as a young man I had picked up the red laterite soil at Grandma Kearsley's graveside and sprinkled it down into the deep hole in which her coffin lay. It rattled on the wood below like the first splatter of tropical rain on a windowpane. I remembered the heave of those body sobs as the gravediggers too hurriedly began shovelling the heavy clods of earth down thudding onto her coffin.

Two senses of loss gnaw at me in quiet times of reflection. The first cannot be appeased in this lifetime. I had answered my mother's call to see her as she lay dying of cancer in a house by a sea loch in Western Scotland, where my parents were living while she underwent that vain period of treatment. She wanted to talk of the future, and I wanted to talk of the past. We had spent much of our life as combatants, so alike that it was like arguing with oneself, taking the opposite side to each other in discussion for the sake of it, knowing that under it all we were of one accord in our view of just about everything and that to love each other was like loving ourselves. In that grey northern winter, the time came for us to part, and I will not describe the depths of my grief as we said our restrained, heart-breakingly inadequate farewells as she lay on the couch in front of the open fire in the company of the neighbour from down the loch who had come to look after her while my father drove me to Oban Station to catch the train that would take me away from her forever. The windows of that train, as it rattled through the thick mist along the shores of Loch Etive, were as wet as my pathetic face as I began my long homeward journey to the South Seas.

'I'm missing you' are the saddest words we know when the object is gone forever. When I signed away the citizenship that was my birthright, in a bureaucrat's office in Suva in October 1987, it was because the Fiji diplomatic passport I possessed would have been of little use to me in establishing myself in some place overseas where I could make a living. By shedding my Fiji passport and obtaining a foreign one, I would be free to leave Fiji when the time came later that month. Looking back on it now, I realise that at that moment I joined the world-throng for whom nations and nationalities, with all their symbols and trappings and restrictions, are just inconveniences to be dealt with as seldom as possible. It is true that passports and citizenship papers are no more than the makings of people, but in giving up my homeland I had given away more than I knew. Those emotionless visits back to Fiji thereafter were what it must be like for long-time lovers who after bitter divorce have to see each other now and then, and know in their heart of hearts there will never be another.

Exile is a state of mind where boundaries are bitter-sweet memories of that which will never be again, and nostalgia is the name of its curse. It is a state of defeat, with subjugation compounded by time's trampling, as frail existences fall before the power of nevermore. And as we fall, one by one, and our years depart like ships over the southern horizon, the acceptance finally sets in that all things do pass, that change is the one constant. Time is running out for this particular organism and the job of defining ourselves is ours alone.

With that lifting of the head, my army of one is now winning something back. For all its insignificant resources, it has recrossed once forlorn boundaries and is infiltrating the old territories. My ears are platoons of stealth recapturing rhythms of speech, the birdsongs of home, the thud of kava being pounded. Loyal nostrils are commandos seeking out the aromas which jolt the senses back across the surrendered decades, and the silent battalions of my eyes are taking in the lay of the land the way they used to move across a mother's face. The campaign goes on, still troubled despite its apparent calm, with all the while the binding trust that victory will be complete only when its hard-won spoil is love.

And I know my soul would depart peacefully from this world, down the spirit path to who knows where, if the last sounds lingering in my ears could be the night-time roar of the southeast trades in the streaming crowns of the coconut palms and the rumbling thunder of that ocean swell, come all the way from Tonga and the emptiness beyond, breaking on the coral reef of our long-vanished Makuluva doorstep.

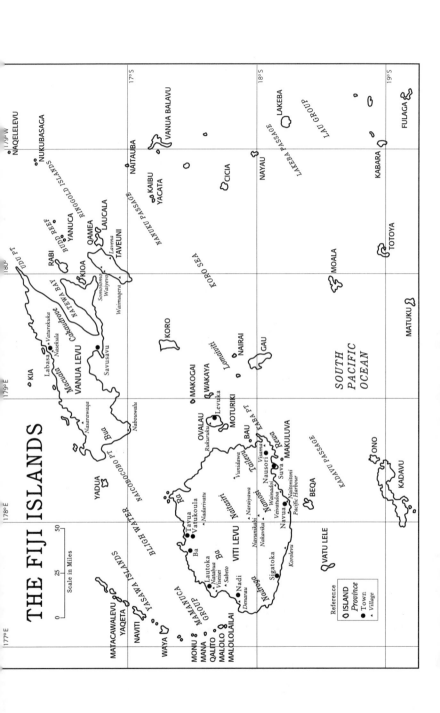

THE FIJI ISLANDS

Scale in Miles

0   25   50

Reference

◇ ISLAND *Province*
● Town
▲ Village

SOUTH PACIFIC OCEAN

KORO SEA

MATACAWALEVU
YAQETA

YASAWA ISLANDS

NAVITI

WAYA

MONU
MANA
QALITO
MALOLO
MALOLOLAILAI

MAMANUCA GROUP

BLIGH WATER

NACOCOBOCOBO PT.

YADUA

KIA

Nasarawaqa

Bua

Nabouwalu

Labasa Vaturekuka
Macuata Nasekula
Cakaudrove
VANUA LEVU
Savusavu

NATEWA BAY

UDU PT.

RABI

Kioa

RINGGOLD ISLANDS

BUDD REEF

YANUCA

QAMEA
LAUCALA
Lavena
TAVEUNI

Somosomo
Waiyevo
Waimaqera

NAITAUBA

VANUA BALAVU

17°S

KAIBU
YACATA

CICIA

NANUKU PASSAGE

KORO

MAKOGAI
WAKAYA

Levuka
OVALAU
Rukuruku

Lomaiviti

Lomaiviti
NAIRAI

GAU

MOALA

NAYAU

LAKEBA

18°S

LAKEBA PASSAGE

LAU GROUP

Tavua
Vatukoula
Nadarivatu

Ba
Lautoka
Natabua
Visesei
Nadi
Denarau

Sabeto

VITI LEVU
Nadi
Natovi
Nasivi

Naraiyawa

Navunikabi
Nakavika

Korolevu

Sigatoka

Nadroga

VATU LELE

MOTURIKI
BAU
KABA PT.

Viti Levu
Bay

Tailevu
Rewa
Nausori
Visama
Wainadoi
Veivatuloa
Navua
Naitonitoni
Pacific Harbour

Suva

MAKULUVA

BEQA

KADAVU PASSAGE

ONO

KADAVU

TOTOYA

MATUKU

KABARA

FULAGA

19°S

177°E   178°E   179°E   180°   179°W

Fijian Glossary

(Meanings of Fijian words in the context in which they are used in this book)

adi	prefix to the name of a woman of chiefly rank
au	I (also me)
baqe	bank
bai	fence
baka	banyan tree
bilibili	bamboo river raft
biu	to throw out
boko	to extinguish
buka	fire (also firewood)
bula	to live (as in the normal 'good day' greeting *'sa bula'*)
bunedamu	orange dove
bure	Fijian thatched dwelling (more properly *vale vakaviti*)
cagi	wind
cakau	reef
caucau	a gentle land breeze
cava	what?
delai	on top of
dilo	a littoral tree with medicinal fruit
dogo	mangrove
draunikau	sorcery
drokadroka	green wood
gone	child
io	yes
ika	fish
isa	interjection of regret or yearning
kaidia	Indian
kaijaina	Chinese
kailoma	person of mixed racial descent
kaimadarasi	South Indian
kaivavalagi	European
kana	to eat

kanikani	scaly skin caused by excessive consumption of kava
kumala	sweet potato
kua	stop
lala	empty
levu	big
lewena	the inner flesh of the stem-base of the kava plant
liga	finger
lovo	earth oven
lulu	barn owl
maca	dry
macala	clear
mai	towards here
mana	possessing supernatural qualities
mata	representative
matanitu	government (also an independent state)
mataqali	land-owning social unit
moli	citrus
na	the
ni	of
nokonoko	ironwood tree
oile	alas
oqo	this
ore	punishment for infringement of custom
purini	steamed pudding
ra	west
rai	vision
ratu	prefix to the name of a man of chiefly rank
reguregu	ceremony of offerings at funeral
rogo	to make a noise
roko	head provincial official
rourou	edible taro leaves
saka	term of respect in addressing superiors
saluka	self-made Fiji cigar (chopped tobacco leaf rolled in a dried banana or pandanus leaf)
sasa	brooms made from the ribs of coconut leaves
sega	no

sevusevu	ceremonial presentation of kava
sogo	to close
sosoko	thick (of liquid)
sulu	loin-cloth
sulu vakataga	tailored sulu
talanoa	conversation
talatala	Protestant church minister
talo	to pour
tanoa	large wooden bowl for preparing kava
tau	to fall
taucoko	all
taukei	the possessor of a thing
tauvu	tribes having the same founder
teitei	vegetable garden
tevoro	demon
tikina	sub-provincial district
toa	chicken
tovo	custom, manner
turaga	chief or gentleman
uca	rain
vagunuvi	to cause to drink
vaka-i-lesilesi	appointees
vakarau	to prepare
vakatunuloa	a temporary pavilion without walls
vakaturaga	in a chiefly manner
vale	house
vale vakaviti	traditional thatched dwelling
valevou	toilet out-house
vanua	land (also a tribe)
veikau	forest
vesi	a hardwood tree, the wood of which was formerly used only for articles which would be used by chiefs
vinaka	thank you (also good)
viti	Fiji
vosa	language
vulagi	foreigner, stranger, visitor

vulavula	white
vuniwai	doctor
wai	water
waka	root of the kava plant
yanuyanu	island
yasana	province
yaqona	kava
yavu	raised house foundations

The Fijian proverb '*Ki Namuka vata ga nikua*' translates as 'We'll all be together soon when we reach Namuka.' Put another way: some of us on this journey may get ahead and some of us may straggle, but we'll all be together once again when we reach our destination.

Afterword

On July 3, 1997, I was standing in our Auckland kitchen mixing yoghurt into the tamarind sauce that friends had recently brought down from Fiji. The yoghurt was needed to tone down the tamarind's tartness, in deference to the more delicate palates of the New Zealanders that would be our guests at dinner that evening. The Fiji friends were Grahame and Pru Rouse and they had been in Auckland to watch the Fiji rugby team play New Zealand's All Blacks in the June 14 Test. Their son Daniel was in the front row of the Fiji team, where he acquitted himself well in battle for his country against the world's number one rugby prop Olo Brown.

I had watched that game in a corporate box seated next to Fiji's prime minister, Sitiveni Rabuka. He was visiting New Zealand to attend the New Zealand-Fiji Business Council's conference, and I was a member of the council's executive committee. It was a special moment for me when at the beginning of the game my former gaoler, the prime minister, came and stood next to me and together we sang the Fiji national anthem surrounded by all those curious New Zealanders. Side by side singing solemnly 'a land of freedom, hope and glory, to endure what e'er befall, may God bless Fiji for evermore'. My heart was full of pride in my country, and I was wishing with every nerve-end that we would beat the mighty All Blacks; it was strange on reflection to no longer be a citizen of the nation for which I barracked.

Anyway, just as I was getting the tamarind sauce right, the phone rang. It was Grahame. 'It's done,' he said. 'The Lower House has just unanimously approved the new Constitution.'

It was a moment transfixed with hope. Coming on the heels of the Great Council of Chiefs' approval the previous month, Fiji's return to reason was now a tantalising reality. We had come full circle, and Fiji would again have a Constitution that would be acceptable to both its citizens and the international community of nations.

Over eleven years have now passed since the year of the coups, and I'm reminded now of a conversation that I had with the Governor of the Reserve Bank of Fiji, Savenaca Siwatibau, just prior to my emigration at the end of 1987. For all our disappointments in that tumultuous year, we agreed that the wheel would turn, and that all through history an extreme position eventually gives way to the powers of reason and moderation. So it would be in Fiji.

The turning of the wheel over the decade after the year of the coups has been an absorbing procession. After the governor general's 1987 resignation and Fiji's exit from the Commonwealth, the interim military government tottered along for a while until Rabuka did a deal with Ratu Sir Kamisese Mara and Ratu Sir Penaia Ganilau whereby Ratu Mara agreed to take on the prime ministership and Ratu Penaia the presidency.

The influence of the Taukei movement had peaked and thereafter it was passé as a political force. A new government led by Ratu Mara was formed and it went on to oversee the promulgation of a Constitution in 1990 which, in accordance with the Fijian stand at the time, was heavily skewed in favour of indigenous Fijians. In 1991 the Great Council of Chiefs approved the formation of the SVT political party with membership open only to indigenous Fijians. In the same year Rabuka relinquished control of the army and became one of two deputy prime ministers, and at the inaugural meeting of the SVT he was elected its leader.

Meanwhile Doctor Bavadra died of cancer at the end of 1989. In 1991 the coalition between the Labour party and the National Federation party, which Bavadra had led to victory in the 1987 elections, dissolved in acrimony. After the 1992 elections, in order to form a government, Rabuka's SVT needed and gained the support of the Labour party, now led by the ever-pragmatic Mahendra Chaudhry. Rabuka became the elected prime minister and Jai Ram Reddy, still leader of the National Federation party, became the leader of the opposition.

At the end of 1993 Ratu Penaia died of his long-dormant leukaemia. Ratu Mara became president. Rabuka, in the face of a strong challenge from a newly-formed moderate Fijian party, won the 1994 elections and continued as prime minister. The 1990 Constitution contained a provision for a review after seven years, so in 1995 Sir Paul Reeves, a Maori and former governor general of New Zealand, was appointed chairman of the Constitution Review Commission. My father was the other person short-listed for this task, and I breathed a sigh of relief when Sir Paul was given the job. At that stage it seemed a thankless task, an exercise which would satisfy no-one and would result at best in some small tinkering with the Constitution. The commission went diligently through its responsibilities, but when the SVT's turn to be heard by the commission came, the SVT tabled an outrageously hard-line submission and the communities seemed as polarised as they had ever been. The commission's report was delivered to the Fiji government and a select committee of Parliament, chaired by Rabuka was set up to deliberate on it.

And then came the dramatic events of 1997. In April Rabuka said he was willing to try out a multi-party cabinet if the recommendations being made by the Parliamentary Select Committee were accepted. The voices of multiracialism started to be heard in support of Rabuka. Grahame Rouse, as national secretary of the General Electors party, was given prominent media attention with his comment that Rabuka was now making decisions focused on what was needed to bring a sense of unity to Fiji's people.

On May 14, 1997, exactly ten years after his first coup d'état, prime minister Rabuka tabled in Parliament the Select Committee's recommendations, sweeping away the racialism of the 1990 Constitution. It was a breath-taking moment. The self esteem and aspirations of so many peoples' lives seemed to have looped back to that place where they had collapsed a decade ago. The battle was far from over, and Fijian nationalists raged loudly against Rabuka's new stance, but when the Great Council of Chiefs met in June and endorsed the Select Committee's recommendations, it dawned on us that Fiji really was at the doorway of a brave new start. At that meeting, Jai Ram Reddy became the first Indian to address the Great Council of Chiefs, and his speech is now regarded as one of the foundation columns in the house of Fiji's nationhood. He spoke of history and the making of history, of fear and the ending of fear, of truth and of a generation's destiny. He called his audience the chiefs not just of the Fijians, but of all the people of Fiji. He called for a society where children of all races grow up with a deep understanding and respect for each other's cultures, languages and traditions; a country in which the security of the indigenous Fijians would serve as the basis for the security of the country as a whole. He described the Crown as a noble and comforting symbol of unity and said, 'May the day soon come when Her Majesty can stand before you – indeed before us all – restored as Queen of Fiji.'

In July, Fiji's Upper and Lower Houses passed resolutions unanimously adopting the recommended changes, and before 1997 was out the new Constitution was law and the fatted calf was feasted upon as Fiji was welcomed, before a bemused but admiring world, back into the Commonwealth. Fiji was hailed as a country which had talked, rather than bloodily fought, its way to a just settlement of seemingly insurmountable ethnic differences.

At the end of October, 1997 the perpetrator of 1987's military coups d'état took his place with the other Commonwealth heads of government as the elected prime minister of a nation with a just Constitution. No longer an international maverick, he was now acknowledged as the man Fiji wanted at its helm.

Amongst the joy of Fiji's 1997 reawakening, there was a nagging sense of déjà vu. The 1987 Deuba Accord that had been brokered by Ratu Penaia had the same effect of a power-sharing government welcomed alike by the nation and the international community. As with the 1997 accord, the Deuba one resulted from intensive dialogue and demonstrations of statesmanship by the elected political representatives of Fiji's communities. What was so different in 1997 that could justify a nation's desultory decade of wandering in a political wilderness? How should that decade be understood and explained to the people of Fiji and the world? Was it just a case of one man's sense of destiny being fulfilled? And indeed, how was it that Rabuka, the man who had ripped apart the covenants of law and loyalty that bound the nation, was now toiling as the chief instrument of their rebinding? What had happened to him and the nation on their long road to Damascus?

Two people I know answer these questions from different

perspectives, and I find elements of the never simple truth in both their answers. The first says the emergence of a man such as Rabuka was increasingly inevitable in the waning of the Mara years. Fijians had always looked to strong leaders, and in 1987 there was no Fijian who looked remotely capable of filling the huge leadership shoes of the tiring older generation. In the old days, such situations called for decisive deeds, like those of the young Seru Cakobau who demolished Bau in 1837 before restoring his exiled father to suzerainty on the island, in due course succeeding him and going on to become the most powerful chief in Fiji. Rabuka, with his courage, guile and willpower, was the Seru Cakobau of the late twentieth century, and the Fijian people were quick to see in him their new leader.

Having taken control and given the Fijians the political security they wanted, Rabuka came to understand, mainly through failed experimentation, that Fiji was on a downward economic spiral if it kept on with the ethos of the 1990 Constitution. Fast-fix economic solutions led to corruption and lack of the certainties necessary for investment. It became clear that non-indigenes were not going to dedicate their hearts and wallets to a country where they were second class citizens, and steady emigration over the decade represented a serious Fiji brain drain, for a disproportionate percentage of the emigrants were the skilled and educated looking for better treatment overseas. The pariah effect of the 1990 Constitution on the inflow of foreign assistance and investment was further holding Fiji back. Something had to be done to stop the rot.

By 1997, in spite of all the tribulations of the last decade, Rabuka faced no serious challengers for the leadership of the Fijian mainstream. He was strong enough to force through the changes the country required, and the follow-up to the Reeves Commission gave him the legal avenue to do so. The threat of Indian political domination had gone, for in the aftermath of the coups some 30,000 Indians had emigrated, reducing the Indian population to forty-four percent of the national total. The mooted concept of power-sharing with the Indian political leadership was one he was keen to try; ten years of running a cabinet made up largely of indigenous Fijians made him keen to broaden the scope of the nation's executive team. Like any astute leader he knew he had to keep making changes to stay ahead of the pack, for to stand still is in fact to fall behind.

The second person says that Fiji's sense of proportion lurched too far to one side between 1987 and 1990 for the situation to remain uncorrected. Fiji had long been a place where tolerance, goodwill and care for the welfare of others prevailed, and it was to a great extent from the character of the indigenous culture that these qualities had emanated. The message of love at the heart of the Gospels guiding Fijian life, sat softly alongside the troubled national conscience throughout this time. Faced with a political aberration of their own creation, it was in the nature of the Fijian people that they would eventually correct the wrongs they had brought upon their fellow citizens. And the latter, knowing of the insecurity of their island existence and with their responsibilities lying chiefly in the welfare of their own families, let it be known that they did not accept their second class status, but had the good sense and patience to bear with this dislocation and give the Fijians time to come to their own conclusions.

Toleration sounds like a pretty mediocre experience, but at the end of the day it was the deep wells of tolerance, which have long been sunk into the ground of Fiji's various and national cultures, that allowed it to survive the storms of 1987 and the decade of ethical drought which followed.

And during the storm and the despair of the drought, hard lessons were learnt. The indigenes took to heart the indispensable economic contribution that the non-indigenes made to the well-being of the nation, and better understood that for them too, Fiji was now home. For their part the non-indigenes had learnt a real respect for the cultural sensibilities and special position of the indigenous people of Fiji. The learning of these lessons needed time, and in 1987 the Deuba Accord provided the answer the nation needed, but not enough time had been allowed for these lessons to have been absorbed in full.

On a visit to Suva in 1997 I heard that Ratu Meli Vesikula, one of the most strident leaders of the Taukei movement in 1987 and a vocal detractor of my position at Government House, wanted to see me. We met at Government Buildings not fifty metres from the spot that the coup d'état took place. He wanted to apologise for what he had said and done in 1987, and gave a moving description of how he had got to the mental position he had at that time, and how in its aftermath he had looked inside himself and not liked what he had seen. And in protracted wrestling with his conscience and his pride, he found a new way of understanding and living with his cultural inheritance. His self-discovery led him to the place where he needed to apologise, and he did this publicly at meetings in Fiji of representatives of the people who had been caused so much anguish by the Taukei movement.

Need I say it, the scene of our reunion was around a Government Buildings *tanoa* from which servings of the *wai ni vanua* were being dispensed. It was with a sense of thankfulness that I saw the end of self-torment in Ratu Meli's face as he talked. I assured him that no apology to me was required, but that I accepted his apology in the spirit with which it was given and we shook hands in friendship. I explained the reason I personally did not need an apology was that, in all sincerity, I was one of the few lucky ones in 1987. Within days of the coup I had been summoned by Ratu Sir Penaia Ganilau, the governor general, representative of the Queen of Fiji and upholder of the laws of Fiji, to be his permanent secretary. As long as I did my duty to him thereafter, my moral and legal situation was an easy one to explain to myself. This was not so for many of my colleagues and for many others in the land, and I can only sympathise with them over the mental loads which must have weighed them down as they struggled through the quagmire of the time.

And what was the answer provided by the accords of 1987 and 1997? It was an end to the politics of exclusion, divide and rule, and exploitation; and the beginning of cultural inclusion and power-sharing for a common good and a common destiny. From Rwanda to Northern Ireland, polarised communities have been unable to share power and to respect and enjoy their cultural differences, and have horrified the world with the consequences of their intransigence. Fiji could have walked that road of hate. In the nation in 1987 there were amongst us a few people who relished the prospect. But sanity and goodwill have prevailed, and the path Fiji now follows, while by no means one free of troubles, is a way along which ears are opened to the words of others and hands are held in national fellowship.

Who knows what the future holds, but when standing back in the next millennium, appraising that which has been hammered out on history's anvil, it will be against 1997's dreams of fullness of nationhood that the swords or ploughshares will be measured. Let the cynics and malfeasants then answer to themselves; for if the path of goodwill that opened again before us in 1997 has proven true, the well-meaning people of Fiji will be able to look each other in the eye and share a smile of understanding, for they will have shown a troubled world a better way.

Ki Namuka vata ga nikua.